The Belief Formula

The Secret to Unlocking the Power of Prayer

The Belief Formula

The Secret to Unlocking the Power of Prayer

Pete Koerner

Bell Rock Press

Bell Rock Press

P.O. Box 5236

St. Marys, Georgia 31558

www.TheBeliefFormula.com

www.BellRockPress.com

Koerner, Pete.

   The belief formula : the secret to unlocking the power of prayer / Pete Koerner.

   p. cm.

   ISBN 10: 0-9799913-0-7

   ISBN 13: 978-0-9799913-0-1

1. Spiritual life—Psychology. 2. Brain—Religious aspects. 3. Mind-Body Healing—Religious aspects. I. Title.

10 9 8 7 6 5 4 3 2

Cover Design by Jennifer Koerner

Cover Layout by R J Communications LLC, New York

Interior Layout and Design by New Vision Graphics

This book was assembled and electronically formatted by New Vision Graphics

1st Printing June 2007

Printed in the United States of America

Acknowledgments

With gratitude and love to: My beloved bride, teacher, friend, and partner, Jennifer Koerner, who has been and continues to be my inspiration in all I do, and without whom this book would not exist; and to our son Jacob, who also serves as one of the main reasons for our continued search for all that can be in this world; My parents, Gerald and Joyce, who gave me an education in this world, without limiting me to a singular expression or set of beliefs, and who encouraged me in all I have ever done; My dear friend and teacher Emmanuel, who encouraged and supported me and this message, and helped me integrate the information in this book into my own life and practice while inspiring a great deal of this writing, and Elaine, whose soft words of kind encouragement gave me the other side of what Emmanuel taught me; Dr. Doug Dennis, who has been, and continues to be, a dear friend, a support and inspiration, and a valuable resource of medical information and encouragement; John Bishop, who also helped a great deal in the final production and editing of this work, and continues to be a great friend who encourages and inspires with his own dedication to the principles of creative living; Dr. Donna Davidson, Ph.D., who offered insight and encouragement from the very beginning of this work, and who continues to be a dear friend and teacher who has helped us bring much of our work to fruition in ways she may never be aware of; Nikki Ross, for offering invaluable input to make this information more accessible and usable; Peter Gallagher, one of the most dependable people I've ever known, who handled most of my business affairs during the writing phase of this work; and Tom and Julie Monahan, who purchased my retail business and allowed me to pursue this work while they continue to build an even more wonderful business than they started with; Bruce Lipton, Ph.D., who encouraged this work, and offered wonderful advice on getting this message across; Rob Williams, Ph.D., for his wonderful work developing Psych-K, which has definitely played a big part in the unfolding of this project; Dr. Tapas Flemming, who has given Jennifer, me, and the world a tremendous gift with the Tapas Acupressure Technique (TAT); Gary Craig, whose Emotional Freedom Techniques have helped and inspired thousands of people, and helped us (and our clients) overcome many obstacles and challenges; Grant Connolly, for creating the Z-Point Process, and whose support and encouragement of this work helped more than he knows; Dr. Ernesto Fernandez, who was instrumental in starting Jennifer and I on our way as teachers of Quantum Physics as it applies to creating the health and life you wish to live – Ernesto helped establish me firmly on the path; Larry Valmore, who teaches Advanced Psychological Kinesiology, and personifies quiet strength and wisdom in his teaching and clinical practice; Jose Silva, for his empowering work in the field of mind development, and for the great gifts he left us with the Silva Basic Learning System, and Silva Ultramind System; Kris Attard, who gave me my first set of tools with which to navigate my mental landscape; Catherine Ann Tipton, my first high school composition teacher, for *making* me think; and finally, Anthony, who gave me a feather and a hint that helped me remember. And thanks again to Jennifer Koerner, John Bishop, Gerald Koerner, Joyce Koerner, Alice Hurley, and Tiffany Dansereau, for editorial feedback and support. Thank you all for your love, kindness, help, support, and encouragement!

About this Book

Simply put, you have this book in your hands now because you need to read it. This book will change your life in amazing ways; and that is exactly what you have been looking for. You know that for some time you have felt like there was something more – something missing, perhaps. And you were right. In fact, you may not have recognized that feeling as being part of a force that was driving you here – and beyond this place and time – to find the answers to your questions and to questions you do not yet know you have. You will find many of the answers you seek within these pages. Whether you are sick and wish to find health, poor and wish to find wealth, or are simply lost and seeking your "self," then you have arrived at this place – with this book in your hands – at exactly the right time.

Whether you believe it or not, everyone prays. When I use the word *pray*, I am referring to the act of focusing your thoughts on your dearest hopes, desires, wishes, dreams, preferences, and questions. Everyone has these; and if they are to be realized or answered, the mind must be engaged. The word "prayer" does carry religious connotations; but this is simply because *all religions use prayer*. But prayer is not necessarily a religious practice; prayer is a THINKING practice – specifically, the practice of focusing thought on that which you most want to bring into your experience.

Religions use prayer because religions are deeply involved with how a person thinks, how they feel, and how they act. But you don't have to go to church to pray; and you don't have to kneel, fold your hands, or go through any other machinations to have your prayers "heard and answered." The idea of prayer is one of "creative thinking," or of working with a creative agency or power we can all access by using the power of our heart and mind.

There are many things one can do with the mind; and all of them are creative. If you are a businessman, for instance, you may pray for successful meetings, deals, or partnerships; and if you are ill, you may pray for an end to your suffering and a return to good health. You may be experiencing debt where you wish to experience abundance and prosperity; or you may be hoping to mend a relationship. These hopes, wishes, and prayers are invisible; but the results they bring will be quite real to you. And, if you do it right, they will even look just like you hoped and imagined they would – but you indeed must first imagine how you want them to look. This is the essence of prayer. If you don't learn to think (pray) effectively, your prayers will still be answered, but you may not recognize the answers as the answers you had hoped for.

There is an art and science to turning the invisible into the visible – to bringing thought forth from the mind into a physical experience. An architect, for instance, draws a plan for a new structure, but only after imagining and thinking about what that structure will be used for and what it should look like. The architect's thoughts are turned into a plan; and, through action, those thoughts take form in the physical world. The building was real before it was constructed; it existed on a blueprint. The building was real even before it was a blueprint – a real image in the mind of the architect. And even before that, the building was a real desire in the heart and mind of the person who hired the architect. We may lose sight of this pathway of creation; but whether you think about it or not, there is always a pathway between thought and thing. The difference between success and failure, fulfillment and suffering, is in how you negotiate that path.

Everyone prays because everyone has things they want to experience and don't know how to create on their own. If you want a peanut butter sandwich, and you have bread and peanut butter, then you probably wouldn't pray for the sandwich – you'd just make it and eat it. But if you are hungry and poor, that same sandwich might represent your fondest desire; a prayer for food may indeed be answered by a passerby carrying a sandwich. Call this chance if you want; but it is truly more like a "dance" – a carefully choreographed and orchestrated process we can either practice and learn to use gracefully, or continue to stumble and fumble with.

If you want to take a more active role in creating and controlling the circumstances of your life, you need to learn how the mind works – and how prayer works. Because when you understand the nature of your existence in this mental universe, you will understand that all things are indeed possible for you – and for anyone who has found the secret that unlocks the unlimited power of the mind. Prayer is simply a word I use to represent the key to that door. If you don't think prayer works, you have simply been misinformed or misguided; and if prayer doesn't seem to work for you, you simply haven't been properly instructed on the use of the mind.

Don't feel bad about this; it isn't your fault. It isn't anyone's fault. But you can learn something from this book that will change you forever and give you the power to turn your fondest thoughts into reality. This is not a book about religion. The "religious" quotes and teachings found within these pages are not unique to any one religion; they are WISDOM teachings common to all religions and all people with minds. Compare the words of the great religious teachers to the words of some of the great business and scientific minds of our own time. You'll see the common thread of wisdom throughout: "Your life unfolds for you according to your thoughts."

This book will teach you how, and why, to think more effectively in order to create more of what you want and less of what you don't want in your experience. This book will teach you the "Secret" formula for prayer, or any form of success you seek. You are ready, or you would not be holding this book. This book is for everyone; the wisdom contained in these pages will help you find the answer to life's great questions and the solution to your problems. Best of all, you will learn to find these answers within yourself – from whence all wisdom emerges.

You may need to read this book at least twice – as is the case with any information that appears to be new, or different. In fact, each time you read this book you will find a different message. Read this book with an open mind and you will be greatly rewarded; you will see a great truth that has the power to set you – and all men – free forever. That power is the power of thinking for yourself in such a way as to become a creator in your own life experience. This is a big task; but who else would you have do this for you? The time is now; the choice is yours. You already have the words in your hands; now read them and use them. You will be glad you did.

This book brings together truths and wisdom from many cultures, religions, sciences, and other disciplines or philosophies, to help you understand how to better wield the power of your own thoughts and desires – your power from within. This book provides you with the key to opening the door between you and your hopes and dreams, wishes and prayers. You now have the information you need to unlock this innate gift many call "the Secret." You now have the key to unlocking the power of prayer.

Table of Contents

Preface

by Pete Koerner

s a child, I used to pray before I went to bed at night. I remember thinking that I was basically saying a poem to God in hopes that He would like me and not kill me while I was sleeping. My prayer was always:

> **"Now I lay me down to sleep;**
> **I pray the Lord my soul to keep.**
> **If I die before I wake,**
> **I pray the Lord my soul to take."**

Then, of course, came the obligatory mailing list; …and God bless Mommy, and Daddy, and so on, and so forth… I really didn't have much of an understanding of what I was doing, but I knew I was supposed to be doing it. I don't remember how I learned that particular prayer, but it was the only one I knew and the only one I ever said.

At some point, as I got older, I just stopped praying. I don't remember exactly when, but it was probably about the time I became a teenager. I think I must have been too lazy to continue a practice that didn't seem to really net any results. I didn't know how to pray effectively, so the only real point in continuing would have been in hopes that I might win some kind of "prayer lottery" and one of my really important prayers would finally be answered.

Of course, even as a child, I realized that unless prayer *did* something tangible, the only other reason to continue the practice would have been for fear of the consequences I would surely reap when God realized I wasn't praying on a regular basis. Even then, I reasoned, if God didn't have the time to answer any of my prayers so far, He probably didn't have the time to censure a child over such a minor transgression.

I was coming from the "Jesus loves me, this I know…" school of thought, as so many children do. I understood a parental God who might be too busy to answer prayers, but I knew that He loved me and I wasn't in jeopardy simply because I stopped bugging Him by constantly asking for things. I didn't understand, at that time, that I was the one missing out. I didn't realize that not asking was a sure way to not receive. Who knows what might have happened in my life if I had truly understood the power of effective prayer at such an early age?

Praying effectively can change your life. It is only our simple programming which inhibits our ability to formulate effective methods of prayer. The manner in which you understand, and talk with, your subconscious mind is a critical factor in effective prayer. If you do not understand how the mind operates, you don't understand the mechanism with which you pray. This is a simple fact; and there are many reasons why this is so.

My goal is to help others achieve a level of awareness which took me years of diligent searching, and lots of help, to acquire. My goal is to share some very simple and basic principles which will help you unlock the power of your subconscious mind to achieve truly effective prayer. Knowledge is power; and the key to unlocking this power is at your fingertips.

As you read, try to open your mind and suspend any disbelief you might have. You can pick it back up when you have finished, if you would like; but approaching prayer action with any degree of disbelief will alter, or render useless, any prayer you might offer. If your prayers are not being answered regularly and reliably, you may already be experiencing this phenomenon ("According to your beliefs it is done unto you…").

Going into prayer with an open mind, and a heart full of belief, will go a long way toward allowing yourself to create any life you desire. It took me a long time to figure this out and then understand it. I know I am not alone; and I believe that each of us has a responsibility to share our experiences with each other when we think it might help. This book is my attempt to share some of what I have seen, and learned, during a very religious upbringing and a subsequent deep spiritual search which is still underway.

When I only knew one set of stories, I could immediately see the differences in any other story I was presented with. But, when I learned other sets of stories, I began to see the similarities between the different stories rather than just the differences. The differences between one set of cultural beliefs and any other are incidental to the cultures; the similarities between all beliefs are elemental to the Universe.

All men are searching for something which they hope will either stop things from getting worse, or make things better. This search is an experience in lifelong learning and as such will never end. There are many treasures, however, to be discovered along the way. The true, creative power of prayer, or thought, is simply one of those treasures.

Teachings from many traditions are used in this book to highlight a longstanding, Universal awareness of the power and nature of thought. This book is intended to inspire and enlighten; it is intended to make you think about thinking. My hope is that you will benefit from this work in every possible way; this is my prayer for you.

*Namasté

*The word **Namasté** can be used as a greeting or farewell, much like the word "Aloha." I understand **Namasté** to mean, "The Divine spark in me recognizes, honors, and salutes that same spark in you."

This book is not a book about religion; it is a book about the Mind and how it can be used to create new realities – just like the great teachers have always told us could be done.
We will do "these and much greater things…"

"As a man thinketh, so it is done unto him."

What are you using your mind to create?

Introduction

here is a great power which lies within each of us. Throughout history, great spiritual leaders, teachers, and healers have been well aware of such power and have gone to great lengths to share the knowledge of this power with mankind. While many of these individuals were killed for their beliefs and teachings, their messages were nonetheless true and enduring.

Despite different religious interpretations of these messages, as well as the obvious problems with translating ideas and concepts from one language to another, close scrutiny of most spiritual teachings reveals a common thread of truth throughout. That truth is that we are much more than we think we are and we are capable of things which most of us can hardly imagine. Even more profound is the fact that such astonishing power is our birthright – our inheritance. We arrive here equipped and fully loaded with miraculous capabilities.

An intriguing point within all of this is the fact that we each possess these powers whether we choose to use them, or not. Also interesting is the fact that you do not have to subscribe to any particular set of beliefs, religious or otherwise, in order to claim your inheritance. Jesus told us that "God sends rain upon the just and unjust alike." No man can *give* you these powers, nor can any man *take* these powers from you – whether he agrees with your beliefs or not. We are bestowed with this power at birth; there is no club or organization to join in order to receive this power, nor can you be denied use of this power for any reason or because you violated some man-made code.

When the Bible, for instance, speaks of belief, it is speaking of belief in this power and in this process – belief in our selves and the capabilities and powers we are bestowed with – and not of belief in a particular religious rite or concept. This is why a single book can be used by so many radically different groups, and individuals, to explain or justify so many divergent viewpoints, judgments, and behaviors. The potential for the truth to show through, and transcend political and religious belief systems, is a frightening proposition for those who would seek to control others. It doesn't matter what you believe in; belief is the true power to make things happen – and anyone can wield it.

It is only natural that after thousands of years of enculturation, and of having those in positions of power directing us as to what to believe, and how to proceed from day-to-day, that we would have lost sight of the truth of this power. The truth is that all men truly are equals and have equal access to this unlimited power. Some use this power to do evil, some use it for good, others simply don't use it at all (though it is constantly at work), and still others will try and take control of this power by convincing the weak or ignorant that they are to surrender theirs.

The only difference between a powerful man and a weak man is not in the man, but in the man's awareness of, and ability to use, this power we are each born with. If a king were afraid of losing his kingdom, it stands to reason that he wouldn't want everyone to know their true nature and power. How could control be maintained then? It is the greed and fear of man which threatens to rob us of our inheritance. Rulers fear a loss of their illusion of control; while the rest of us fear death at the hands of tyrannical rulers.

We have been trained to allow and accept this type of system, whether by giving control of our health to a medical establishment and pharmaceutical companies, by giving control of our liberty to the government, by giving control of our intellects to an educational system which no one is satisfied with, by giving control of our spiritual lives to a particular church or individual, or by giving control of our minds to various forms of media and other entertainment.

But whose teachings are we following, anyway? Did you ever stop to think about the extent to which any, or all, of these statements may be true for you? Honestly, if you have thought about it, what have you done about it? Are you really content with having other people – each of them already having lives of their own to live – direct you as to how to live yours? It might not have occurred to you, but you really do have choices about your health and what kind of life you live.

Knowing this, some people are still willing to give up control of their lives to anyone they can pay to take it from them – be it a doctor, clergyman, politician, lawyer, or whoever. A life of fulfillment really can be yours if you simply ask for it and let it happen. You really do possess this kind of power; we all do. What we need are teachers, like Jesus, to show us how to use our gifts – not men who would tell us when to use our gifts, or what we can and can not use our power for. These men often cite "the common good" as the reason we should follow their judgment instead of our own. The common good, however, is really only good for those making the rules; and they certainly don't lead by example.

Christians, for instance, believe they are being "good Christians" if they go to church, pray, tithe, avoid using profanity, and abide by other codified behavioral edicts. I am using Christianity in this case because that is how I was raised. This scenario applies to any religious person, of any race, color, or creed, with perhaps only small modifications to the rituals or beliefs practiced. The *process* of learning beliefs, however, remains the same for all; and everyone believes what they believe.

Unfortunately, there are times when some of these religious beliefs lead us to judge others simply because they have a different idea about life. Trust me; if you find another person's belief to be strange, or even offensive, there is a good chance that they find yours equally unfamiliar. Keep in mind that a belief is simply that – a belief. Each person has their own beliefs and no real understanding of the beliefs another may hold in their heart. They may think they have some basic agreement as to the general characteristics of a certain thing, but how can you know what someone else really thinks and feels?

True knowing does not come from any book, but from the heart. If a belief is the tool you use to draw lines in the sand in order to set yourself apart from the rest of God's creation, you might want to consider why you would want to do such a thing. And, you might also want to reflect and seriously evaluate what you believe, where you learned it, who told you to believe this way, why someone might want you to think like this, and how this belief is actually working in your life.

Believe me when I say that this belief is definitely working in your life – all beliefs do. If, however, a belief causes separation, in any way, it is probably not working the way you expect it to. If you believe, for instance, that "in God, all things are possible," then you will need a pretty small definition of *ALL* if you wish to exclude certain possibilities – like the possibility that you may be wrong about the whole thing, for instance. Who knows? And if you are in the habit of qualifying those things which may or may not be possible in the eyes, or kingdom, of God, you are a braver soul than I.

It never fails to amuse me when I hear declarations such as, "That's not possible!" or people engaging in telling others what God means by, or feels about, a certain thing. For example, to isolate something as being impossible, you must have an awareness of all things that are, in fact, possible so that you can check the list and see if this presumably impossible item is there. The only such reference that I am aware of would be biblical: "In God, all things are possible..." What thing is not on this list? And what man knows the mind of God?

Many people have glimpsed the reality of our inner power. My true purpose here is to awaken minds and souls to this great power within. I have seen it. I personally use it. It absolutely works. Opening ourselves to new learning, however, requires the awareness that there is much we do not know, and a desire to find information that might improve our situation. New learning is the key to evolution – spiritual and otherwise. Televisions and toaster ovens come with owner's manuals, but the machine which imagined, designed, built, and flew the space shuttle – the human mind – came with no such instructions. We have tremendous capabilities but we must learn how to use them if we are to benefit from them. This book represents a step in that direction.

Prayer is the key to unlocking the power within each of us. Everyone prays, in one way or another, because everyone thinks. Some part of each of us believes that we can simply ask for what we need and it will be given unto us. If we could simply unite that part of us with the rest of us, we might then be able to find more effective means of prayer. I am not simply suggesting that we will find more elaborate poems and praises, but prayer techniques that actually bring about definitive and rapid results or answers.

This power within us is not imaginary, nor is it unreliable like a car that may or may not start when it is cold outside. This power is always there and is only limited by the amount of energy that you put into it and the amount of belief you possess. I am indeed saying that if you truly believe, and truly understand the mechanism with which you pray, you will better understand the entire process of prayers, and the manifestation of the answers to those prayers. You will also find that you are praying more effectively, realizing tangible results much more quickly and profoundly than ever before, and seeing the miracles of God everywhere you turn. Prayer works in a very real sense.

Read the following pages with an open mind and an open heart. The information here may be new or perhaps only arranged differently than you are accustomed to, but it is certainly not harmful. If you find yourself doubting, or afraid of anything you read, consider what benefits doubt and fear bring you, and compare those with the abundance brought forth with belief, faith, and trust. You don't have to believe anything you don't want to; and you shouldn't – that's the point of this book. But you should start thinking about what you believe and why you believe it.

There is nothing I can do about the doubt and fears of another, apart from warning them of the lack which will surely follow. I can, however, share inspiration and insight others have shared with me. The things presented here are not presented as one truth that is intended to supersede any other truth, but simply offered as one way of looking at some things we have long looked at in many other ways – some of which bore fruit while others did not. Life is a process and I can attest to the fact that this process bears fruit when approached faithfully. Trust in the process and your faith will sustain you.

What do we really know?

We each live within a comfort zone of beliefs and knowledge we have been given thus far by people in our lives. If you're not creating a life you love with the recipe you've been given, you may need ingredients no one told you about yet. Did you think you've already learned it all? Those ingredients exist; but you have to look outside that very small comfort zone of "What I Know" in order to find them. The answers to your questions, and the solutions to your problems, are *not* inside your comfort zone.

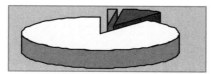

- □ What you "Know," or Believe
- ■ What you know you Don't Know
- □ What you don't know that you don't know

---

*"Belief consists in accepting the affirmations of the soul;
unbelief, in denying them."*

— Ralph Waldo Emerson

Chapter One

Why Pray?

L ike everything else in this existence, prayer can be used effectively or ineffectively. Prayer is a part of our existence, just like riding a bus to school is part of many young children's existence. But just because it is part of our reality doesn't mean that we won't miss the bus. In fact, many people don't pray simply because they don't have time, while others don't pray because they don't believe it will do any good. This is like not going to the bus stop at all just in case the bus doesn't come.

Still there are many more that do pray, but do so in a constant state of mild frustration because, if their prayers are being answered, they aren't able to see it. Unfortunately, these people were simply told to go to the wrong bus stop. If your prayers aren't being answered in a way that you can see, there is a reason and we can find it, and correct it, so you will be able to reclaim your birthright and make use of one of the tremendous powers at your disposal. You will be able to get the answers and the help you need, as well as manifest the life you always wanted. You will be able to do all of this with effective prayer.

Think for a moment about when and why people typically pray. They either pray before bedtime, before meals, during church, at funerals, or in other ceremonial or ritualistic expressions of gratitude, recognition of, or obedience to, a Higher Power. There are also those times when we really want something, or are afraid of the possible outcome of a particular situation. So for the most part, we pray for pretty simple reasons – fear and desire. We will see that fear is not only the wrong reason to pray, but it may be the reason why most prayers seem to go unanswered.

You see, fear comes from thinking, which we do in our heads; and our truest desires, like love, come from our heart, which is where we derive the true power behind any effective prayer. A desire to change your experience is the beginning of an effective prayer. Face it, you wouldn't pray if there wasn't something to ask for – even if you are just praying because you think it is something you are supposed to be doing. The only difference is that if you ask for these things you ask in prayer, and you do it *sincerely* and *believing* that it is so, you will receive these things. If you don't believe that, then why pray in the first place?

Even if you are praying out of fear of judgment, ask yourself what you think the realistic outcome of your prayers will most likely be. Ask yourself what you really think will happen when you pray. It is unfortunate, but the various systems that were built by us and for us aren't really always for us – even belief systems and other systems and methods of thinking. Ironically, those who most often encourage prayer frequently do so in ways that actually inhibit the realization of those prayers. No one else can tell you what is best for you – they can only tell you what they think is best for you (and them) according to their own personal beliefs and agendas.

There is an effective way to pray, and if you use it, you will no longer be dependent on others to tell you how or what to think. You will have "access to all knowledge" and the answers to all questions. Also, if you use effective prayer techniques, you will no longer be dependent on others for your survival, or enrichment. So, why pray? Well, to get what you want out of this existence would be one good reason. To see yourself for what you truly are and to experience God without having to jump through a world of hoops held by other people with no more right to live freely and fully than you have. You are a powerful creation of God; and prayer can unlock your powers.

You are not simply a ship adrift in this world. You emerged into this existence through and with the power of creation. If you went to a fast-food drive-in and ordered a hamburger and soft-drink, you may not have cooked the food or poured the drink, but you are the creator of that moment, nonetheless. It was your desire and thoughts which set in motion the events that would ultimately see your desire fulfilled.

It is understandable that so many people simply write this off, along with so many miracles of manifestation, because they don't understand and haven't been shown the significance of such acts. The fact that you can become aware of a desire and then experience the

14

fulfillment of that desire through simply thinking about it and doing what comes naturally, is an important piece of information in unlocking the power of prayer.

If you begin to look closely at such events in your life, as well as in the lives of those around you, you will see a pattern emerge. You will see that all of these things, no matter how simple or insignificant any of these things may seem, happen through the same process, follow the same pattern, and utilize the same principle and mechanism. Manifestation is manifestation; whether you want a cheeseburger, vibrant health, or a new job, this is your gift. Why would you not use such a thing to your benefit, or to improve or enhance your experience here?

Obviously, the answer is because you do not know, don't believe, or don't care how to use this power effectively, or at all; so you simply don't. None of these reasons are your fault. We only know those things we are told, or experience in some way, and we only understand to the extent we are taught. As we will discuss further, the teacher and healer Jesus was here for that very reason – to teach us and help us understand our true nature and power.

Once we have the awareness that there are things we do not know, which could make our lives better if we knew them, it is our responsibility to find those things and learn what we can about them – assuming we were taught how to learn new things. If you do not pursue better, fuller, healthier, and happier living, you should be asking yourself why you are not and what is so much more important to you. What is it about your current situation that you would choose to cling to?

The nature of the universe is change; trust me when I tell you that you are definitely experiencing change. You may not, however, be experiencing forward progress in your life. If you seem to be stuck in one place, or at one level of your life, there is a reason for this and you will probably be well aware of it by the time you have finished reading this book. It is natural to want to claim your inheritance and use it effectively. Don't let some petty fear or judgment keep you from experiencing the life of fulfillment that you deserve, and probably desire at some level. This is your time; and there is a way for you to get the most out of it – to realize any dream or desire.

Whether you believe in God, or not, and whether you believe in Jesus, or the Bible, or whatever, there is absolutely no reason to not try something that is free, easy, and takes only minutes, when it could save your life, or influence it in a positive direction instead of in a negative way.

If you only had to take a few minutes and try some simple techniques which have been documented for thousands of years as having amazing potential, in order to achieve any desire you could possibly imagine, wouldn't you want to know about that? Wouldn't you want someone to give you that super-power, if they could? Well, you already have it. No one can take it from you, but they can program you to forget how to access it; and this is exactly what culture does via mass consciousness. You can't keep pieces in a machine if the pieces are all aware that they have the same power as the machine – especially if the pieces don't like the way the machine works!

You have as much power as anyone, or anything; you need only realize this and unlock your hidden power. There are no special abilities or requirements one must possess before accessing this power, for "He maketh his sun rise on the evil and the good." One need only accept their birthright; it is earned at birth and learned through use. There is no such thing as not being good enough, or not being worthy. We are all creators; and this is our power.

When I refer to these methods, or techniques, I am not simply referring to prayer, or meditation, or affirmations; I am addressing effective ways of thinking. Regardless of what label you place on thought, it is still thought. If you believe prayers can be answered, then you believe that there is something that responds to thoughts.

This process isn't limited to thoughts that begin with, "Dear God," and end with, "Amen." There is a process, and there is a mechanism, so to speak, that you access with your every thought. It is the mechanism through which prayers are answered. Call it what you want, but to focus on the name, to the point of being distracted from the true meaning, is folly.

In other words, stop worrying about how other people pray, or talk to God, or whoever they talk to, or whatever they believe, and start thinking about what you believe and what you want in your own experience. Just look at people who are always "nosing around" in other people's affairs; do any of them appear to be truly blissful? The time it takes to judge others is time we could use to think mindfully about what we want. There is only so much time in a day; are you spending it allowing spiteful thoughts and words to become your reality?

16

Praying for three minutes at bedtime doesn't undo an entire day's worth of negativity, but it is a good start. Praying for three minutes at the end of a day of positive thinking and acting, however, is even better. Every moment of thought adds to some future moment; and you have the freedom and ability to choose what thought you will contribute to your future reality. Learn how to use this tremendous power – and then use it. Your whole life will change for the better.

If you are not religious, don't worry; praying doesn't require you to start acting like an evangelist, or a "Bible-thumper," or any of the things that may have turned you away from church. You don't even have to be a Christian or believe in the Bible in order to pray and be heard. I realize that may sound controversial; but Jesus wasn't preaching the Bible – and He wasn't a Christian. The Bible you know didn't exist then; and the people He taught already had a set of their own beliefs and religious texts – the same belief systems Jesus grew up with.

Jesus was teaching techniques for effective thinking and living – new ways of looking at and THINKING about those teachings which were ancient even in the time of Jesus. Jesus was teaching ways to make old teachings produce new fruit – simply by changing the way you think about those teachings. Everything Jesus taught had been taught before, and has been taught since, in many different ways and in many different languages. Some of these teachings made it into the Bible and some did not; but they are *all* still within us.

There are variations of these techniques which are backed by scientific observation, and principles of quantum physics. There are clinicians who do not believe in God, or Jesus, but use hypnosis techniques which basically resemble guided prayer and follow principles that are outlined in the words of Jesus. In other words, if the reason you have avoided finding an effective way to pray is because of the words used, or the religious connotations, or superstition or disbelief, then you are letting the programming others gave you keep you from discovering and unlocking your innate powers. I am telling you that if you learn how to pray effectively, there is nothing you can imagine that will be beyond your grasp.

Throughout this book, I will make reference to the words of Jesus (as found in the King James Version of the Holy Bible), but bear in mind, these are only translations of the words of Jesus. If I see a phrase differently from the way you have traditionally viewed it, this too would represent two different translations of the same words. A translation is simply a re-writing in a way that another will understand in the same way the translator understands.   As such, every translation changes the original word.   Keeping true to the **spirit** of the word, and learning from the context of the word what possibilities exist, will narrow your search for your own truth.

If I read a passage a certain way, therefore, and your response is, "That's not what that means!" ask yourself how you know what anything means.   Then ask yourself if your translation is producing miraculous results in your life. If you are basing your existence on a text, the reading and application of those principles should be true to their words – "Wherefore by their fruits ye shall know them." Scriptures you live by mean one thing to you; if your application of those words bears no fruit, then either the words are wrong, you are reading them wrong, or you are applying them incorrectly, inefficiently, or inconsistently.

Just because you are doing it exactly the way you were told doesn't mean the way you were told is the easiest, or even best, way to achieve your desires. Observe the person who told you what and how to believe and see for yourself how their beliefs are working for them before you decide whether you want to bring such things into your own life. Being open to a new approach to an old question is essential to growth of all kinds, but especially spiritual evolution.

I don't just accept things just because the "Bible tells me so," or because some other person told me to believe it. And I am not asking you to accept my beliefs, either. I accept what I feel as true, and what I see working effectively. But it is important to know that there are two aspects to believing – what you believe and how you believe.

When focus is placed on verifying historical facts and events, the value of those events has been lost. It isn't important to know when, why, and how Jesus, or any other religious icon, came to be; what's important; is what He said while He was here. Does it matter if you get His birthday right but never figure out what He meant by "judge not," or "As a man thinketh…?"

The truth of practical teachings, or wisdom teachings, can only be known by the fruit they produce. If you have studied the great physician for years, and still suffer, you haven't truly understood. There are many methods, techniques, and rituals throughout the Bible and religious texts from all cultures. They all work when faithfully applied, or they wouldn't be worth remembering. There are many scriptures which I believe hold valuable answers to unlocking our powers, but there are techniques elsewhere available, also.

There is an acupressure technique, for instance, which contains most of the components of the Lord's Prayer; and the methods and settings for saying affirmations, or meditating, are similar to those set forth by Jesus for prayer, or communion with the Creator. There are many new ways to look at traditional texts. Every new version of the Bible offers testament to this fact; and there have been hundreds.

I am not challenging tradition or religion; I am simply opening eyes and minds to the meaning of "all things, in God, are possible." If God is limited in your life, then you did it, or allowed others to teach you how to do it. If your life is not abundant, your thinking has been limited somehow – by someone. You can let go of those ideas which are keeping you from experiencing fulfillment; you can find your inner power. It is always there, waiting for you to allow it into your life.

You don't have to believe in anything in particular, nor do you have to subscribe to any particular religious sect; the powers you have were with us long before we created religions. We need only believe that we are worthy of any gift God would choose to give us – including the power of creation. What better way to show your appreciation for such a wonderful gift than to use it?

Why pray? Why not pray? Call it whatever you want to call it, but your life is shaped by your thoughts; and when you put time and energy into shaping your thoughts, it is reflected in your life. This is a plain and simple fact. Mindful thinking and living will produce positive results in your life; meditation will produce results, prayer will produce results, and so will many other practices. If it works, is it not of benefit? If it is, was it not created in the same manner which you were created? If all things are possible, why not open up your heart and mind to the infinite possibilities your belief will bring? You have free will; you have choice. You also have a life to live and, believe it or not, you can live it any way you'd like.

But be aware; if you resist new learning for the sake of living your life "the way you want" (which often translates to: "the way I'm used to living…"), you are not living life to the fullest, and are therefore not *really* living life the way you want. You are living life the way you are currently programmed to live it – complete with limitations and beliefs about what is not possible in a universe of infinite possibility. You are, of course, one of **those** (of which there is only one); and you will always do, of course, that which one of **those** always does.   Ponder that for a moment.

You are unique; you are the only one who has walked your path, and experienced your life. There have been others along the way, but you came here alone, and will leave here alone. You are the only one who has walked your path and, as such, are uniquely qualified to live your life. No one else knows what a person who was born to your parents on your birthday, who lived your life and has your knowledge and experience, and is in your current situation, will do next. There is only one of each of these types of creatures; and each one will always do what that exact one of those would always do in that exact situation. How could any of us presume to judge another?

There are multitudes of ancient writings warning against passing judgment. There are definite negative affects which are brought about by passing judgment. Scriptures that warn us to "Judge not," or to "do unto others," are intended to help us avoid activities which will weaken us, shorten our lives, or hamper our ability to effect changes in our life through this very natural mechanism of prayer. These are exhortations for us to strive for the best we can achieve in life – to be the best possible person we can be and to achieve the best possible existence.

Prayer, or mindful, directed thought, is the key to achieving these things. So, why pray? Why not pray!? It is your life and it is your choice; build the life you want in your mind, and then live it in your reality. The only limitations are those in your mind.

"We're all speaking the same *different* language."

We may all have a unique story to tell; but we all have a story. We all want to love and be loved; though some were not taught, or cannot remember how. Each child loves its mother; and every mother loves her child. We all believe in different things; but we all believe what we believe. We all came from somewhere; yet none of us knows where that is. None of us likes pain; but some seem to enjoy suffering. And we all want whatever we want – even if that is nothing.

If we stop and think, we might realize that we are all experiencing the same things in different ways; and we are saying the same things in different languages. We are all thinking, and seeking our desires. Some understand how to believe in their dreams (like the Wright Brothers, etc…); and some do not. Perhaps we should stop arguing over which language and stories are the "right" ones and start learning about who we are and how to think of, and believe in, those things we truly desire or wish to experience.

Chapter One Key Points and Afterthoughts

- We live in a mental Universe where thoughts are things; and all prayers are answered in one way or another.

- Your thoughts determine your experience; if your thoughts are chaotic, your life will be chaotic; while peaceful thoughts create a peaceful life.

- Likewise, if your life is chaotic, stressful, or miserable, then you know the thoughts you are having are creating these experiences – and you can change the thoughts you are thinking in order for them to be more in alignment with what you want.

- All religions deal with the human mind and thought. All religious teachings give advice on how to think in order to create certain conditions – ideally a life you love.

- Prayer is simply thought concentrated on a specific desire; we are always thinking, but we are not always specific with our thought – which is why our lives are scattered and unfocused.

- There are many things you can do with your mind, effective prayer is only one of them; and it requires a concentrated awareness of the thoughts (prayers) in your mind.

- The more you learn about your mind, the better you will be able to operate it. It is the mind with which you pray and create your future; if you know how to use it better, it is only reasonable that you could do better things for yourself, or be more effective at the things you currently do with your mind.

- Fear, negative emotions, stress, and other forms of resistance, impede the flow of information through your body and mind; these things impede the sending and receiving of thought energy – or prayer.

- If your mind is not functioning properly, or you haven't been properly trained in its use, it simply will not produce the effects you are hoping for.

- Everyone has thoughts, and always has; therefore, everyone prays. Thinking/praying preceded all religions; and religions were developed through the use of thought and prayer. Religions were also developed as ways of teaching large groups of people about the nature of thought, and the nature of life and the Universe in which we live. All of this requires constant thought in order to extract true meaning and value from ancient writings and teachings. Prayer (thought) is automatic and continuous; effective prayer (effective thinking) is a learned skill.

"A mind is a terrible thing to waste."
— UNCF campaign slogan

"To accomplish great things, we must not only act, but also dream; we must not only plan, but also believe."
— Anatole France

Chapter Two

The Courage to Rise Above

any great minds of our time, as well as those from ancient times and since, have pondered the questions of our existence. Where do we come from, where we are going, and why are we here, are but a few of the unanswerable questions our great thinkers have tangled with over the millennia. The common consensus is that we just don't know.

We have had several tremendous insights as to our basic nature and how things appear to unfold before us, but anything more is merely speculation. The one thing which seems to be obvious, however, is that whatever we are here to do – and that is different for each of us – we are meant to learn from it, and transcend.

Transcendence is simply rising above one's current situation, position, circumstances, etc. This drive to transcend is an essential part of us and can be seen in each of us in many forms, or manifestations. We have the ability to learn from our experience, and improve. In life, just as in school, or any other learning environment, the ultimate outcome would be one of learning all that was necessary or available from a particular experience, or level of existence, and moving on.

We do not know where we are going, but we can be assured that we are indeed going. Furthermore, history is heaving with warnings of those who, not knowing of their history, have doomed themselves to repeat it. Perhaps the word "doomed" is a bit dramatic, but the point remains. After you leave this place, if you have learned nothing of humanity, you will not have accomplished much for having been here. So, for those who believe in reincarnation, you may very well have to spend another tour of duty here learning your lessons that were neglected the first time around – just as a school child in the same circumstances would perhaps be required to repeat a grade in school.

Whether you believe in reincarnation, or not, we still have no shortage of examples where we have ignored lessons of the past, only to repeat painful experiences. This pattern repeats itself continuously throughout our history, and at all levels of existence. For those whose journey doesn't include a high degree of awareness of the human condition, the pattern will certainly continue into the future.

Transcending, in this case, involves an open-minded search for the truth; for it is only in uncovering the truth of our past, and of our basic nature, that we can find the power to rise above past "mistakes" and onto the next step in our spiritual evolution. I use quotations around the word "mistakes" simply because our standards have become so out-of-sync with reality that we have become comfortable labeling experiences as successes or failures, good choices or bad choices, correct responses or mistakes, and so on, rather than recognizing that each outcome leads us to the next experience regardless of how we choose to judge the outcome. Is a mistake truly a mistake when it is simply one step, maybe even the critical step, on the road to wherever you currently are? Mistakes, as we so often label them, are often the critical events which result in a change of direction, or focus.

Babies, for instance, fall down many times before walking, and have their way with our language for months before we are able to understand them. These events, however, are simply viewed as a natural part of the learning process and not as mistakes, or failures. The child will eventually transcend his life of crawling around at our feet and take his place among us; perhaps one day raising children of his own.

This transcendence is in our nature – this is our purpose, goal, and reason for being. We record information from each experience and create the next experience from that – gradually changing the landscape of trial and error with our palette of experience, knowledge, and possibilities, and our paintbrush of free will. There are no limits placed on our success or creative powers other than those which are self-imposed. We are powerful beings with unlimited potential. We arrived here with this potential for creation and transcendence – it is our inheritance; a gift from our creator.

It is quite easy to see children move from one step to the next. Over a relatively short period of time in a child's life, we may observe the child give up a life of crawling for a life of walking. In a similarly brief period of time, this same child can learn to communicate quite effectively with language – perhaps even multiple languages. Over the next few years, skills are learned that make the life of a child more stimulating. These things happen naturally. Unless an adult is operating from a place of extreme dysfunction, and intentionally harms the child, most of these early stages of life unfold naturally over the course of early childhood.

The word *dysfunction* is not used in this case to judge anyone as a failure, or as a bad person, but to account for those who operate from a dramatically divergent view point than most of their culture or society. In some cases, these individuals are simply expressing a certain level of genius by breaking societal molds of enculturation to allow for the potential of unfettered spiritual growth in their child. In other words, some of these parents that "don't raise their children the *right* way," according to social norms and mores, may actually be giving their offspring a tremendous advantage on the journey to fulfillment.

These aren't the parents I am referring to, however. In this case, I am referring to those parents who were either not given the proper tools with which to raise their children, or more precisely, have had those tools largely disabled by events within their own lives and culture.

For instance, a society of violence begets violent children; who in turn become violent parents unable to freely dispense love, especially in the direction of the responsibility which they see as the source of their problems, or fears, in life – their child. These children of violence, having no early model for unconditional love or transcendental behavior of any type, will most likely live a life where "getting-by" is not only good enough, but most likely the only choice that any of them are aware of having a "realistic" hope of achieving.

Added to this is the programming of futility and hopelessness which often permeates the environment these children are raised in. Besides having parents who act as models of anger, frustration, depression, or fear, these children are often recipients of verbal programming which works at a deep level and, lacking any therapeutic intervention (from any source), will operate as subconscious programming – forever limiting the experience of the child.

Frustrated parents at this stage can often be heard saying hurtful things to their children. "You'll never amount to anything; I wish you were never born!" is an example of the kind of hypnotic suggestion often passed down from a fearful, angry parent to an innocent child. It can be shocking to many of us when we hear such verbal abuse in public settings, like the grocery store, or at the park. But we must realize that the problem is not one of a lack of a censoring mechanism; but that these individuals most likely have only one parenting model to reference and they do not think they are doing anything wrong, or even unusual.

The purpose of this writing is not to provide an in-depth exploration of the mechanisms I am referring to here, but simply to highlight the tremendous interplay of every moment of each person's existence in determining not only who we believe we are, but also how difficult it might be to claim our inheritance of power. The fear and anger, passed down from one generation to the next, serves to perpetuate a culture of submission, whether intended by the parents or not.

As mentioned before, most people are unaware of the part they, and their various behaviors, play in the continued enculturation of a population of *survivors*. Surviving is only a part of life. Survival is the most important goal of humanity, but is hardly fulfilling in and of itself. Most of our lives are not spent in the active pursuit of survival; though every aspect of our life is completely dependent on our survival. There is an underlying part of all of us which maintains our survival even when we are unconscious. In the event of an emergency, such as a fire, survival may become an active, conscious, exercise, but only for a short time. It would be impossible for a human to indefinitely maintain an active struggle against a lethal, and unyielding, foe. Ultimately, there will be an outcome on which the next events of life will be constructed.

Our technology has "tamed" our immediate environment so most of our time can be spent in the pursuit of happiness instead of running and hiding from predators, or fighting with enemies until one or the other is terminated. The latter are fear based activities that exist to ensure the survival of the species, and still make up a large part of what happens on this planet. With the exception of scattered pockets of people, as well as individuals spread throughout society, our culture has largely transcended this level of survival; although the vast majority of individuals on the planet occupy the very lowest level of this schema.

To transcend this life requires a certain power (which all humans possess), and an awareness of that power. The awareness is that which leads to the exploration of such powers and any possible limitations of these powers. Unfortunately for most, those who have power have tended, throughout history, to act as if they alone were entitled to this power. Insomuch as this power is often misused to control the spiritual growth of others, it can be a dangerous thing to all of humanity, while simultaneously providing all of humanity with the spark of life that keeps us going. Understanding the nature of this power reveals the nature of our environment – and vice versa.

Jesus spoke of our "divine inheritance" as being one of, "the kingdom, the power, and the glory of God." This, He told us, is our inheritance – our birthright. He also spoke of those who sought to build their own, personal kingdoms here on earth, invariably, at the expense of others. This group of individuals seeks to profit from the labors of others, and place personal gain and power as priority number one in order to insulate themselves from the fear that comes with such positions. Jesus spoke of this "power" as being in all of us, however, and what we do with it – if anything at all – is a matter of free will.

Those who choose to misuse this power, as well as those who simply aren't aware of the dynamics of such power, often receive some degree of financial, or "earthly" success; meaning that these particular behavior patterns are designed to elicit a materialistic benefit from our environment – the acquisition of riches and worldly (of the earth) goods. This, Jesus often reminded us, was to be their reward. Just as those who adorn themselves in those earthly possessions and take their relationship with God out into the public to be "seen of men" have their reward – they are indeed seen of men. Is this, however, the reward we are seeking?

And if we have inherited the kingdom of God, the omnipotent, omniscient, and omnipresent, then this would include all things – not just the earthly goods so often sought after with blind abandon. An inheritance is a gift, or a birthright; not a reward to be worked for or earned. "Verily I say unto thee, they shall have their reward" is a lamentation for those who have abandoned true power for a proverbial quest for gold or worldly tokens which have only temporal existence and value.

The multitudes to whom these messages were delivered either failed to understand, or remained (as do their descendents) too afraid of those who are aware of, and proficient with, their own power, to lay claim to any sort of equality – especially one based on the possession of a largely unknown power. These fearful masses usually simply turn themselves, and their inheritance, over to the first authority that comes along and assumes control. Any resistance will be met with such violence as to discourage further uprisings. The meek, then, become subjugated by the forceful – a fate sealed by their own paralyzing fear.

The surrender of power typically results in a life of drudgery, or the Life of Survival, examined by George Jaidar in his book, *The Soul: an owners' manual.*

This life can be transcended, however, which is a fact that has not gone unnoticed by those who have assumed dominion over their fellow men. The promise of such transcendence through "hard work and long hours" is a false one that drives this machine of culture and keeps those who would, and often do, use force against us firmly in control. The relegation to a life of drudgery, striving to acquire more, simply to regain what you never really lost, is yet another example of losing sight of the transcendent nature of *"who you really are,"* and settling for a worldly inheritance. The meek shall indeed inherit the **earth**. The **kingdom**, however, is a much different place and it is not so easy to access.

Our culture, like most cultures, is one of fear and control. The transcendence of fear, the breaking of our bondage, is not a journey to be taken lightly, nor is it a journey to be embarked upon by the meek. The quest for transcendence is largely one of rediscovery – the rediscovery of an inheritance long ago surrendered to authority at the end of a sword.

We are all descended from those who survived to at least child-bearing age. The skills that this long line of descendents had to perfect in order to survive have become our "false inheritance." These survival skills are what humans weave into culture and pass down from generation to generation. Our "true inheritance," or divine inheritance, is one of power and a comforting bond with the Creative Force which connects us with unlimited resources and places all of creation at our fingertips.

This power, unknown to most due to its being replaced with fear and false hope, has been all but lost to this world. From time to time, enlightened ones arrive among us to awaken us to the truth underlying our temporal reality. These bringers of knowledge are often subdued, murdered, or ostracized by not only those of authority, but sometimes even by their own people. Remember, it was Jesus' own people who sent him to his death; the Romans merely performed the ceremony. Neither the legal authorities, the religious authorities, nor the majority of the people, were ready to deal with this revelation of inherited power and equality, so the messenger was quickly dispatched and the message lost or, at least, severely damaged.

According to accounts in the Bible, Jesus knew of this, often spoke of what his fate was to be, and He knowingly faced death at the hands of those who didn't understand, anyway. The courage required for such an undertaking is tremendous. Jesus' deep understanding of whom and what he was, and the subsequent knowledge of the absolute peril faced by a largely unaware population, resulted in the manifestation of behavior that far exceeded mere courage in its power to change the world. It resulted in the display of pure, unconditional and unselfish love for all of humanity.

"Things always happen that you really believe in; and the belief in a thing makes it happen."

— Frank Lloyd Wright

Chapter Two Key Points and Afterthoughts

- There is no way to get through an entire human life without thinking; and there are many things to think, and many ways to think about them. The vast array of human thought reflects the vast array of human experience – and vice versa.

- You have no choice but to pass through this world and this life; and you have no choice but to learn and grow along the way. The extent of that living, learning, and growth are a matter of choice; and choice is limited to what you are aware of.

- Your journey through this life is not unlike a child's journey through school; the more you learn, the more capable you become and the further you advance. As your capabilities increase, so does your responsibility; as responsibility increases, so do potential rewards.

- It is only natural to want more out of life – more health, more happiness, and more prosperity. Moving from one level to the next, however, seems anything but natural; transcendence is sought after, learned, and practiced.

- Transcendence is change; change requires faith and courage, and most of all – incentive. To end suffering is a common motivation for change. Seeking pleasure is another common motivation for change.

- To change is to be something different, or to be somewhere different; different is, by its nature, new and unknown. Most people fear the unknown and so they resist change of any kind.

- Life is a constant learning opportunity. In every situation, we either succeed, or we learn and grow.

- Fear is the enemy of growth, and therefore, the enemy of life. Fear robs the body of the energy it needs in order to continue living and disrupts the reception and transmission of the nerve signals that guide and control our every action. Fear is not really a thing; it is the absence of courage, or love. There is no getting rid of fear; there is only overcoming the misperception of fear. This is easiest done by loving the thing you fear – or facing it courageously. Love and courage always dissolve fear.

Chapter Three

The Power of Prayer

n October, 2002, a friend of ours (who at the time was a senior BodyTalk System™ instructor), Dr. Ernesto Fernandez, introduced Jennifer and I to a book titled, *Messages From Water,* written by Dr. Masaru Emoto. This book contains hundreds of pictures of frozen water crystals; Dr. Emoto was the first to ever be able to photograph water crystals. He did this by freezing water samples, and then photographing the crystals with the aid of a microscope.

Dr. Emoto's work involved exposing the water samples to various words (which were printed on the sides of the containers), pictures, sounds, and even thoughts (prayer), before and/or during the freezing process. The results of this work are so profound that most human minds – including mine – may never be able to fully understand how deep the implications of this work may extend.

Basically, Dr. Emoto observed that water exposed to words or thoughts of love, gratitude, and kindness, would form beautiful crystals when frozen, while words of hate, or discontent, elicited no such response from the freezing water – the water would not crystallize! This phenomenon extended through all levels of Dr. Emoto's work.

For example, beautiful works of art, pictures of saints and angels, and praying to or for the water, also resulted in magnificent crystalline displays. Pictures of death and destruction, killers (such as Adolf Hitler), and the issuance of hateful words in the presence of water, again result in a failure of the water to form crystals. Water placed between speakers playing heavy metal music failed to crystallize, but water that was frozen while "listening" to classical music, such as Mozart or Beethoven, formed some of the most elaborate crystals of all. Interestingly, the name of an evil-doer like Hitler, written on a container, produced similar responses to a picture of that same person.

Furthermore, many of these experiments were conducted with a common, pure water source which was exposed to various stimuli; but some experiments began with polluted water, that would not form crystals, and involved exposing that water to the power of prayer alone. The once-polluted water formed crystals when frozen. Further experiments showed that this polluted water source would form crystals when exposed to the "positive" imprinting mentioned above. The inescapable message from the water in these experiments is that water is in agreement with us as to the value and quality of the concepts it is presented with. Or is it?

Clearly, that we see beauty in the shapes created by water in response to those things that we believe are good, indicates that at some level, our concept of beauty correlates to our concept of good. Further, although we have no way of knowing by what mechanism water seems to "think" with, its actions definitely appear to correspond to our ideas of good and bad. Keep in mind that we are mostly made up of water and water was here long before we were and will remain long after we are removed from this place.

While we are here, however, our spirits carry with them "physical" bodies comprised mainly of water – much like the planet we live on, and every other living thing here. If the water is responding so as to appear to agree with our concepts, how did we manage to supplant water's dominion over this planet so that it is OUR concepts that WATER (which is a very large part of us) must choose whether or not to concur with?

In other words, if water responds to love, or any stimulus, in a particular manner today, it probably always did – even before WE were here to agree with it. It certainly will after we are gone, so which part of this equation seems to be irrelevant? Apparently, that would be *us*. Is it possible that we think the way we do because water thinks the way it does?

Also, it is a fact that we are what we eat. We are comprised of the food we eat, the liquids we drink, and the air we breathe; these are the only "physical" things we put into our bodies. When disassembled and reassembled within us by that innate intelligence which creates and maintains us, these small pieces of the world in which we live (food, etc.)

become living pieces within us – directed in this miraculous transformation by our inborn intelligence.

Knowing that the water you drink will replace water that is currently inside various cells within your body, allowing that water to be released, carrying with it waste products no longer needed inside the body and allowing the cells we are made of to be replenished with fresh, life-giving water, wouldn't it make sense to use the best available replacement fluids – especially when we can create such fluid with the power of prayer alone?

The fact is that if we can change the structure, or consciousness, of water and then integrate it within our own structure, then our own form would thereby benefit from such an addition. The wisdom of the ancients reflects an awareness of this concept with the tradition of praying over, or blessing, our meals prior to eating them; basically thanking the food for what it is about to become – a part of our living bodies.

I was so intrigued by the implications of Dr. Emoto's work, I ordered *Messages From Water, Vols. 1 & 2,* as well as the accompanying video featuring Dr. Emoto (through a translator) presenting an explanation of his work to an audience. A more relevant message, it would seem, is that this work basically demonstrates the power of prayer. This power is a power we each have within us, not one that is waiting for us if we can survive our sins and make it to "heaven." This power is available to us now; it is a gift given to us by our creator.

After Ernesto shared this amazing book with us, I was immediately struck with an idea that such super-charged, "prayer-water" would have to have a rather dramatic influence on all that was exposed to it. I even entertained the thought that Holy Water must have, at one time, been created and used in this manner as a bona fide implement for spiritual cleansing. I mentioned to Ernesto that I would like to perform an experiment where I used several identical groups of plants, each group watered with water "imprinted" with various messages – some positive, some negative – to determine if there was some observable difference in the growth of the plants. Ernesto echoed my curiosity as to the possible implications to agriculture. This project, however, was not really a priority of mine and, though not forgotten, went unaddressed for several months.

"Blessing" your Water

After reading messages from water, Jennifer and I began peeling the labels off the bottled water we drink, and writing messages *to* the water using a permanent marker to write on the plastic bottle. The messages were simply words, such as: *Peace, health, joy, happiness, trust, faith, courage, love, God, prosperity,* and other words which have all been demonstrated to produce a positive effect within the water. These words also represent qualities, or characteristics, we would like to embody; as the water seems to take on a more beautiful shape as it embodies the essence of the messages written on the container. The idea is that we can impart these qualities to the water; and then incorporate these qualities into ourselves as we consume the water with that intention. Try this experiment yourself; I believe you will notice a difference almost immediately.

In August of 2003, I mentioned to my mother, Joyce Ann, during a discussion about the power of prayer, my earlier discussion with Ernesto. My mother is very talented with plants – a fact that I have been aware of as far back as I can recall – and told me that she would try the concept, if not the entire experiment, on her own plants.

A week later, she told me that she couldn't bring herself to feed her plants with "hate," but that she did indeed imprint the water she used for her plants with love and prayer. She excitedly led me to her enclosed patio to show me what had happened with her plants. She said she was amazed at the growth and color change in all of her plants and that her ferns, which apparently had been maintaining a relatively constant size, were huge! She estimated that they had increased in size by about 25-30% and appeared much healthier.

She showed me two other plants that produced long, segmented leaf-structures. These plants, she said, would add a single segment every so often, but that was all. Each one of the plants had not only added new growth, but each existing leaf-structure had added a new segment – every single one!

My mother's experiment was not scientific, but that is hardly the point here. Dr. Emoto's work can and has been verified by many people in a variety of ways. If serving no other purpose, my mother's experiment validated the power of prayer and love, as well as supporting, in at least our minds, Dr. Emoto's work. The implications of her application of this concept, however, are tremendous. The plant that added all the leaf-segments is a variety of cactus – not exactly known for rapid growth. If adding nothing but thoughts of love and gratitude, to the water used for the plants, could increase the growth rate and production of these plants, then what of fruit, or vegetable, bearing plants?

I believe that Dr. Emoto's work, and subsequent applications of his concepts, not only prove the power of prayer, but open many doors to the future that could change the face of the planet. For instance, if you were growing vegetables and, without adding any other nutrients except for prayers of love and gratitude for the water you provided the plants with, you were able to greatly increase the production of those plants, what you have shown is that you could literally feed the world with love.

Blessing your Food

This ancient ritual existed even before recorded history; but ideas about this practice have changed through the years. Some ancients recognized that they were literally consuming a part of God – manifest as bread for their nourishment. There has always been an emphasis, however, on imparting the energy of gratitude, reverence, and love to the food. Based on principles of quantum physics, as well as on the clinical observations of Dr. Emoto and others, there is every reason to believe that you can raise the nutritional value of food by raising the energetic frequency of that food; and that raising the vibration of the food can be done with a thought, or prayer.

The mechanism of creation has always existed. We have planted seeds and harvested crops for ages. This process has not changed that much over the years and the way my mother cultivates plants is largely the way plants have always been grown. Creation seems to operate much like a machine, however, that merely processes thought, or intelligence (not to be confused with intellect, or learning), so that what goes into the machine of creation as an idea emerges in the three dimensional world we seem to live in.

There is no shortage of examples of this process, as all things that have ever happened started with a thought. You, in fact, have never done anything without first thinking it. Keep in mind that creation is not a machine, nor is it something that can be understood, or even explained, in linear terms. We speak of creation in this way to reduce it, for sake of discussion, to terms that we can understand, or at least visualize.

We seem to create things with our hands, our minds, and our voices. I say that we *seem* to create things because it appears that planting a seed makes a tree grow. We can not, however, realistically take credit for a tree growing. Likewise, if we write a beautiful piece of poetry or music, this creation really happens through us. The music, for instance, has always existed in a field of potentiality, we have simply been given the thought and impetus and the music emerges, colored by the palette of our own personal experience.

Playing a piece of music on a piano can be a demonstration of manual, and mental, dexterity if you are reading and playing the music. This ability is trained into a piano player; and, much like a computer, a human has the ability to execute programmed commands such as reading and playing music. Of course, computers are like humans, and not the other way around. We humans designed computers, modeled them after ourselves and the way we think (process information), remember (store processed information), and operate (execute stored programs).

But even when reading and performing music written by someone else, the creator within you is still an active participant; for instance, there must be some inspiration within the player to perform. Even playing the piece from memory is somewhat different than witnessing creation happening through you. There is still the need for an inspiration to begin any movement at all, but the mechanism at work here involves recalling past experience, and reliving it to some extent. In this situation, however, there is the potential for one to become lost in the music and truly experience a continuity of spirit, or a sense of "oneness" that comes from a moment of expanded consciousness. This oneness is the requisite state, often referred to as "the Zone," for manifestation to occur.

By this, I mean to say that when you experience such a state, big things happen. It is in this state that effective prayer takes place — prayers you can literally watch unfold before your eyes. This is the state necessary to transcend all perceived physical limitations to whatever extent your higher self deems necessary to accomplish its goal of manifesting the answers to your prayers; whether it means performing a flawless solo in front of a crowd, or receiving guidance in a spiritual matter, there is no task too big, or small.

Truly creating music, however, involves a completely different process. Though every writer is different, most share an underlying commonality when experiencing the creative process. The music seems to come from somewhere and, through mind and hand, emerges from the piano to be experienced by the hearer. In this case, the creator and the hearer are experiencing through the same body.

In many cases, on hearing the creation, we judge it, apply what we "know" about music to the sounds, rearrange the sounds and the spaces between the sounds (which are equally important to the music), and polish the creation to meet our human standards. We, in effect, take an active role as co-creator. We allow for the creative to flow forth from the oneness we experience as a result of a love for, and belief in, our task at hand, but then our judgment enters into the picture and that critical part of us takes the lion's share of responsibility for the outcome.

This isn't a bad thing; but it is important and useful to realize that different aspects of your essential nature are always engaged in a power-play of sorts, and all of it colors creation. It may even appear at times that this critical factor completely blocks creation; but that state, or belief, is also a manifestation of the creative force channeled through a particularly doubtful aspect of you.

Now, as a product of every thing or event that has ever happened to you – colored by the events of your experience – there is much doubt that you are responsible for even your conscious input to the resulting sounds. Truly these touches are yours; they are a product of you that could have only occurred if you had experienced the exact set of experiences which led you to this point. Each of these experiences is built on the experiences before and, at some point, we were much too young to be steering our own vessel.

In fact, we have each had several years of programming from a number of outside sources before we begin "making our own choices." It is easy to see, in this context, that by the time we start making these decisions for ourselves we have been programmed with a number of cultural parameters (that are not the same for any two people) with which to guide our decision-making process. It is our computer, so to speak; but we aren't the ones who program it. Our culture programs our computer for us in order to insure the continuation of our culture. And before you think about blaming your parents, try to understand that the same thing happened to them in one way or another.

The point is that everything we do colors our perception of creation. There are, as demonstrated by Dr. Emoto, things we can do to influence, or paint our own mark on, creation. The simplest of these things available to us is prayer. Prayer is potentially the most powerful tool we will ever know in this existence. This may sound like religious nonsense, but trust me – it is not.

Doubt in the realistic efficacy of prayer is prevalent these days, for several reasons – one of which is religion itself. Perhaps the most common reason for this disbelief is the simple fact that all of us have had prayers that have gone unanswered. This, in fact, is an errant assumption. But coupled with a belief in a vengeful and arbitrary God, it is easy to imagine that we are the victims of a merciless God – tormenting us because we do not live up to His unrealistically high standards, and arbitrarily dishing out rewards. We are, after all, only human.

This is a primitive way of thinking that has long since lost any practical appeal to all except those who still seek to control and dominate by playing on our primal fears, and our need to find favor in the eyes of God. This need to find favor is so strong, in fact, that our focus is drawn away from God and directed toward those humans who are actually the ones issuing the edicts of religion and society. We fail to realize that we are actually seeking the approval of humans who *say* they speak for a god we can not see or hear. Whose judgment are we actually submitting ourselves to, anyway? Are we to continue to pretend that we are unworthy, so that a few can experience feeling powerful or righteous – or both?

The mixed messages in the Bible, as well as from our religious and political leaders, create a paradox which is virtually inescapable. The turmoil and fear created in the face of such confusion are practically insurmountable obstacles in our quest to reclaim our inheritance. Such distraction all but eliminates our ability to clearly see the truth in any message, or to remain clear enough spiritually to exercise our birthright in a practical, or useful, manner.

Prayer has always been a practical tool; you need only understand how to use it effectively, practically, and safely. Prayer is an inherent power of all humans. Prayer is our bridge between the invisible world and the formed world – between our desires and their manifestation.

Though it appears that religions have rendered prayer all but useless, the fact is that no one can affect the value or effectiveness of prayer. Religions have simply taught us ineffective methods of praying which not only seem to produce less-than-hoped-for results, but also seem to have seriously undermined our ability to truly believe in anything. This has been a grievous problem for all of humanity, for it is the power of belief which unifies the Trinity; and it is the Trinity that is our key to manifestation, or the answering of all of our prayers.

"To succeed, we must first believe that we can."
– Michael Korda

Chapter Three Key Points and Afterthoughts

- Your body is mostly water; and water has been shown to configure itself based on ideas, concepts, thoughts, and other energies directed at it.

- If your thoughts can affect water, and you are mostly water, then what are your thoughts doing to the water you are made of – and you?

- Food also contains water; which should be an adequate basis for blessing food before consuming it. But more to the point, water is just Hydrogen and Oxygen – energy in a specific relationship – and it is the relationship and energy which are affected by thought and other forms of energy.

- We all run on, or operate with, the same power from the same power source. We simply use, or resist, this power in many different ways.

- Though holy water and baptism have become religious practices and symbolic rituals few people truly understand; water has always cleansed us, quenched us, sustained and nourished us, and help us change the shape of our world. Apparently, acknowledging and appreciating this fact can increase the beneficial effects of water.

- We either create ourselves, and our world, with thought and activity, or something created us and our world; and all we create or do is actually done through us by that creative force. In either case, all creation consists of the joining of energetic forces and matter by a power capable of intelligent planning, design, and communication – among an infinite variety of other capabilities.

- When we observe matter, or order, there is an underlying plan, or thought, around which matter is assembled, or order is established.

Chapter Four

Unity, Duality and Trinity

ractically every culture speaks of duality – whether they realize it or not – when speaking of religion, science, philosophy, or any other observation of nature. Duality is the nature of everything we experience; it is a basic characteristic of the physical universe. Good and evil, night and day, hot and cold, and so forth, are common manifestations of duality.

We often speak of duality as the existence or relationship of opposites, but that is not exactly accurate. In fact, such definitions only serve to illuminate the shortcomings of words in describing most concepts. Duality did in fact give us our concept of opposites, but then we defined the word opposite to mean, "in opposition or opposed to, or in conflict with." Of course, each word used to describe opposites also has many definitions which lead us further off course. Night isn't actually in conflict with day, for instance; they coexist and are dependent on each other. Without one, what would we call the other?

Keep in mind as we speak of duality, and the trinity, that we are speaking of concepts which are much deeper than the scope of this writing. These concepts contain many more facets and levels, but are much more manageable in this simplified format. Simplifying life in this way is like summing-up the life of Albert Einstein with the formula: $E = mc^2$.

Einstein's life was much more significant and complex than any of his theories; just as his formula is the simplified representation of a much more complicated concept. The point to remember, throughout, is that everything we speak of can be represented conceptually, and for the sake of clarity we have kept to familiar terms and ideas that can be viewed from many aspects. Duality isn't the deepest way to look at existence, but it is a very effective way to describe apparently oppositional forces in nature.

Duality represents two sides of the same coin, so to speak. You couldn't experience good without knowing of bad, for example, any more than you could spend one side of a penny. Nor could one side of a penny exist without the other side. Duality, it seems, is an absolute requirement for holding together our **very small** concept of a physical universe.

Positive and negative forces, mediated by a neutral force, represent the triune nature of the Universe. The building blocks of our physical world are atoms, which also happen to be a union of a positive force (protons), a negative force (electrons), and a neutral force (neutron). This triune nature is evident throughout creation, from the smallest particles to the concept of time itself.

We speak of gravity (G) as the attraction between two heavenly bodies. We are all heavenly bodies existing in the heaven of perfect creation; it is only our fear and judgment which would have us see ourselves as any less. As heavenly bodies, it is a natural attraction, or gravity, that is the force which exists to pull opposites together; it is the power which holds existence together. If you can see that a *force* we can call gravity (or strong force, or weak force, or magnetism, etc.) seems to hold the protons, neutrons, and electrons of an atom together, and these atoms are the building blocks of what we see in the Universe, you will see that this attractive force is a force which seems to sustain the triune nature of existence.

You don't have to look very hard to see that the equivalent force on our scale of existence is *love*. We refer to the gravitational attraction between living creatures "animal magnetism," "love," or some other term which speaks of the union between the various aspects of our emotions. The lower Chakra energy, spoken of by many cultures, will provide a gravitational attraction based on survival at some lower level; but it is the energy of the heart that forms lasting bonds like those between atomic particles.

When love is present, unity exists; and opposites join together to form a trinity which is far greater, and stronger, than the sum of the two parts. This is clearly evident in our own species. The euphemism, "You can't live with 'em; you can't live without 'em," is a tribute to the fact that neither man nor woman can create life without the other. If we are to continue to exist at this physical level, we must unite at this level. This is true of all formed things.

Humans were given a unique situation in which to exist. We are absolutely spiritual beings; yet we seem to exist in a physical realm, or environment. You may think that everything exists within a physical realm, but this could not be further from the truth. You need not look very deep to unravel that particular brand of logic, yet many people continue to act and speak as if the physical is all that really exists. The mere ideas that you entertain emerged from the non-physical; and it was ideas which resulted in all you see around you in the so-called physical universe.

All things that are physical emerge from the non-physical; all formed things were formed out of the formless. Emotions, for example, cause physiological responses which often result in physical phenomenon, yet emotions themselves are not physical in the sense that you can not hold them in your hands. Thoughts and emotions are only two examples that are easily within the grasp of human minds, but what of the mind itself? No man has ever located the mind, nor does any man truly understand how the mind works. Even the mind, with which we argue for or against such concepts, is another non-physical reality we must relate with on a daily basis.

Humans are simply a physical expression of the boundary between duality. We are basically the glue that holds duality together – at least in our case, anyway. This is a very difficult, if not impossible, concept for a human mind to grasp, but there is no shortage of metaphors that highlight mankind's awareness of this phenomenon. If you consider the *space between* the past and the future, you will see (even though it may give you a headache) that this is where we live – *now*.

Also, it is always NOW and, paradoxically, now occupies no space. We can not march through time and step into the future. The future must come to us. We can not experience the future until it becomes *now*. Similarly, we can not hold onto, nor can we reclaim, the past. Neither the future nor the past exist in any physical reality.

It is easy to look at an architectural icon such as the Great Pyramids and think that you are looking at the past, but rest assured, the Egyptians didn't build aged and weathered pyramids. The time-worn pyramids we know exist only in our *now*; just as shiny, new, smooth pyramids existed for the culture which built them. They are similar, yet different. Their Great Pyramids lacked the effects of time; whereas our Great Pyramids lack the newness they once reflected. We did nothing to create or deserve a reality that includes new pyramids that will endure thousands and thousands of years. Our architectural icons are flimsy by comparison and have relatively limited durability – surely a reflection of our modern consciousness.

We, and our thought processes, represent the *now* we experience. Remember, the future doesn't exist yet and the past doesn't exist anymore. There is only now; and now has no qualities or characteristics of time – NOW exists *between* time. This, at first, may seem strange, but it is absolutely true. The future passes into the past through a thin veil that we call "now." This veil has none of the common qualities of time; for if *now* lasted one-second, then the first half-second would become the past and the last half would be the future until experience makes it the past. This would remain true regardless of how short a duration you attempt to assign to this moment.

This may be confusing, but it is nowhere near as complex as a human being. In fact, we create our concepts of time and Einstein proved, to the satisfaction of the entire scientific world, that such concepts as time are relative and are created within our mind simply to give existence some sort of scale by which it can be measured. The nature of *now*, or of "living in the moment," is tantamount to finding the proper balance within duality. To fully experience *now*, one must find the proper balance between past and present. We must learn to release all that no longer serves our highest purpose and hold onto only those things we will be able to integrate into our continuing journey toward fulfillment.

Furthermore, we must only consider the future in the context of our higher purpose, and not as something to be afraid of. Likewise, to experience a life of fullness, one must find the balance between the two sides of humanity. Unfortunately, this can not be done by denying that side of us we choose to judge as bad, or "dark." This, in fact, represents a breaking of the trinity; and it is the trinity that holds the key to unlocking our infinite potential. This discussion of past, present (now) and future is merely to lay the foundation to understanding the nature of duality, and what it means to us in a very real sense of practical applications. We must still come to understand the trinity in order to make use of any such practical applications in our own lives.

You see, we can view our *self*, or that which we intellectually consider our self to be, as the veil between our Higher self and our Lower self – the two aspects of our mind which conceive of heaven and hell, good and evil, or God and devil. Being the proverbial glue that holds us together in the middle, like the line between night and day, or the present moment (NOW) between past and future, we don't really exist except as the union of two apparently opposing forces.

Oppositional, or dependent on each other, is only a good / bad judgment we make between things we view as different, but which are joined together in some way. The fact is that these two aspects only exist together – in unity – as one. Our existence is the product of the union of these two distinct aspects. Our existence *is* the union; and the union itself becomes a third individual aspect that wouldn't exist without the first two. It is no accident that all life models itself in this way.

A baby, for instance, is the product of the union of man and woman. The baby, in essence, *is* the union – a third individual aspect that couldn't exist without the first two (mother and father). Man and women aren't opposites; they must coexist and to do so, there must be a union of the two, for with no union, there is no trinity and no existence. We have no identity except as the union of two distinct forces and we exist in a timeless, dimensionless realm between two distinct aspects of time (past and future), neither of which actually exists.

Both future and past are necessary, however, in order to experience *now* in a physical, or "real," way. To experience now, there must be a field of potential from which to draw experience, and a place where these experiences are archived after they have been experienced. This is a very difficult concept to grasp, but understanding the nature of what is, and what we are (or at least seem to be), is important if one wishes to consciously direct the power that lies within each of us.

True, there are some who quite easily move in and out of various states of awareness (which allow for very reliable manifestation) without really understanding what it is they are doing. They simply use the principles they know because these principles are a part of them and because they work; they achieve certain desired results. As stated earlier, if you are getting the results out of life that you desire, then you need read no further. On the other hand, if you can't seem to get a handle on your health, finances, relationships, or any other area of your life, there is a reason for this and only a paradigm shift will correct it.

It is the life you have lived, and the ideas you were given about life (and therefore naturally cling to), that have led you to, and created, the situations you are currently experiencing. Basically, it is through a disconnection of the trinity that life seems to unhinge itself before our very eyes. We must look at what this means if we are to correct it. If things do not flow smoothly for you, or if life is a struggle, then you have masked your power with a belief system which is limiting your expression. When someone else experiences success in an area where you can not seem to, they simply don't share your limiting belief system.

When most people think of the word *trinity*, they think of religious descriptions of "the Father, the Son, and the Holy Spirit." Sadly, it is through translations, misunderstanding, misrepresentation, and perhaps fraud and deception on a monumental scale, that most of our current religious practices have been derived. When I say, "sadly," I am referring to the obviously unfortunate state of religion in general, as well as that of many religious people. Face it; if you are doing everything your religion has told you to do (regardless of what religion that might be), yet you still suffer or experience lack, you are simply using a system that doesn't work. It is not a case of you not being good enough, or not being smart enough to use religion effectively; the problem lies within the system itself.

Remember, you are a perfect creation. Anyone selling a product that doesn't work will be forced to contrive some excuse as to why it doesn't work – usually blaming it on the purchaser for some mishandling of the product to some degree. Jesus and his disciples were healing people now, not later. Jesus taught that we all have this power, and equal access to the kingdom. It was us who, well after Jesus was gone, began arbitrarily drawing lines in the sand denoting who we thought should have power and who shouldn't.

Jesus wasn't teaching that you had to be a scholar, or particularly intelligent at all, to access this power – this power is your birthright. Nor was Jesus advocating that religion was the key to unlocking the power within. Religions typically focus on a God outside of us (which is no different than denying the God within each of us) we need "qualified" assistance in order to communicate with; and it was the religious establishment (the church) that killed Jesus.

Jesus was teaching the same thing that spiritual teachers have always taught. He was simply misunderstood; and the world, it seems, was not ready for such great leaps in awareness. Jesus understood the power of the trinity, and used it to great effect. His message is clear, albeit unbelievable for most: This power is in each of us. Jesus never said that there were levels of miracles you had to be granted the use of by some outside agency, or religious hierarchy. He said that we were all born with this power, and all we need to do is believe we have it and accept what it brings us.

Aligning the trinity is the key to this power. Throughout all cultures, human nature has been observed and divided into three aspects. There are many systems of classification and many ways of breaking down human behavior, but systems using divisions into three parts are perhaps most common. The Greeks identified the body (soma), mind (psyche), and spirit (pneuma) as the three distinct aspects of a human. Keeping in mind that the body, or soma, is the physical embodiment of the union of two other forces – parents, or male and female, for instance – we can see that Jesus represented that "embodied" part of the trinity; but so do each of us.

The paternal input, in this equation, or the *Father*, is aptly representative of the wisdom, or intelligence that unifies all. In the overall schema, this would be called God; and in our case, this is our mind, or psyche – that part of us with which we are capable of conceiving of such concepts as God and mind. The spirit, or pneuma, is that life-giving force within us and all of creation.

Obviously, no individual part of this triune can exist apart from the other two. Of course, the outward reflections of this triune are limitless. Our sciences and medicine (in the western tradition, anyway) address the physical, soma, or body. Psychology and philosophy focus on the mind, psyche, or intellect, while religion and spiritualism attempt to address the spirit, or at least the spiritual aspect of the mind. In fact, all outward appearances are somehow products of, and ruled by, this triune.

Dividing a person up, only to focus on one distinct part, is a direct reflection of a misunderstanding of the trinity. This occurs throughout all levels of culture and society and applies not only to the human being as a whole, but to each individual part of the human. As all we know – of any of these things – comes from the mind, it is in the mind where we must begin any healing, or reunification of the whole.

Sigmund Freud labeled the three observable parts of the human persona as: the Id, the Ego, and the Superego. Practitioners of Huna, an ancient Polynesian religious practice, refer to the Lower or Basic self

(Unihapili), the Self (Uhané), and the Higher self (Amakua), as the three aspects of man. "Me, myself, and I," is another commonly used aphorism denoting the triune nature of man, and the delineation of the inner child, the higher conscience, and the logical mediator of the two – the conscious mind, or intellect.

Even the physical structures of the human brain are representative of these three aspects of mankind. The innermost structure of the brain, the reptilian brain, is the oldest part of our brain. It wasn't replaced by subsequent layers because this is the layer that keeps us alive and allows for the newer parts to exist. The reptilian functions include such tasks as maintaining our heartbeat and respiration, and ensuring our survival by responding to threats. In fact, the functions of this part of the brain are basic, but necessary for development of further functioning – just as the actions of a child are necessary for the development of an adult.

The middle layer, or limbic brain, represents evolutionary advances which mediate our survival behavior – like emotions, for instance. Being able to reproduce (reptilian function) may allow for species survival, but nurturing the young (limbic function) – rather than eating them – practically ensures continuation of the species and that evolution will proceed indefinitely.

The outer layer of the human brain, or the cerebral cortex, supplies the majority of our intellect and reasoning capabilities – the responsible father, so to speak. It is through the development and cooperation of three distinct parts of one greater whole that we observe the miracle of modern man and all of his accomplishments. These structures are located within the human brain, function within the human body, and are reflections of the human mind – which is definitely not the same as the brain. If we consider the teachings of Jesus, and references to the trinity, in the context of the human mind, these teachings become much more practical than hypothetical, and more real than ideological.

In our own time and language, there are many allusions to the triune nature of man and the importance of maintaining the integrity of the trinity – lest you create a completely untenable existence for yourself. All human souls recognize the disintegration of the trinity when it appears to be happening to another. When we speak of someone "coming unhinged," or "breaking down," what mechanical pieces are actually disconnecting from each other? Similarly, when things are falling apart, or when you are having trouble keeping "it" together, what is "IT" that seems to be separating from "itself?"

We seem to have a bit more trouble recognizing this phenomenon when is occurs within ourselves. We are empathetic, however, when we witness it in another. We offer such advice as, "Pull it together!" or, "Pull your self together!" even though we may be largely unaware of the significance of our words. It is easy to observe when some one is freaking-out and letting their frightened *inner child* run the show because their *intellectual self* has been overwhelmed and has essentially "left the building." Our admonitions to "get it together," are essentially helping hints from one soul to another that the aspects of the trinity have, for one reason or another, become separated from each other and that the "Father" needs to take a moment to calm down and "get His *house* back in order." In essence, put the three-sides of the triangle back together before things "really get bad!"

This is an absolute reflection of our inner knowing that simply reunifying the trinity will bring any undesirable situation to a favorable close, but continuing to let the inner-child run things will bring no good. There is always a realization that, when things are going bad they are "falling apart," or "breaking down;" and to restore order, the trend must be reversed in order to bring things back together. A reunification changes the effects brought about by a disconnection. Relationships, as all life, work in the same way. A union is formed by the coming together of two separate entities which together form a third. When things "fall apart," there are obvious symptoms of the disconnection of the two sides which had to join in order to give life to the third.

A marriage, for instance, dies when the man and woman separate. When couples speak of working on keeping "it" together, they aren't actually worried about pieces of their physical bodies falling off; the "it" isn't really an "it," it's a triune, or trinity. It is the union itself which they must come to an agreement in order to save. Love will restore harmony between the various aspects of all living things. Activating the wisdom of that higher self living in and through our hearts will restore the union and its orderly function.

Activating your higher wisdom and intelligence will also bring the other two sides of your own being to an agreement to work together for the highest good. In fact, the disruption of a union on the scale of a marriage between two people usually reflects a disruption of the union of forces within one, or both, of the individuals involved in the relationship.

Only the strongest relationships, built on love, can withstand the disintegration of one of the essential components.

Even then, the marriage is not the same as it was when both sides were whole. How many people have warned their married friend, "You'd better pull yourself together if you want to save your relationship."? This awareness is natural. Pretending it is anything less than it is, or ignoring it altogether, simply limits ones ability to benefit from the inner strength, power, and knowing that such awareness brings. If we keep our eyes open for such warning signs as discord and disharmony, and recognize them as such, we can quickly restore the natural order of things.

Each of us is free to believe anything we choose. Voicing these beliefs, however, may lead to death as it did in the case of Jesus – who wasn't killed for His beliefs, but for sharing them with others. Our brain, in fact, has given us an interesting survival mechanism that is designed to protect us from harm that may result from others who judge our beliefs as contrary to their own, or as a threat. We call this mechanism, which some have evolved into a very efficient survival skill, *lying*. Jesus, at practically any point in his ministry, or during his persecution and subsequent prosecution, could have saved his own life by renouncing his beliefs. His beliefs, however, were not simply beliefs.

Jesus demonstrated these principles on a regular basis during his ministry. Therefore, as the only reality Jesus knew, these principles proved impossible to deny. Denying reality is one of our most popular methods of breaking the trinity. Jesus, above all others, knew the consequences of this. We must all surrender our flesh and return it to the earth from which we took it. Whether we do it today, or next year, is of little consequence; but denying reality could bring with it great consequences for the soul. A coward dies a thousand deaths, as they say. Jesus was indeed a man, but realized that even a man is much more than the flesh we all cling to so desperately.

Keep in mind that while Jesus was in the process of being murdered – a process which took several days to play itself out – He knew it the entire time. Yet Jesus remained steadfast in honoring something that was in His mind and His mind alone. Where else would any of us possess any thing – especially a belief or concept – other than in our minds? To honor the mind, we must know the mind. True understanding of the functioning of the mind of man, and the power contained within the mind, was the gift Jesus tried to give humanity.

Sadly, humanity was not ready for such revelations and culture was driven to terminate what it perceived as a threat. Indeed Jesus was a threat to culture insomuch as government and religion – the two power structures of the time – would surely not be tolerated by a world of people able to create their own destiny, health, wealth, or any other desire, by coming to know God through the inner power Jesus spoke of, and by unleashing this power with effective prayer practices based on the very simple principles Jesus taught.

These principles are alive and well today, though we have ignored them throughout the ages. These principles can never die because they are as much a part of the universe as anything else we observe. Science, Medicine, Religion, Spiritualism, Philosophy, and other disciplines, each contain their own truths but none contain all truth. The principles on which the teachings of Jesus were based fall evenly among each of these disciplines and will require a unification if we are to save ourselves and our world. We can each begin this process by turning within and unifying the trinity. Only by unifying our selves can we ever hope to form genuine unions with others.

Even if you can't see the trinity as existing within yourself, look honestly at the principles outlined here; they are effective on the order that Jesus spoke about. Considering that man knows God only within his mind, and our mind seems to be clearly divided into at least three distinct "personalities," take a moment and entertain a new paradigm.

The *Father,* or the logical intellect that monitors and mediates our activities, is but one part of us. The *Son,* or our inner child, is that aspect of us which seeks instant gratification, but also, being a fearful, and not very mature, personality, does its best to keep us alive by avoiding threatening situations. The *Holy Spirit* is that higher aspect of us that infuses us with life, love, right action, and the guidance to transcend. When these aspects are in harmony, the trinity is whole, and manifestation becomes instantaneous.

It is the Holy Spirit which makes us whole – hence the name. The Holy Spirit, however, is a loving parent that, while always having the right answer, will not just step-in and run our lives for us; we have to ask for this to happen. By the same token, the Son, being a typical child, will take the ball and run with it if left unchecked. We must direct this child in its efforts lest it run amok with our lives. It is the Father that must monitor the Son, and appeal to the Higher self (as a Father would appeal to the Mother for help with the kids…) for any assistance that may be needed. Perhaps the best visualization for this that comes to mind is that of the little devil on one shoulder and the angelic apparition on the other – both mediated by you, the conscious mind, caught in the middle.

Keep in mind as you read about the nature of thought and prayer that ancient Toltec wisdom divides everything (GOD) into the *nagual* (everything that exists that we can not perceive) and the *tonal* (everything that we can perceive with our common senses). *Intent* is the force which links the two together – turning the unformed into the formed. In an existence where all things are possible, it is our appeal to this force of intent (prayer) which shapes all things as they emerge from the unformed into the formed. This is indeed ancient wisdom and it shows up, in one way or another, not only in the teachings of Jesus, but in most world religions – regardless of their name, or the names they use to describe various aspects of existence. Those who give us this wisdom understand it; those whom carry this wisdom forth do not always share that understanding. It is up to you to seek your own level of understanding, as it is from that understanding that your future will emerge.

Of course, most religious people have their own imagery that is called up when they hear, "…the Father, the Son, and the Holy Spirit…," but where did this imagery come from? Where does any imagery come from? The same place all of our awareness comes from – the mind. When the three levels of mind are in harmony, each doing its own individual jobs in concert with the other two, the trinity is said to be complete and life is experienced as such – complete and fulfilling. I believe this, and have proceeded in this way, for some time now, with absolutely amazing results.

It doesn't really matter to me if these words have different meanings for different people. In fact, I don't see how *any* word can have entirely the same meaning for any two individuals. What I consider important in all of this is that what feels right to an individual is right for that individual; and results speak for themselves. Jesus performed miracles to get this point across to a population that had done things completely different for many generations. They saw these things, and still didn't believe. They missed the point, they missed the kingdom, they lost out on their own life full of miracles, but they escaped the Jesus era with their religion intact. And look at the world since that time…

We have literally thousands of new religions, each claiming to be the "right" one. Baptists fight Baptists until some Muslims come along for the Christians to unite against. This isn't God-like, or Jesus-like, and reflects true misunderstanding and a lack of belief that God is *all things*. It takes belief to seal the trinity. Even if that belief be "no bigger than a mustard seed," whatever you ask in prayer will be given unto you. Unfortunately for the "faithful" masses, saying you believe is slightly different than actually believing. The way our religions are set-up, it is very difficult to truly believe the whole package. This splinter of doubt is all it takes to burst a bubble built on hope. When events in one's life go sour, our doubt is compounded and belief becomes an even more precious commodity.

There are many interesting viewpoints concerning the trinity. The original trinity of humanity would be Man, Woman, and the Sun. If any of these three entities disappeared, humanity would disappear. It is interesting when you consider that Christianity came from Judaism, and Judaism only emerged after this people had left Egypt. All original cultures realized the importance of the Sun in the survival of all life on the planet, and they all worshipped the Sun as the only source of light, energy, and life, in this solar system.

In fact, when Emperor Constantine created what we now call Christianity, he established the day of worship as Sunday, not the Sabbath, as the Jews (even Christ and those who followed his ways and traditions) had always observed. And if you consider a line from an Egyptian prayer, "Oh Amen, Oh Amen, our Father who art in heaven…," you may begin to realize that Judaism and Christianity inherited a little more than the day of worshipping the Sun from ancient Egypt and other "nature-based" religions.

There is not much in the Bible, in fact, that doesn't appear in other cultures which predate Judaism; and the Bible has undergone continuous change ever since it was first assembled. In fact, the line of the Nicene Creed that makes reference to the "Holy spirit" was added in 381 A.D., 56 years after the church had decided what the "official" definition of the trinity would be at the Council of Nicea. When the church establishes such things by decree, after years of fighting, arguing, and bloodshed, and then, as recently as 1897, goes so far as to forbid any further research into the source of the doctrine of the trinity, I think you owe it to your soul to follow your own inner guidance and arrive at your own conclusions.

Listening to the authorities, or the "powers-that-be," is not the same as seeking the truth in your heart. The measuring stick left to us by Jesus comes to mind again: "Know them by their fruits…" If thinking of the trinity one way doesn't produce any results for you, considering some of the views held by some other great minds – those not supported by the Roman Empire – may bring you greater insight and understanding.

Remember, the people who gave us the "Official Trinity" didn't know Jesus any better than you do; but they were the folks who brought us the crucifixion of Jesus and countless others. Isn't it interesting to think of the brutality in which they [the Roman Empire and the religious/political establishment] murdered this Savior, and then the tireless efforts they seem to have undertaken to reassemble and preserve His doctrine and teachings?

Even if you have fundamental doubts as to the validity of these concepts, doubt remains, and is indeed diametrically opposed to belief. The problem with doubt is just that – it kills belief. It takes belief to unify the trinity, or to bring into agreement the various aspects of mind, and "what any two agree on in prayer shall come to pass." If this means that if any two aspects of mind are in agreement on an issue then it will come to fruition, then why not try it and see? We must experiment with various meanings of words simply because of all the translations that our ancient literature has undergone. Especially in light of the fact that results, or a lack of tangible results, seem to indicate serious shortcomings in our current religious practices.

I asked a deacon at a local church if he had asked God to relieve him of an illness he had been suffering from for a number of weeks. He said, "No." The implications within his admission are tremendous. How many of us don't pray because we don't believe? How many of us do pray, but don't truly believe? How many people think that blindly accepting the stories grown-ups once told them is the same as having true faith and belief? I truly believe that it is nothing more than a simple lack of faith, or belief, which has led to a breaking of the trinity for most people; and it is precisely such a disconnection which renders prayers marginally effective at best. Trust the process and the process will support you. You must believe.

Chapter Four Key Points and Afterthoughts

- Our experience – including the experience of our "selves" – is made up of three obvious components: A guiding principle, such as a plan, thought, or idea (MIND); An animating force with which to creatively express that which arises from Mind (Spirit); and A physical, or material, expression (body), of MIND and Spirit – through which creation is expressed and experienced.

- The MIND, within which the "seed" of experience is "sown" as a thought, is expressing desire – through Spiritual animation – into form, and then back into the MIND in the form of *impressions*, or feedback from the physical, sensory experience of the *expressions*.

- We experience *"Experience"* in this triune nature; all things are experienced in the context of the contrast between what things ARE (Present/Now), and ARE NOT (Past/Future). In/Out; Up/Down; Good/Bad; Front/Back; Left/Right; and Positive/Negative represent some of the dual-expressions of our experience. The third part is that which binds the two apparent opposites together – that which is neither positive nor negative, but neutral and "in between."

- Thoughts are often called "Inspirations" because they have enough Mental Energy to generate an Emotional, or Spiritual, response – a movement of your body, in other words. When action (Spirit) follows thought (MIND), a physical expression results (body). The pathway is MIND – Spirit – body – MIND. "As we thinketh, so it is done through us and to us."

- Gandhi expressed this pathway thusly: "Our thoughts become our words; our words become our actions; our actions become our habits; our habits become our values; and our values become our destiny." Your destiny is the results and experience found along the path you have chosen to walk. Observe your thoughts; for as you sow them in your mind, you will surely experience a resulting physical experience – perhaps strong enough to dramatically alter your experience.

- All parts taken as one represent the whole (holy) trinity; by only considering one part – fixating on the past, for instance – you are dramatically limiting your experience with limited awareness.

- You will know the results of your thoughts by the fruits they produce in body, MIND, and Spirit: PEACE of MIND; Joy of Spirit; and health of body. These are the true fruits of Life; and they can not be purchased – only cultivated in the MIND.

"I am tomorrow, or some future day, what I establish today. I am today what I established yesterday or some previous day."

—James Joyce

Chapter Five

The Importance of Belief, Trust, and Faith

It can not be stressed enough how important belief, trust, and faith are in making prayer an effective mechanism versus a hollow ritual. The way a person lives their life is often indicative of the degree of faith and trust they possess. A person's actions also betray the truth of their beliefs – not the religious affiliations they proclaim, but what they truly believe in the deepest part of themselves.

The simple truth is that a little belief goes a long way toward seeing what you would like to see. Effective prayer depends on belief. When Jesus spoke of belief, He was referring to a belief in the *process* He was teaching, not of belief in any particular dogma or doctrine. This process Jesus was speaking of is the natural process of God, or the Universe; and the principal component in its operation is belief.

Prayer is the vehicle to achieving whatever one desires. The process of prayer works without exception as long as you follow the process and believe in it. "Ask and ye shall receive;" it is as simple as that. If you don't believe this is possible, you have found the root of your problem. You may not consider that not having all your prayers answered is a problem, but it is.

You see, prayer is a natural part of the universe and a natural part of who we are and how we operate. The fact is all your prayers are answered, or at least responded to or acted on in some way. The problem is that if you aren't the one operating the mechanism, it is operating on a "default setting" of sorts – you are like an airplane on autopilot doing only what you have been programmed to do.

It is your subconscious mind which is always operating to create your reality. As such, your subconscious mind is subject to anything it has been fed, for it believes with the faith of a child. It is, in fact your inner child. Since your subconscious has no problems with believing, it manifests everything that you do not manifest through conscious thought, effort, and careful programming of that subconscious aspect of your mind.

By not consciously engaging in the active process of prayer, or affirmative thought, you are not using your power of manifestation. To not use it is to be less than you can be; for what you truly are is a creator and the mechanism of creation is prayer. If your prayer action or conscious thought processes are minimal, and your belief is minimal, then the product of these two variables of creation will be minimal, indeed. The product of these two variables, by the way, is your life and everything you experience as manifest in your life. In the next chapter, we will look at another aspect of prayer – the fact that all thought is basically prayer – but for now, just consider the nature of belief and how it relates to the act of prayer.

Your subconscious, as we mentioned above, believes everything that enters it. It is normally the job of the conscious mind to mediate what enters, but even if you logically reject a certain fact, there is a good chance your subconscious has accepted it; and having accepted it, it will act in ways that will bring this thing to pass. The critical factor here is belief. That which you believe will be given to you will indeed be given to you; you must only believe. The Bible says that "as you believe, so it will be given unto you." Also, "according to your faith, so it will be done unto you." For example, if you have no real belief that you will win millions of dollars, there's no sense praying to win the lottery. By the same token, there is no thing so great that it will not be given unto you if your faith that you will receive it is equally great.

Skepticism is so prevalent in our society that few prayers, it seems, have much chance of being answered. In fact, the Bible makes reference to God not having patience with those who challenge Him. It would appear as if people have always been skeptical of the nature of prayer. But God isn't some petty deity just waiting for us to violate protocol so He can punish us. That is an aspect of our own personality that we assign to God.

The simple fact is that by challenging God to prove His existence by showing you some arbitrary miracle, you have created a double-bind of sorts, and most likely have neutralized your prayer action. That is, of course, if you made one in the first place. Most people that pose such challenges to their creator never actually ask for anything. A vague challenge to simply, "Show me a miracle..." has already been met. Ask God to show you a miracle and then simply open your eyes; miracles abound everywhere you look. It's as if God is laughing at you, returning the challenge by asking you to show Him a place where there are no miracles. The fact is, no human is sophisticated enough to come up with a request which can not be met by God. Our lack of sophistication may limit our ability to understand the answer when we see it, but rest assured; in God, all things are possible.

Another simple fact often overlooked by the skeptical is that effective prayer requires belief. An attitude of, "Show me," or "Prove it," betrays an outright lack of belief. In essence, "I will not believe it unless I see it with my own eyes" is a trap you set for yourself. If you refuse to believe until you see your prayer answered, you will never see. It takes belief, which you are so stubbornly withholding, in order to see the prayer answered. Keep in mind that all prayers really are answered. Sometimes, however, the answer is not what you imagined, or hoped it would be.

This is rarer than you might imagine, however. The answer will likely be "No" only if what you are asking will be contrary to your higher good; and even then the answer is "Yes," but in some form you recognize or judge to be negative. If you do not believe, the answer is more likely going to be, "As you believe, so shall it be given unto you." The most important thing, though, is that belief is actually the energy powering your prayer. Belief is a necessary component in the mechanism of prayer and manifestation – a necessary variable in the equation, and a necessary ingredient in the formula.

To effect physical changes in our reality, we ultimately must go inside our mind. It is an obvious fact that all change begins inside our mind and emerges into reality from that place. If we become ill, symptoms interpreted by the brain are responded to by the body, which eventually alerts us via our brain. We may experience a thought compelling us to go to the doctor's office so we can listen to what he says, change a current thought pattern, and hopefully through actions inspired by the doctor's words, our reality changes from one that includes us being ill into one that does not.

Where does this renewal take place? Deep inside the mind and only after we ignite this new thought pattern with belief. At the doctor's office, you probably already believe that you won't die; you've seen things like this before and they usually go away pretty quickly. In fact, you came to the doctor because you believed that it would improve your situation a bit quicker, and definitely ensure that it wouldn't get any worse. When the doctor, as a trusted authority figure with your best interest at heart, tells you that you'll get better in about a week, he is telling you something that you already know and believe. The doctor is affirming to you that which you know deep inside, and probably even at a conscious level – that these things usually go away in about a week and this will probably not be any exception to that rule. In fact, he's going to give you this "wonder pill" which will just make double-certain that your body doesn't decide to get it wrong this time and let you wither away and die.

All of these things take place within your mind; you interpret all of these suggestions and predictions logically, and subconsciously, and your body responds accordingly. You take your medicine three times a day because you had a suggestion, or program, installed by the doctor that inspired you to take the appropriate actions at the appropriate times – like setting an alarm clock. You even act out the recovery on or around the appointed date – depending on how much fuel you provided this idea. The fuel you use to bring this idea into the physical realm is belief. Belief in all the requests, or prayers, and subsequent answers we receive is the major determinate of how quickly we receive our outcome, and what the outcome will be.

If the doctor told you that, this time, you had something fatal and only had one week to live, you would probably – if you believed him – be dead in a week. This happens all the time. Most miraculous recoveries are only miracles to the doctors who failed to convince their patients to die. The patient, at some point, decided to "fight it," as they usually say, and begins this combat in their mind. They begin telling themselves that they are better, and they encourage those around them to act as if they are perfectly fit and healthy. Then they make the changes in their thinking and lifestyle which will produce the kind of person they desire to become – a fit and healthy person who isn't suffering from life, but is thriving in it. If the person believes, they will live. But they must believe in their desire. They must believe that they have free will to see any future event they choose. They must believe that the process of asking, believing, and receiving (prayer) really works and they must make the decision to do what is necessary to allow this new reality.

60

I do indeed mean *allow* this new reality – not *force* it. Trying too hard indicates that you do not trust, or believe, in the process. Let things you have asked for unfold for you. You have already created them with your desire and ensured their arrival with your belief; you need only allow what comes naturally without resisting. Most people get into trouble here because they ask for something and then assume that they know how the Universe goes about creating such things. When things happen that they wouldn't have expected to be part of the plan, they lose faith in the process. As belief dies, so does the realization of our desires. God works in mysterious ways; you simply have to get out of the way.

You see, all of this battle takes place inside you at various levels of your mind and consciousness. If you could bypass your logical "thinker" during times of need or crisis, you would in fact be turning over your prayer to your inner child. When the Bible speaks of having "faith as a little child," the implication is clear: Get out of the way and let it happen. If you can not accept a new belief logically, all you have found is that you haven't yet encountered anyone to give you that particular form of programming.

For example, very few people believed in heavier-than-air flight before they actually saw an airplane. Even then, it was probably said to be, "Unbelievable!" After seeing an airplane, however, future encounters with people speaking of such things would result in curiosity, interest, or numerous other possible responses, but disbelief would no longer be among them. The program would be in place and belief would be based on the fact that the logical mind has seen it, or has been programmed with an awareness of a new addition to reality as it is known to the logical mind. Mindful living and diligent observation of all things may lead to belief in this same way, but it is not the only way to belief.

The Wright brothers didn't have the experience of witnessing a manned, heavier-than-air flight to buoy their faith in flight; but they certainly did believe it was possible. Without their belief, they wouldn't have proceeded. And without proceeding, they never would have realized their dream. Belief was a vital ingredient to achieving powered flight just as it is in achieving anything. Once this milestone was achieved, the awareness of the entire world was raised and many people began designing, building, and flying machines that "couldn't possibly fly!"

It doesn't take a genius to see what happened to the entire world in the relatively short period of time since then. For thousands of years, men have watched birds and dreamed of flight. Of course, one dreamer here and one inspired thinker there hardly amount to much of a movement. After some period of time, diligence (faithfulness) to the vision paid off – despite the widespread disbelief. So you can clearly see that a few souls, here and there, can achieve great things; but when you can show the world with a miracle, like the Wright brothers did, or like Jesus did, then you swing the pendulum of belief in the direction of achievement and the realization of dreams. Thousands of years of a few individuals dreaming against all hope, but believing, produced a rickety contraption that flew several feet, but less than fifty-years later a flying machine dropped a single bomb which destroyed an entire city and led to the end of a world war. Then, roughly forty-years after that, we saw shuttles that fly into space and return to land on a runway in California or Florida. The time in between saw airships, helicopters, hovercraft, hang-gliders, and even rockets that carried men to the moon.

Once powered flight was a reality, and men began to have belief in it, they proceeded to paint creation with the brushes of their own imagination. What was once impossible now offers options, features, and first-class upgrades! It is amazing how quickly things change when the whole world believes in something – when humanity is united by a common belief. The major accomplishment of the Wright brothers, it seems, is that they shifted awareness and turned disbelief into belief – opening the door to the light of possibility. The Wright Flyer is not much of an aircraft by today's standards, but it carried an entire species into a new world full of possibilities; and it did it fueled by the belief of two brothers.

Our beliefs are programmed into us from birth. Everything that we experience becomes a permanent part of us and we use these experiences to build a sort of database with which we judge subsequent experiences. We are told about God and, depending on what we were told, we either believe in Him or not. If we were told there was no God, for instance, we would believe that until we had an experience that convinced us otherwise, or until we had acquired enough knowledge to form some contrary opinion based on what we have come to know and believe. These beliefs become who we are and control everything we do and experience. They are basically the computer programs that are loaded into, and control, our autopilot system, or subconscious. When we aren't consciously acting on some thought, our subconscious is driving the car for us, in a manner of speaking. Our beliefs tell our subconscious mind how, and where, we want to be "driven;" and they operate our control systems according to those parameters. If you believe you will never amount to anything in this life, then even when you aren't actively doing anything in particular, your subconscious is making arrangements to help you never amount to anything. You have to take an active role in programming your beliefs instead of simply accepting beliefs from someone else; you never know what those beliefs will lead to. Why not believe in something you truly want?

It is difficult for us to believe sometimes. We try to do the right thing, we follow all the rules, and things still don't go the way we would like them to. This still doesn't seem to wake us up to the fact that occupying ourselves with someone else's agenda is no way to live the life you want. You must pay attention to your own existence if you want to get anything out of it. Instead of simply staying busy doing things or spending your days dreaming about that one day in the future when everything will be a certain way, why not try something new? Why not try something that you haven't tried, and see what happens?

Why not try to believe that you are safe and everything is going to be the way it should be? We have been overwhelmed with paradoxical teachings that confuse us and make us doubt the reliability of anything we see or hear. You need to be able to see that you have created the life you are living by the programs you have been holding onto and running in your subconscious mind. You need to recognize this in order to be able to release any such programming which may have been producing less than favorable results for you.

In many cases, we are able to empower life-changing paradigm shifts without an abundance of preexisting belief. In these cases, we simply surrender to the process. The act of surrender produces similar results as believing because surrendering implies that you have realized you are not in control, and have absolutely no conscious idea how to handle a given situation. Admitting this is tantamount to saying, "If I get out of this, it is by some power greater than me." Essentially, it is like pleading "no contest." You simply get out of the way and allow whatever happens. There is a realization that you aren't the one in control, yet things are happening anyway and before you know it, you are on a completely different page in a completely different story.

If you simply can not make yourself believe, you are not alone. It may sound strange, but churches across the United States are full of people who just can't seem to make themselves believe. They keep going to church and hoping for a miracle, but they just don't believe, deep in their hearts, that *their* miracle is coming, or that they are even worthy of receiving a miracle. They do all the right things and never miss a day of church – or work for that matter – but still their lives aren't easier; life just seems to get harder and harder. In fact, some of these people are at the breaking point – ready to just give up. The real problem for these individuals is two-fold: They can't bring themselves to believe; and they don't know when to surrender.

It is important that we learn and remember where it is our beliefs came from in the first place so we can keep ourselves out of this double-bind people often find themselves in. We are told, taught, or given our beliefs by other people – sometimes people we don't even know. These beliefs rule our lives and are largely responsible for conscious decisions we make as well as unconscious decisions that are made for us by our subconscious mind. If a part of you believes something that another part of you doesn't, there is an internal conflict that projects itself outwardly as conflict, confusion, illness, negative emotions and situations, and dis-ease of all types, in your external world. The only thing worse than doing this to yourself, is when you tell the "white lie." Pretending to believe something that the inner parts of you know to be a falsehood, or acting like you believe something you logically reject, will always bring you results you don't really want – even if you think you do.

If, for example, you have been going to church and going along with a group-belief that, at some level, you just can't reconcile with what you know, think, or believe to be true, you are damaging your ability to pray effectively by damaging your ability to believe. We do such things as *going along with the group* because we fear the judgment of others. We fear the judgment of others because we don't completely accept ourselves. When we lie to ourselves so others will not reject us, we are denying that which is within, to attain that which we think is without – acceptance.

Every human on this planet has a slightly different, if not completely different, idea about the way things are. In fact, the only reason beliefs are so similar within groups, but dissimilar amongst outside groups, is that we make agreements within our own circles as to what we all will believe and disbelieve. This is where our problem starts. We believe we are separate from God, which is impossible if God is all things and all places (omnipresent); and the fear that we experience drives us to seek security within a group. To be accepted by the inner group, or family, we learn their beliefs and customs and wear various masks (like the good, little child with perfect grades...) in order to be accepted. Then, as a group, we decide where we will go to church. The family may have always gone to a particular church, or never have gone at all.

If you do go to church, you pick from the many available by trying to match what you have been told so far with what they believe. This simplifies your indoctrination into the new group, but it also gives you a welcome feeling, as if you have found others that you had been long separate from – a homecoming, of sorts. Everyone in this place believes in God, but we also believe that the people in the other church, down the street, have it wrong on at least a couple fundamental points. So we have our agreement within our group that *they* aren't like *us* and thus we have more in common with each other. The family, as it were, is stronger via another unifying bond.

Then it becomes clear that a hundred different voices create a din, so we should have one person speak for all of us and, since he is the one speaking, after all, we'll let him tell us what we've already agreed to believe in by joining this group. It is so much simpler this way! But the minister isn't really deciding how to interpret church doctrine, either – in most cases.

We go to this particular church because it's a little different from that other church; but then, representatives from our church, and the other church, get together at a conference to decide what new things we all are going to believe this year. Our representatives return from the conference and tell our congregation that, for our group to remain under the protective umbrella of the "Convention of Churches with Similar Names," we must now believe that a certain other group among us, perhaps people of a different religion, culture, or perhaps even gay people, are different from us and we are supposed to separate ourselves even further from humanity by ostracizing this new foe.

I say, "...new foe," because there was a time when these other groups were not necessarily our enemies. In fact, it is almost as if new individuals are placed in leadership positions and their own fears and judgments come out in the form of new policies against new enemies to the group. Where did these fears come from? Like every other piece of information in your head, they were programmed into you; and they are programmed into those you choose to lead you. The only difference is that you can never tell what programs may be running in another person's mind – even if you have placed them in a position of authority over you.

Now you have some new beliefs that you didn't know you had when you signed-up to join this group. But all of a sudden, you aren't really sure that you agree with this particular thing they are saying. Your personal experience in life has shown you, for instance, that this group that is now on our bad list, isn't bad at all; they are just different. You may even be entertaining ideas such as, "Isn't it neat how many different ways God expresses Himself in this world?" But you can't say that out loud, or you just might find yourself at odds with your group. This means rejection, isolation, abandonment, or many other things that take away the very reason for joining a group in the first place – security and communion. So now you have an internal conflict, but your fears keep you rooted firmly in the place you feel safest and keep you from open, honest expression of your heart.

It gets worse the deeper you look at it, too; because most *group beliefs* are based on various interpretations of the Bible, where Christian churches are concerned (each religion has their own foundational documents), and the Bible has some catch-all's in it that put all such new rules to a test that they can not withstand. "Judge not...," for instance, doesn't say, "Try not to judge, unless you see someone who is clearly different from you, then it's acceptable to ostracize them." It is really quite simple, everyone is different and it is human nature to think that *they* are different from *you*, and not that *you* are different from *them*.

Also, it is said that "In God, all things are possible." So, when you base your existence on a book that says, "...all things are possible," and "Judge not...," it pretty much shuts down any petty human differences; anything can happen, everything is possible, and you are only human and have no knowledge, experience, or authority with which to judge the works of God (other humans, for instance). That part is pretty simple; I just can't seem to find the part about boycotting people and businesses because they refuse to judge others. Are we saying that we should follow the Bible's teachings, except for where the Bible got it wrong and there is clearly a need for someone to step in and render some judgment? Or, have we simply decided to use the "love thy neighbor" policy when we are in a good mood and the "hellfire and brimstone" approach when we have had a bad day, or week – or life, or marriage, etc?

When these things happen, we can pretend anything that we want, but a paradox is a paradox; and our subconscious minds know this without exception. Have you ever had a computer refuse to do what you wanted it to do because you had attempted something that is not possible, or something that it deemed an "illegal operation?" Computers are modeled after our brains and our brains do the same thing when faced with paradoxical situations, or lies. The part that locks-up, however, is that part that creates our existence. We go into a sort of default mode and those things that have already been accepted as true continue to play themselves out.

I am not singling out any particular religion, or any particular belief; I am trying to speak plainly of the workings of the mind. It works a certain way; and when we try to force it to do things contrary to its programming, it doesn't always respond in the way we would like it to. We must decide for ourselves what is truly important and set our own priorities. We must choose our own beliefs according to what we feel in our hearts. I am not suggesting that your beliefs are wrong, I am suggesting that you do some serious reflection and determine if your beliefs are really *yours*. Then, take an honest look and see if those beliefs are really leading you down a road of happiness and fulfillment, or if they are keeping you in a place of fear and judgment. You have to decide for yourself; but there is a very real threat to accepting someone else's beliefs as your own – the threat of lying to your subconscious and crippling your ability to believe anything new.

If you are not sure what you believe, and you have reached that place where you feel like giving-up, now is the time to trust the process. If you can't find faith at this stage of the process, then surrender. You will find it frightening, at first, but the realization that you had about not being in control is accurate – you aren't in control. When you are driving down the road with the kids in the back seat, does it matter if one of them says, "That's it! I'm not driving this car anymore! We'll go wherever it takes us!"? No, it doesn't matter, because they were never really driving in the first place – even if they were pretending they were. You aren't driving your car, either; and even if you think you are, isn't it time for a break? I mean, if you are to the point of giving-up, it is a result of the way you have been driving, or think you've been driving, your body and life thus far; taking your hands off the wheel may be a great idea!

Years ago, when I was learning to fly airplanes, they still taught student pilots how to recover from spins by putting them into spins. Picture an airplane with its nose pointed straight at the ground spinning like a top. Now imagine sitting in that plane. This is how some people's lives actually feel to them – completely out of control. The planes, in which most people learn to fly, are innately very stable. Like a human body, they naturally seek stability if you just take your hands off the wheel. So I learned, in the seat of that airplane, that out-of-control means that *you have no control.* Manipulating the stick and pedals are attempts at controlling your destiny. When you are out-of-control, you have put yourself there by your manipulation of the craft or vehicle you occupy. The solution, when you have demonstrated your ability to lose control, is to simply take your hands off the wheel and let balance return naturally. When balance returns (the spinning stops), you simply lift your nose (or chin, as the case may be) and select a new attitude.

It still takes a bit of faith to just let go and take your hands off the wheel, but don't worry; we have a built-in mechanism that will take us out of the driver's seat when the time comes. After that first time spinning an airplane with an instructor, I would go and practice spins for fun. Can you believe it!? Surrendering to one of the scariest things that can happen in an airplane turned a fear into a source of joy. Facing a fear is indeed one of the quickest, most effective ways of building faith.

When I learned to just "let go" of the controls – a scary thing to do in an out-of-control airplane – I learned how to immediately stop the out-of-control spinning; which meant it wasn't really out-of-my control – the plane was simply responding to my inputs. Regaining control simply required more focus and faith – and less effort. Once the spinning stopped, however, I was still pointed at the ground; it was up to me to choose a new direction of travel! People often use prayer, or other techniques, to "stop the spinning" in their own lives, but then fail to ask for what they'd rather be experiencing. Letting-go stops the spinning; but you have to change direction and decide where you go from there. If you crash, it is only because you waited too long to change your attitude.

In life, true surrender usually comes from utter desperation. When you reach this point, you'll know it. Unfortunately, some people have programs running that tell them to respond to adversity and desperation in self-destructive ways. There is little that can be done unless they first realize this, and then seek a better path; for if they seek, they shall find what they are searching for. You must believe in the process; and you must trust that you will not be forsaken. For God can not leave you; God has nowhere else to be.

Learning to *Let-Go*

Practices such as meditation are designed to help you let-go of those thoughts which upset your health by causing noise and stress in your nervous system and stimulating the systems of your body in a chaotic and disruptive manner. Medical science has estimated that perhaps 95% of all trips to the doctor's office are due to stress-related complaints; and stress is caused by our perceptions – the way we think about our lives. In other words, by simply learning how to release, or let-go of, thoughts which upset your nervous system, you can eliminate stress and the health problems it causes – such as unwanted weight gain, high blood pressure, diabetes, Fibromyalgia, and most other chronic pains and illnesses.

Remember; you are not your mind and you are not your thoughts. When meditating, thoughts arise just as they always do for all of us; but you can look at the thoughts which arise, and notice that they are only thoughts. No matter how distressing a thought may be, it will not upset you if you have learned how to release it and allow your mind to rest, or settle on another, more pleasant thought, or a thought of peace, love, joy, kindness, compassion, health, or gratitude. When you become aware of a distressing thought, simply stop and say to your mind, "Thank you for sharing!" and then put your mind at ease by thinking about something worth thinking about. A relaxed mind will lead to a relaxed body – and a relaxed life.

"You can have anything you want if you will give up the belief that you can't have it."

– Robert Anthony

Chapter Five Key Points and Afterthoughts

- If you don't believe something's possible, why would you spend time thinking about a thing (praying) – or doing that thing?

- If you do something you do not believe in, or something you do not believe will succeed, then you are doing it half-heartedly – without the power of the belief in your heart.

- Our degree of belief determines the extent to which our plans unfold; though belief does not make an incomplete plan complete.

- All thoughts are creative. You can consciously participate in each moment of your life; or you can take your chances with the creations of your unconscious thought patterns – your habits.

- Beliefs are the result of the continuous thinking of a thing, or the acceptance of a reality based on authority, evidence, or experience; BELIEF, is the Energy of Faith we put into our beliefs and thoughts. Enough BELIEF will generate movement, action, and manifestation of that in which we believe – to the extent we believe.

- Beliefs and BELIEF are not the same. Once we have accepted a thought as a Belief, we will act on it. Everyone has different beliefs; some of them lead to violence and suffering while others do not. "It is by their fruits that you will know them." Not all beliefs are beneficial.

- As Einstein said, "Nothing happens until something moves;" belief makes things happen by making things move. Things move because of belief (growth, play, expansion...) or fear (decay, withdrawal, contraction...). When the motivation for movement is fear, or the avoidance of what we do not want, then action is inefficient and often painful and unsuccessful. When the Inspiration for movement is the belief in the possibility of the acquisition of a desire, action is often effortless and is never thought of as burdensome or painful.

- Beliefs determine and outline the path; BELIEF determines how – and how fast – we travel that path. Not all paths are the same; but they all begin and end in the same place – regardless of the scenery along the way.

- By what agency do you wake yourself each morning? You are not responsible for your being here; and you do not keep yourself here – though, with courage, you can choose to leave at any time. Have faith that something put you here and sustains you until you can no longer be sustained – until such a time, relax and believe in your dreams.

Chapter Six

Surrender to the Process

What are you going to do now? You have come as far as you can come on this road. You have pushed this plan to its limits and you have gotten nowhere. Things are hopeless and you don't know what to do. There is some wisdom in knowing when to fold your hand and walk away. In life, walking away could mean walking away from a situation that you have realized you can no longer tolerate, or control; or it could mean walking away from a belief that you have found to be limiting your progress and holding you back in your efforts to experience a fuller life.

Either way, or any way, surrendering means to give up on a course that is not taking you where you want to go. Surrender typically follows a period of desperation and is equivalent to admitting defeat, admitting failure, or acknowledging that you are not the one in control of your life; you are simply the creative director of this particular production. This can be a very liberating moment, but it is typically experienced during the worst moments, or lowest points, in a person's life.

People are very vulnerable and fragile at these times and sometimes seek alternative means of escape. Escape, however, is not the answer. When you are up against the proverbial wall, or even when the wall is real, you still have options or free will. True, you could end it all, as some people do; or you could simply run away. These are both escapes, of sorts, but you are only "escaping" a place or situation – not your problems. The thing that is driving you to acts of desperation is a conflict within you and, as such, will follow you wherever you may roam. It may surface at any time, in any number of ways, but this is an internal conflict that you were only made aware of by the external circumstances and appearances of your environment. If you do not change the way you see things, the things that you see will not change. If you have run out of options, it's time for a change.

Every one of us has, at some point, been in such a predicament that the only resource left to us was an attempt to make a deal with God, or our Creator. At one time or another, most people have probably uttered something like, "Oh, God, if you just get me out of this, I promise I'll never...," or "If you just make this pain go away, I'll..." These prayers are basically attempts to bribe God. "For a hamburger today, I'll gladly pay you Tuesday," as Wimpy used to say in the old Popeye cartoons.

Each supplication contains an important element, however, that has the potential to make it successful. There is, in these efforts to seek mercy, an obvious surrender to the process and whatever Force operates it. There is an appeal that is offered to an implied Higher Authority – albeit one asked for "on credit." The implication is that through surrender, you have shifted your disbelief to a belief that an appeal to God is your only way out. This is evidenced, obviously, by the fact that you acknowledged that you must ask to receive, and that you would have to put some energy into your side of the equation. Sacrifice, it seems, would demonstrate belief; it may even seem to demonstrate this belief at a very deep, almost superstitious, level. Surrender, therefore, seems to be no different than belief, except for the extra punishment that you put yourself through on the way to acceptance of what is.

History is full of individuals that have reached great heights through acts of sacrifice, and surrender. The story of King Solomon and the baby is an example of a mother, surrendering to the loss of her baby in order to save her child's life. King Solomon's suggestion to the problem of one woman claiming another had stolen her baby was to cut the child in half – giving each one-half. The mother, facing the death of her child, was indeed desperate. Rather than watch her child die, she proclaimed that the baby should be given to the other woman, while the thief was indifferent and willing to have the baby cut in half. The wise king knew that the true mother would rather lose her baby than see it die.

Surrendering to the process, the mother not only saved her child's life, but was restored custody. Do you not believe that this was her fondest prayer? Do you not believe that if she hadn't surrendered, the baby would have been cut in half? She surely did. Now, can you see that the prayer didn't change at the moment of surrender, only the answer did? The prayer, powered only by grief and fear, had little effect. Only when the mother surrendered her attachment, was the request granted. There are obviously many components to this story, but which one do you think you could change and the story still have the same outcome?

The story of Abraham and Isaac is another example of an individual being induced to surrender and sacrifice that which he loved. These stories each end with the child being saved and restored to the parent, but so many stories reflect the tragedies that follow a lack of faith, or an unwillingness to surrender. Quitting and walking away is not exactly the same as surrender and really only changes or postpones the ultimate outcome slightly. Surrender means acceptance of what is and whatever outcome God gives you. The expression of faith inherent in a pure demonstration of surrender provides enough energy to see us through most any adversity in our lives. The Bible is full of such stories, and it is these stories that are meant to underscore the importance of faith, and the importance of surrendering to what is.

If you view life like a river, you would see that it basically flows in one direction. If you are in the current of life, you are weightless, surrounded by life, supported by it. If you struggle, you change the dynamic by making that which supports you your enemy. You are biting the hand that feeds you in a very literal sense. If you try too hard, you are saying that you can do it yourself. In a universe that takes you at your word, your efforts to "do it yourself" are met with an invitation to do just that. When you lose the energy of love, and faith, that fuels the creation of all you see, you begin to see the deterioration of your surroundings; your creation begins to wither and will soon die if not rejuvenated with love and faith. In the river, any resistance you feel is caused by your efforts.

If you feel resistance, you created it. You have either put your feet down in an attempt to slow the passage of time, or you have turned around in the current, facing the past – from whence ye came – in an apparent effort to hold onto, or recapture, a fleeting feeling. You can not capture creation, you can only ask and receive; you need only allow what is. The past is not a *thing* that can be recaptured; but just as you created the moment that you long to recapture, you can create other moments even better than past remembrances. You are no longer in the past; and you are no further downstream than you are. You are right here, right now. This is what is; surrender to *that* reality.

If, instead of dragging your feet, or facing the current, you are actually trying to *swim* upstream, you are still going to find yourself going downstream; it will just take you longer, you won't see where you are going, and you're going to be too worn down by the river to enjoy any of your experience. Life isn't here to fight you, why would you fight it? You can not swim into the past; and you can not live in the past — no matter how hard you try. Go with the flow. You're going to get there when you get there; so enjoy the ride!

Some people look as if they are trying to see how much punishment they can get out of life. The unfortunate thing is that most of them really do think that life is "attacking" them and that they are a victim. Well, if you can't beat 'em, join 'em. If you are under attack, and you know you can't win, you have two choices: Surrender, or die. I will tell you right now, no human has ever survived an encounter with life. So, knowing you can't win by fighting, and that you are going to have your chance to die either way you choose, why not surrender to the current and see where it leads?

Anytime you feel resistance, anytime you feel like you are making an effort, let go. If you are trying, you are fighting what is. The reality is that life is going where it is going and we can not change that physical reality with physical force alone. You would be up against a force that swings an entire solar system full of planets around a star, for starters. Ask for what you want, unambiguously, and then let go of your illusion of control. You will be surprised at what happens if you can really do it — and you *can* really do it. We all can — it's our inheritance. When we relinquish control of our thoughts, miracles happen. Of course, they aren't really miracles; it's really the way things are supposed to work. But we recognize these events so rarely anymore that they seem like miracles. In fact, St. Augustine once said of miracles, "Miracles are not contrary to nature, but only contrary to what we know about nature."

It should be clear that you never could control nature, so there was no physical control that you ever had to let go of. Your "control" is an illusion; that is, it exists only in your mind. It exists there as a thought, or belief, that was formed by other thoughts or experiences. Maybe someone told you they were in control and, when you assumed their role in life, you thought that was what control is. There are many sources for this very common belief, but they are all dubious. You are in control only in the sense that you *think* you are in control; and that is only because you *think* (believe) there is such a thing.

74

All you need is a middle-school-aged child to demonstrate how flimsy your illusion of control really is! You are definitely not in any sort of physical control over this realm of existence. You can't manage it with force; you can only surrender to that fact. You can surrender your false belief of control and free your mind of the burden of holding onto a thought that is responsible for most of your inner turmoil.

When you free your mind of illusions, and the doubt and fear that sustains them, all that will be left is belief; and that is what drives the mechanism of manifestation. You would be surprised at how many people will hear such a thing and dismiss it immediately out of *disbelief.* There is nothing for sale here, you ask for it, believing, and you get it. Disbelief is self-sustaining; it doesn't need any extra help from you. If you don't start, right now, believing in the things that you want, then your disbelief will keep you from ever having them. Until you come to terms with this, life will continue to feel a bit heavy at times.

"Boxer 'A' and boxer 'B' were engaged in a boxing match. After fighting for some time, boxer 'A' thought to himself, "I am so tired I can't throw another punch;" while boxer 'B' continued to affirm, "Just one more punch!"

—Paramahansa Yogananda

"The future belongs to those who believe in the beauty of their dreams."

—Eleanor Roosevelt

Be of Good Cheer; it's Good for You!

It is now a scientifically established fact that your psychology and physiology (mind and body) are inextricably linked. A sharp, middle-school aged child can describe for you the way our thoughts reflect in our bodies through nervous, chemical, and mechanical energy and the subsequent changes these energies cause. The hormones released when you are in a state of stress, anxiety, anger, grief, worry, and other negative emotional states, make you feel bad – not figuratively, but quite literally.

When you are nervous, you may not have real "butterflies in your stomach," but your stomach really is quivering as a result of the stress hormones it is experiencing. When the thoughts are different, the electricity and chemicals are different, and the feelings, or emotions, are different. Frustration may make your neck sore; while anger may give you a sharp pain in the area of your gall bladder and fear may make your knees or bladder weak. Every thought has some emotional response; some thoughts and emotions are subtle and calm while others can be intense and painful.

The hormones released by the body during the stress response are great in times of emergency – when your life may really be at stake. But stress hormones are harmful to your body at other times – causing weight gain and an estimated 95% of all trips to doctor's offices. Stress – which is caused by thinking about things that make you feel bad – weakens the immune system, shuts down the reproductive system, and slows or stops digestion among other things; all of which lead to other problems – some of which are quite serious. Stress also makes you dumb by robbing your thinking centers of blood and oxygen.

Happiness, on the other hand, turns off the stress response and releases chemicals which are beneficial and healing to the body – boosting the immune system, and all the systems of the body. When you can change your thoughts, you can change your physical condition. The ancients spoke of this mind-body connection, and the benefit of positive thought, often with saying such as, "Laughter is the best medicine," "Fear not; be of good cheer and you will be made whole," "Your faith has healed you," and "As a man thinketh, so it is done unto him." Think healthy and happy; be healthy and happy.

I often use a flashlight to demonstrate a point about focusing on your problems. I'll shine the light on the floor, in a narrow beam, casting a small circle on the floor. I tell the client to look at the spot of light, and that the spot represents their problem. Now, keep your eyes focused on that spot of light, and tell me if you see the answer to your problem, or if you still just see the spot of light that represents the problem. In a dark room, the message is even more dramatic. There could be answers lying all over the floor, but if you don't shift your focus away from the problem, you may never see one of them.

Even if an outside party tells you that there is a perfectly logical answer just beside you, unless they can convince you to take your eyes off your problem and look toward the solution, you'll likely never see the answer. You may even find that your problem remains, even after you close your eyes, just as a spot of light will seem to linger behind your eyelids. This is very often the case in life. Fortunately, focusing on one problem long enough will result in dead batteries, a new mission in life (changing batteries, perhaps), and a fresh, brighter perspective on life. Some people have ways of relocating their problem, or replacing it with a new one, but life gives you many opportunities to refocus your outlook.

Imagine this as a game. After a while, you say that you give-up; you can't find the answer. Just like any game – and all games are inspired by life – when you give-up, or surrender, the answer is given to you. "Ok, I give up. Where is it?" I can almost hear the answer now. "You were so close! It's right there. Do you want to try something harder this time?" We learn a little more every time we play – just like lion cubs learning to hunt. Playing teaches us about surviving; playing teaches us about life. Sometimes we are very pleased with our outcomes and sometimes we feel as if we have failed; but either way, we learn about life if we just pay attention. Anytime it gets too difficult, or too frightening, we can surrender and we will be shown the way to safety. Imagine the way you would like it to be and then surrender to the process. Life will carry you. It always has.

To surrender means to stop trying and start allowing. Joseph Chilton Pearce relates stories of what he calls "un-conflicted behavior" in which doubts give way to a knowing or belief that the task at hand is already accomplished. The outcome is a foregone conclusion so there is nothing left but to experience the asked-for situation. By surrendering your thoughts to the moment, you surrender any doubt or fear, along with any illusions of control. Things unfold as they have been created and feedback is experienced that lets us know which direction our thoughts and prayers are carrying us. When experiencing un-conflicted behavior, we are experiencing a place where the beliefs and programs that we carry around with us can not harm us or hold us back.

For humans, un-conflicted behavior is quite rare, but very illuminating. Fear is a contractive energy that keeps us from venturing too far outside our comfort zone and keeps un-conflicted behavior at bay. By surrendering this fear, we can see what our true capabilities are in any given situation. By surrendering our fears and opening our hearts, we can get a glimpse of what our true power really looks like. By surrendering our fears, we are letting go of our illusions of control and allowing our future to unfold the way God would have it be for us.

The fear of failure, or death, keeps most of us from exploring the limits of this behavior. The times in our past when individuals were able to accomplish this, or were driven to this state by desperation, are marked by momentous events that apparently changed the course of history. Jesus transcended fear and walked into history with a cross on his back and a crown of thorns on his head. President John F. Kennedy, when asked once how he became a war hero, stated, "It was unintentional; they sank my boat."

Heroes are born when fear dies. We all seem to recognize when someone has transcended, even if for just a moment, the limitations of their beliefs of mortality and weakness. We admire these individuals, for they remind us of our transcendent nature. We are comforted somehow to know that we all possess such capacity for greatness and that ours, too, will be waiting on us when we need it most. This greatness is real, we have seen it in all types of humans, but the idea that it is waiting for you is misleading. Greatness waits for no person, but falls on he who seeks it. Greatness is only waiting for you to invite it in, believing, and allow what comes. When I speak of greatness, I am speaking of fulfillment in any endeavor you choose with your heart. I am speaking of surrendering to the heart and following wherever it may lead you. I am speaking of letting go of fear and replacing it with thoughts of faith, gratitude, trust, and courage; for it is these thoughts that will bring these things into your life.

Chapter Six Key Points and Afterthoughts

- That which we resist – persists! "Let go and let God."

- "There is nothing to fear but fear, itself." – Winston Churchill

- You can influence any situation; but you can not control it.

- Surrender doesn't mean giving-up on your dreams, but opening up to new possibilities. By giving-up our illusion of control, we open up to new, possibly easier ways of getting what we want. By releasing our attachment to a plan that may not have been working, we open ourselves up to newer, better ideas.

- We don't have to be the cause of everything we want to experience.

- Whatever makes things happen in our lives makes things happen in all lives; and it was here, making things happen, before it made *us* happen. It will likely continue making things happen after we are gone, so lighten-up; and let-go of your burden – the burden of an illusion of control.

- What is – is. You can accept that fact and learn to live with it and use it to your benefit; or you can continue to experience the painful experience created by your conflict with reality. Learn to Love what is.

- Experience simply is; Life simply is. You can experience it with or without resistance; but any resistance you experience is created by you. More specifically, any resistance you experience is created by your fear of letting go of something, or your fear of receiving, or accepting, something. Resistance is resistance.

- Disbelief is actually a belief that something will fail to happen, or that something can not happen. There is only belief. What you choose to believe in is your business; but you should know it is these choices by which you form your experience.

- You can only think of one thing at a time; if you are thinking of illness, you are not thinking of wellness. Regardless of the context in which you are thinking of illness (such as the removal of illness), you are still thinking of illness; start thinking of wellness instead. To get what you WANT, you must let-go of all thoughts about what you don't want.

"The environment you fashion out of your thoughts, your beliefs, your ideals, your philosophy is the only climate you will ever live in."
—Stephen R. Covey, First Things First

"Prayer is a thought, a belief, a feeling, arising within the mind of the one praying."
—Ernest Holmes

Chapter Seven

Prayer is Thought

ake a moment and imagine you are in church. Even if you don't go to church, just bear with me; you'll get the point, I'm sure. The minister directs the congregation to bow their heads in silent prayer. Imagine you are in that congregation, bowing your head, and praying. What do you imagine you'd be doing in that moment? What do you imagine you'd be thinking?

Just consider for a moment what you would actually be doing to perform the act of praying. The answers all lie within these questions. What you would be *doing* is *thinking*, and *imagining* – **period**. What else could you possibly be doing in your mind, anyway? That is, after all, where you think you are praying from isn't it? Whether in church or not, think about the act of prayer for a moment and how you learned to pray.

During the act of prayer, in this scenario, you respond to a directive or an invitation to pray. Each person will do this in their own unique way, but for the most part, they will all go through very similar motions. You close your eyes, perhaps; and maybe lower your head by dropping your chin toward your chest. You might take a breath and begin to organize, and issue forth in the form of a thought, various ideas of requests for assistance, or for the acquisition of some thing or some situation. You may attempt to visualize that thing you desire, and you may simply think the words that represent the content of your request. This may be in the form of a mental "letter" being read in an imaginary voice that you can only monitor in your thoughts.

You may even hear your own voice quite clearly – just as if you were reciting the prayer aloud – inside your own head. The various ways we issue these thought forms, and transmit them to that power with which we aspire to communicate, could be completely different for each person; but each way will simply be variations of the form of prayer we were taught by our parents, or by whoever first introduced us to prayer. We'll discuss this last point later. First, it's important to recognize where and how we were programmed with the information on how to communicate with our Creator.

At this point, let's simply remember that the whole point of the exercise of prayer would presumably be to establish communication with the Source of all creation — that Power that, having created us and everything else, could certainly create the answer to our request. Upon establishing communication with the Source from which we hope to receive an answer, we would then appeal for our particular form of relief. After a review of the request, perhaps to validate its appropriateness, an answer would be received and a part of our life, or some part of someone else's life, would get a little better than before. Isn't that the point?

Of course we exchange a little gratitude for the various blessings that we are aware of in our lives, and then offer our genuine thanks for that which we are about to receive. By the way, there is a verb-tense problem with the phrase "...for which we are about to receive..." that may be neutralizing some of these prayers. We'll look at this in a moment, as well; but for now, just consider that the first thing all humans do in order to get what they want or need is to start thinking about it in one way or another.

So, we have just closed our eyes and bowed our heads, decided what it was we were going to ask for, and formed our wish-list into a letter of request which we then recited, mentally (or even aloud), to our Creator. And we did all this, presumably, because we believe that it is possible to receive an answer; and, we don't know of anything else to do, or any other way to achieve our ends without divine intervention. At any rate, most everyone has prayed in one form or another. And each time, it has followed a similar format — *"Dear Creator, Thanks for that. Please give me this. Thanks again. Amen."* This is pretty much the way it works for most people. Of course, this is just a very simple model of a very basic format for a prayer; but if praying is at all necessary, or worthwhile, then a prayer would consequently require at least these components. So now let's consider the many important implications within this process.

Basically, a prayer is a thought (prayer = thought). You say many thoughts out loud; just as you can pray out loud. But speaking a thought requires that you think it first. All things you consciously do, or become consciously aware of, arise from a preceding thought. In this case, you think about what it is you want to happen, or what you would like to receive. Then you think it in the form of an address to the Creator. Before you did any of this, you first thought, "I'm going to pray for this…" This thought was preceded by an awareness of a need, or desire, for something or for something to occur. So there is obviously an underlying implication that if you think about something in a particular way, it could actually happen – that somehow your mere thoughts could change the course of future events.

Actually, you might be thinking, "No, I think God changes the course of future events for me. I just ask Him to." Either way, we certainly are at least aware of, if not worried about, the possibility that things might not go a certain way, so we appeal to a higher Power to help us out. Would He have done such a thing (correcting a future situation for you) anyway, had you not asked? Are we just hedging our bets? Either way, if we take the time to pray, that is simply one form of thought we have attached a hope of manifestation to.

But what makes that any different from any other thought? What special filtering device do you possess that ensures only those thoughts addressed to God actually get sent to, or read by, Him? You have to consider these questions if you wish to achieve mastery of your thought processes, and take control of your life to some extent. Your prayer actions (or thought processes) will surely benefit from a little attention to detail. After all, in some cases, prayer may be the most important thing you could possibly do; in certain situations, it literally may be "your only prayer," so to speak.

Do you really think that those thoughts that you *think* of as prayers actually get routed to a different place than all the others, as if they had been addressed like a letter? Well, if you do, that's great – you are at least aware that you possess many very powerful attributes of the mind. Do you think that, in addition to answering all these prayers, God has time to sit around sorting your mail (thoughts) for you? Do you also believe that this mechanism only works in time of dire need? Where would these rules come from, anyway? "Ask and ye shall receive…" is not attached to a long list of conditions and restrictions – just try it and see. Later, we'll discuss ways to really do this effectively, but they require a greater awareness of certain attributes of Mind, so let's continue to look at the mechanism of prayer for now.

Every prayer is a thought and every thought is a prayer. The point is, we have thoughts traveling through our heads all the time; those we dwell on – those that receive extra attention and, therefore, extra energy – become manifest more quickly than those we ignore. If you pray, this is the mechanism you are counting on working for you. This is why you highlight these particular thoughts in the form of a prayer. You may have the imagery of God actually listening to you, waiting for you to need something bad enough to go to the trouble of asking Him for it, so He can swoop in and save you at just the right time.

In that case, you would at least have to believe that in those sequences of events, which just happened to end up with you going through the motions of a prayer action of some sort, you did one particular thing to attract God's attention, at least on most of those occasions, and a certain percentage of the time things worked out your way. He either didn't answer, or He did and you either realized it when it happened, or you didn't. Either way, why not ask for what you want? If this mechanism works at all, it works because it is supposed to.

And it does work; I simply can not imagine the extent, or magnitude, of the implications of having so much power at our disposal. Most people can't; yet many still seem to have some special insight on what is and isn't possible – or at least they think they do. Until you can figure out how to build a human, don't pretend to know what parameters may or may not have been placed on those things we have the power to do. All things are possible.

Quite simply, every thought you give energy to is a prayer. And every prayer is acted on in some way by this mechanism proportionately to the amount of energy placed into the thought. Noticing the thought is giving it energy; but releasing it quickly will likely not allow enough energy exchange for the thought to grow and become manifest. Obviously, some thoughts require much more time and energy than others in order to become manifest. For instance, if you really need to speak with someone, and address this thought in the right way, the phone may ring and you will catch yourself saying, "I was just thinking about calling you, and the phone rang, and it was you!" This frequently happens with many of us; and there is a reason, and a very reliable mechanism, which causes this to occur.

If, on the other hand, you think about being an airline pilot, you might also want to think about looking for a flight school – this is one of those things that requires time in order to become manifest in a manner that would be safe and realistic for you. Learning how to direct the necessary energy into a thought, or prayer – or learning how to streamline your thought processes – will result in better, or more effective, use of this mechanism. If you don't believe it, don't do it; and you will definitely *not* be bothered by any of those pesky miracles appearing abundantly in your life. If you do believe, however, then you possess the very fuel on which this mechanism operates; for the mind operates on belief – no matter how small.

When Nothing Seems to Work

There seems to be a million different self-help, self-improvement, and life-enhancement books and programs out there; and oftentimes, none of them seem to work. As long as people have talked about the power of positive thinking, there have been people who have said, "Bah-humbug! This doesn't work!" Have you ever wondered what makes a cynical scrooge an expert on positive thinking?

There are two components to making your thoughts really count. First, there is what you think; this is your prayer, or the plan you are "trying" to make work. Remember; if you're trying too hard, you are not relaxed. The other component is HOW you think, or more specifically, how your thinking is polarized – positively, or negatively. If your perspective is negative, the only way the Universe can respond is to bring you that which you greatly fear. If you can't seem to think positively, release the negative thought patterns by putting your attention on serving and blessing others. When you begin giving from the heart, you will begin thinking with the heart; when you learn to think with the heart, you will soon learn to believe with your heart and your life will unfold for you "as you believeth in your heart." When you can't seem to make things work, *let them.*

The Bible says to dwell on those thoughts that are good. This, indeed, is the key to observing only good in one's life. The mere fact that we all pray, or think, about the things we want – in every case – before we actually have them could be reason enough to take this advice. It is clear that, to some degree, we are able to appeal to a Power that is privy to our thoughts, to assist us (or simply do it for us…) in creating a reality we would prefer over our current reality.

It seems that, in cases where we seem to really think it counts, our thought-requests bring forth better situations and outcomes. We must be keenly aware of the reliability of this process, at some level, because we continue to fall back on it; and we pass it down to our children. People tend to drop those practices which do not work, or which no longer serve them. After at least thousands of years, however, we still pray. Why? Because prayer works; and if we just look around us we will see the great differences between the lives of people who either don't pray, or don't pray effectively, and the lives of those who do pray effectively.

Interestingly, effective prayer doesn't require that you realize you are praying. Conversely, many people who do realize they are praying, and are quite devoted to the process, aren't actually praying effectively. In many of these cases, prayers never seem to be answered, but the same ineffective methods are adhered to out of a deeply-rooted fear and a fairly common resistance to change things in one's life.

The fact is there is a mechanism through which prayer actions seem to be processed. This mechanism doesn't require that you use the word "prayer," or any form thereof; but it does require a certain mindset, as prayer (thought, meditation, contemplation, etc…) is a wholly mental activity. There are indeed conditions within which thought seems to manifests itself perfectly, and therefore conditions outside of which prayers will appear to go unanswered. Realize that there are many things to consider within the simple act of prayer; and if your prayers aren't getting answered to your satisfaction, you need only take a few moments to think about and try subtle variations to what you are probably already doing. This is important to each of us because we walk around thinking all day, and each of these thoughts are being acted on as if they are prayers.

If we are careless and dwell on our problems, then these are the kinds of things we fill our lives with. Our negative thoughts are receiving the attention that our prayers deserve, and are manifesting in our lives. If you don't believe this, then you probably believe that the negative things in your life are being thrown your way by a malevolent God out to destroy you – or at least torture and torment you with a life of frustration. While it is true that you may have been taught these kinds of things about God, you alone have the power to see the God that is in your own life. No individual outside of you can describe your God to you. If you see the world as a dangerous place, then you probably see God as the biggest danger of all. Could anything else be logical?

This is the result of programming, or a deteriorating set of thought patterns, and needs to be addressed if you truly wish to live a life of fulfillment. God is not out to get anyone; and if you think you are a victim of life, then you are indeed a victim – but only of your own thought processes and of those who programmed you to think this way. Prayer works. Thoughts are things. Take a moment to learn how to use this unlimited power. Turn the page.

Chapter Seven Key Points and Afterthoughts

- All knowing is only possible through the mind.

- What you know about God, religion, science, yourself, and even your own mind, you can only know within your mind.

- If you do not understand how to use your mind, you do not understand how to best communicate with that power you believe created you and all you see. How could you?

- If you do not understand the nature of mind and thought, how do you know what your thoughts are doing? Do you think your life, and your experiences are completely unrelated to the tone and nature of your thoughts?

- Praying, meditating, contemplating, dreaming, planning, obsessing, thinking, wondering, remembering, focusing, and concentrating, are all mental activities. These aren't the only words for the things we do with our minds; but this list should be long enough for you to see that there are many different mental activities that we would simply consider to be "thinking." What do you think the big difference between praying and obsessing is? What do you believe to be the filter between one kind of thought and another – the "switch" that makes the Universe listen to some thoughts and ignore others?

- Praying is thinking; prayer requires using your mind. The more you know about using your mind, the more effectively you will be able to use it. If I understand that my cell phone doesn't work very well in a certain part of my house, then I will make sure I am not in that part of my house when I am making a very important call. This may be the best I can do to ensure that my call is heard clearly and completely.

- Like a computer, the mind has many functions and capabilities – most of which remain untapped and unexplored. As with a computer, the results of your mental activities depends greatly on your ability to "use the system;" the variety of human experiences, success, and failures, illustrates the reality that your mental life is variable, but not automatic.

- Success is not guaranteed, though participation is indeed required; success depends on the degree to which you participate – mentally, spiritually, and physically.

- The more you know about the game you are playing (Life), and the equipment you are using (your body and mind), the better your chances of victory. Learn to think positively and focus on your goals and desire – allowing, blessing, and quickly releasing any negative thought energy.

Chapter Eight

Right Thinking and Right Living

inally, brethren, whatsoever things are true, whatsoever things are honest, whatsoever things are just, whatsoever things are pure, whatsoever things are lovely, whatsoever things are of good report; if there be any virtue, and if there be any praise, think on these things." This passage from the New Testament contains excellent advice for setting up the conditions of right thinking, which naturally leads to right, or Dharmic, living. Every living thing knows what is right and what is wrong, or those things which support life and those things that shorten it.

The above passage is not only good advice, but contains an implicit warning about the power of your thoughts. Those things we dwell on will most likely come to pass. This is the nature of prayer, and it is the way of our world. We must become masters of our thoughts, or at least make an honest attempt to spend our time thinking pleasant thoughts, thoughts that are positive, and thoughts that we would like to see manifest in our lives – because this is exactly what happens with those thoughts.

When you think about this, you will hopefully come to an understanding of why right thinking is so important. Also, you should come to the realization that thinking any other way really makes no sense at all. Why dwell on that which we see as being negative or that which we do not want in our lives? If you don't want to spend time experiencing it, why would you want to spend time thinking about it, anyway?

When we truly open our eyes and begin to see, it is clear that all things are intricately woven together. Form follows thought and we attract into our lives those things that resonate with us. Increase your resonance, your life energy, or "Spirits," and your life will surely reflect this positive change. If our thoughts do become things in our reality (which is what you presumably believe if you pray), why spend time projecting negativity into our path, when we could instead be paving the way for ourselves with bliss and joy?

We often do things out of spite – sometimes just to spite ourselves. When we are feeling better about things, we usually come to regret those moments when we acted out of some negative feeling or patterning. What good comes from banging your head against a wall? Have you ever seen someone become so angry that they actually punched a wall? Later, while nursing a broken hand, what seemed to you, at the time, like an excellent way to vent your frustration is no longer such an appealing option.

In fact, anything you do while operating in an *"I'll show them!"* mode, or mindset, is coming from a part of you that you definitely do not want running your life! These angry outbursts often seem like genuinely righteous acts of vengeance; but think about that for a moment. There is no such thing as righteous vengeance. Vengeance, for any reason, is harmful to you – whether it accomplishes its intended goal of harming the other person, or not. Is that really how you want to be living your life? Does that really sound like a good plan to get ahead or to get anything that you want out of life?

I hear that "living well is the best revenge." Well, life shouldn't be about revenge, but if you are a "wall puncher," you may want to consider this alternative. The fact is that living well is the only thing that makes sense. Why else live? Stewing in negative thoughts and emotions is an absolutely ridiculous waste of one's time and life. You have this one life, right here, right now, and you have free will to do with it as you please. You can choose to spend it being mad at the world, or at those you love; or you can spend it loving the world and the people around you. One leads to joy and fulfillment, one leads to disease and death. That is a well-known, well-documented, medical, and scientific fact, not just some ideological philosophy.

Imagine you are standing in line at a fast-food restaurant. When it is your moment at the counter, you have a choice to make. You can ask for what you want, or you can ask for what you do not want. Whatever you ask for, however, is what you get. Like it or not, it is your choice. Who can choose for you? Life is actually a bit more to the point, or a bit more attentive to your "order," than the person at the fast food restaurant – not wasting anytime creating what you have asked for, and not holding back on the variety of manifestations it shows you.

In other words, people who spend their days stewing in the misery, anger, and depression that only perpetuates itself in the absence of some positive intervention, are people I imagine stepping up to the counter and saying, "I'll have the rotten garbage, with a side order of despair. And make it quick, I haven't got all day! Oh, and give me a large diet cola with that, too." You get what you ask for; and in life, spending time thinking about something is indeed asking for it. That is the nature of thought and prayer. Be careful what you ask for, you will most likely get it!

This moment, right now, is one of those rare moments when you can know something for a fact. It is a fact that doing something nice, kind, generous, or loving, makes you feel better, not worse. This is proven to reduce stress, thereby lowering the risk of getting any illness. The neurotransmitters and hormones released while experiencing *love* (in any of its forms) are better, in every possible way, than the drugs people take recreationally in order to induce euphoric states. So basically, it's like this: *If you deal with others from a place of love, you will be happy, healthy, feeling as good as you possibly could emotionally, and psychologically; and you will actually have a healing affect on people by simply being near them.*

Also, as a bonus, pretty much everything that ever happens to you will be good, and you will lead a nearly perfect existence in every conceivable way. This is a fact. There are very few humans willing to make the effort to live from their heart at all times, but for those who do, there can be no greater reward than life itself. For life itself would be total bliss. It's really only fear that keeps us from having this experience of bliss. Fear causes us to armor our hearts against possible harm. This closing of the heart steals our ability to experience such blissful realities, as bliss is achieved only through an open heart. Armoring the heart further stifles our ability to believe, or have faith in anything new. Not being able to envision new realities leads to stagnation and decay. This is the way to death. Right thinking results in right living; and right living is the way of the heart – the way of life.

The true power of the Bible is that it displays the ability of people throughout time to put their minds on thoughts, believe that the thoughts have already occurred, and then experience a new reality. The authors of the stories in the Bible are simply sharing with us a warning that, in life, all kinds of "stuff" is going to happen to us and as soon as you think you've seen it all, there will be something new facing you.

But, whenever it gets really bad, you can simply picture a new reality, and have faith it has come to pass. Jesus helped people learn how to not be oppressed. He showed people that you can use the power of belief to heal yourself and create any life you desire. You can even change the political power structure if enough of you believe it. In fact, if enough of you wanted Rome to fall, and you spent your days thinking on that, only God knows how that might come to pass – but come to pass it will. Who would have thought that an idea, like Christianity, could ultimately lead to the fall of Rome? Prayer works. And prayer always works for you, not against you. If you are thinking worrisome thoughts and they come to pass, it is not my worries, or the worries of another, working against you; it is prayer working *for* you – giving you exactly what you spend your time thinking about.

Gandhi, Martin Luther King, Jr., the Wright brothers, Nelson Mandela, and countless others have empowered people to see what they wanted for themselves, not what they were suffering; they helped us to believe in something new. They were able to describe, to some extent, the simplicity that is so elusive. See where you wish to be, not where you wish not to be. Jesus simply asked people, "Why do you suffer, why do you complain? How do you wish it to be? Well then, if you believe it, so shall it be."

In plain and simple terms: "If you just tell me what your problem is, I'll help you understand why you are seeing it that way and how you can find a better way to look at it. If you believe that this new way is better, and you believe that it can be a reality, then it is." It's up to you to change your reality; and you do it simply by changing your mind. Pretty simple, huh?

We have made it so much more complicated, but creation really is just that simple. Jesus was trying to show people what they could do for themselves, but the people didn't understand and thought they were seeing a God performing miracles, rather than a teacher of *the Way*. Most people came to "see the show," rather than to listen and learn.

The point of Jesus' ministry wasn't, "Hey! Look what I can do!" His ministry was about, "Hey! Look what YOU can do! All of you – you were all born with this power." He wasn't trying to impress people with parlor tricks; he was educating them to the *Way* it is really supposed to be – the *Way* nature really works. If it can be done, it can be done;

you either believe that or you don't. You can change any situation by changing your mind. Spend your days thinking about the good things in life – the things that make you happy – and you will know joy. Spend your days doing those things you love and prosperity will follow. You will see the things in your life you wish to see. This is the recipe for right living.

We get so preoccupied with enforcing what we believe to be Biblical mandates for all to adhere to, for all-time, that we miss the point of the whole thing. The bottom line is that a group of people with a common belief can change the world – and they frequently do for better or worse. It helps if you strive to be a good person, but this is just the way it is. From time to time, there will be those among you who figure out how to use this formula for manifestation, and who seem to attain some degree of mastery.

Sometimes, it will be a bad person who visits misery on mankind, but good will always triumph, because nature always has a failsafe survival mechanism. Either people will find the power within their hearts to rise to the occasion with courage and faith, or they will be pressed to the point of surrender or die. In the past, those people who surrendered not only lived, they ultimately triumphed over their oppressors without resorting to violence. In the act of surrender, they found freedom – a broken heart is also an open heart.

We are not here to judge others; we are here to experience our own experience. If you are making the most out of your experience, how do you find time to judge others in theirs? The best way to save the world is to leave people alone. This is akin to the proverbial, "If you don't have something nice to say, don't say anything at all." Work on yourself. Matthew 7:1 reads, "Judge not, that ye be not judged." As if this needed clarification, Jesus compounds this statement FIVE times in the next four sentences. There is not one other place in the Bible where a point was more clearly expressed – there can be no clearer expression of hypocrisy than judgment.

You know that you don't know everything, none of us do; we only know what we know. So stop pretending that you know something about how another person should live their life. You couldn't know how to be them anymore than that person could know how to be you. Everything has a purpose. Pretending to know things can lead to an unwillingness to learn new things; so learn all you can. If you must pretend, pretend to know nothing. That way, it will seem natural to want to learn new things. You will do yourself a big favor by becoming the best *you* that you can be. If things in life bother you, make you mad, or push any buttons for you, then you are a victim of your judgments and this is a sign for you to take a moment and work on yourself before you start experiencing physical symptoms because of these emotional triggers. This is basically where all dis-ease is born – in the stress caused when life doesn't match our beliefs about life. Your salvation lies within your mind.

You can choose to occupy your mind with harmonious thoughts, and you can choose to believe in any reality you wish, but the one you believe in is the one you get. If you are not choosing thoughts that serve your highest good, you are not thinking right. You are not bad, you are simply experiencing less than your share of something you are entitled to, and that's not the way it is meant to be; it's just the way it is. You deserve so much more than that; you are entitled to so much more out of life than you can even imagine right now.

Right living is the result of right thinking. You project *right* thoughts out ahead of you on the road of life, and then you experience the reality of living in those *right* thoughts when you have arrived at them – or more specifically, when time has delivered them to you. If you are experiencing turmoil, you are experiencing the result of at least one stray negative thought, or maybe an intentionally placed negative thought. The thought, which you may have long since forgotten, has come to fruition as an obstacle in your path. By redressing the original thought, or by creating a new thought to replace the negative one, we project better realities into our path and then we live the *right* thought.

The right thought leads to the living of that right thought – right thinking leads to right living. Any obstacle is but a moment of your life, unless you prolong the experience by dwelling there in your thoughts, instead of allowing that moment to fall into the past. Allow your mind to let go of the negative so it will be able to take hold of your next experience – hopefully one created with peace and joy in mind. Fill your life with pleasing thoughts of the reality you desire. Do not dwell on the negative. It takes right thinking to project positive experiences for ourselves, so get in the driver's seat and get in the right lane to right living. It's not that difficult, and your life will surely be a better place to live.

Chapter Eight Key Points and Afterthoughts

- Psychology equals physiology; our thoughts produce the electrical impulses which produce the chemicals responsible for creating the physiological changes we experience as emotions, or feelings. Feelings are indeed us FEELING electrical, chemical, and physical changes occurring inside our bodies as a result of thinking. When we think happy thoughts, we have happy feelings; sad thoughts cause us to feel sad, etc.

- Coincidentally, or not, the chemicals that are good for us make us feel good. When we think a thought, we can tell whether or not the thought is good for us by the way we feel. If the thought released chemicals that are bad for us, we feel bad, or uncomfortable, so that we might make the association and stop thinking the unproductive or harmful thoughts which have caused our physical suffering.

- You are free to think whatever you wish; but each thought is a seed which produces after its own kind. Each thought will bear fruit. You may think you were right, or justified, in a particular action; but if it does not add love to the world, it will only add pain to your experience.

- "As a man thinketh, so it is done unto him," is a statement of the Law; ignorance of this Law does not excuse anyone from the natural operation of this Law. In other words, the people who are rude and violent in the world, or who are victimized by life, are thinking negatively without realizing it in many cases. Nonetheless, their negative thoughts are just as creative as anyone else's negative thoughts.

- Open your mind to the greatest possibilities; no one knows what they don't know they don't know. All possibilities wait in the unknown; do not waste precious time with negatives. You can't afford the luxury of a negative thought; all thoughts are creative.

- Following rules does not necessarily make a person happy; only choosing to be happy guarantees happiness. Do what makes you happy; and do what your heart tells you is the right thing to do. If it is right, and makes you happy, you have found something worth doing.

- "Do unto others," and "Judge not," are good advice because they help you as much as they help others. The nature of these teachings isn't to protect others from your wrath and judgment, but to protect you from the harmful effects of such mental activity.

"Belief creates the actual fact."
— William James

"…whatever you ask for in prayer, believe that you have received it, and it will be yours."
— Mark 11:24 (The New Testament)

Chapter Nine

The Belief Formula

he essence of prayer is to effectively create, or see, a change in the way things currently are. Your wish, or desire, is your prayer. Obviously, we don't pray for those things we do not desire, but dwelling on a thing will certainly bring it to pass. This illuminates one of the most important aspects of effective prayer — mindfulness. We must be ever diligent in our thought and word as it is these things that become manifest for us.

It is apparent everywhere we turn that those who dwell on the negative live their lives mired in negativity and stressful conditions, and situations. It is said that a man who can see the good in every situation will always be grateful. It is this gratitude that empowers us to bring more good into our lives. Life is too complex for most people to always side-step adversity; but once you have found yourself there, dwelling in that place is the best way to ensure a long stay. Seeing adversity as a lesson, challenge, opportunity, or a reminder to be more mindful, on the other hand, will keep your mind in the proper place from which effective prayer can be rendered.

By *effective prayer*, I mean that, while each thought is a prayer of sorts, and will be acted on in some way; we can effectively manage our energy and direct more of it in the direction of those thoughts that would bring the most beneficial effects into our lives. If we are thinking anyway, why not think *creatively* instead of destructively. Even when negative thoughts arise, there is no reason that we must focus on them. If we simply let them go, they will be replaced with new thoughts. If we focus our energies on positive thoughts, they will ultimately become our dominate thought patterns. If we achieve a state where the only thoughts we ever experienced were positive, or good, thoughts, then these are the things we will find filling our lives.

Effective prayer begins with mindfulness and awareness that each word was first a thought and each thought is essentially a prayer. With this awareness, and the further understanding that we exist within that which always tries to accommodate us and answer our prayers, we would see how counterproductive entertaining a negative thought for even a moment can be. This is what is meant by the saying, "You can't afford the luxury of a negative thought."

In Ecclesiastes 5:1-3, the author warns us to, "Keep thy foot (*"watch your step"*) when thou goest to the House of God, and be more ready to hear, than to give the sacrifices of fools; for they consider not that they do evil." And, "Be not rash with thy mouth, and let not thine heart be hasty to utter anything before God: for God is in Heaven, and thou upon the Earth. Therefore let thy words be few." Again, being careful what one asks for seems to be the theme here. This basically means to be mindful when you go into prayer, or meditation, or wherever you go to communicate with God, and seek silence rather than listening to the noise of the day; for it is in the silence that we will hear the voice of God.

Our "vain repetition" or utterances of scriptures and prayer, without understanding or emotion, is considered the "sacrifice of fools." Most people do not consider the fact that this type of prayer is far from what the masters have taught us about prayer and the use of human thought processes; and are unaware that this is the reason for the conditions we find in our lives. We would do well to think *and* feel before we issue forth our prayers; because we know God will answer, but we do not know what form that answer may take in the physical world.

With careful attention to our thoughts, we can also begin to see how quickly the pattern of manifestation unfolds. If you pay attention to the thoughts you entertain, and then observe the world around you closely, you will begin to see more and more of what you once believed to be coincidences. The more you notice these events, the easier they are to unravel until the original, underlying thought becomes visible to you.

Once you have achieved this level of awareness, things will start to happen pretty quickly. It may begin to seem that practically every time you think of someone, your paths will cross in some way, or whenever you ask for something, you receive it in a very short period of time. Then you may find that the variables in these equations, like how long it takes, or how big it is, are proportionate to the energy and belief that you put into a particular thought or prayer action.

Things seem to happen quicker for people with stronger belief in the process. Now, if you are sitting there thinking, "I go to church three times every week, I tithe, I do everything I am supposed to do, and my prayers don't get answered like that!"; you must realize that performing rituals, and having an absolute belief in this process are two completely different things. There are many people who do all of those things, but don't really believe they can have whatever they want. In fact, most people that do all of those things probably don't really believe that they are *worthy* of having their every desire fulfilled. This is very common.

How many times have you called yourself a "sinner" in an effort to seem appropriately humble and unworthy of the greatness of God? "God is perfect, and I am just a sinner. It is only by His 'amazing grace' that a 'wretch like me' could be saved from Hell." If you believe in this way, get used to disappointment when it comes to prayer. God doesn't create wretches, and He certainly doesn't save them. God helps those who help themselves.

If you want something, ask for it. If you truly think you are an unworthy wretch, you probably won't bother asking for what you want; which is an excellent way to ensure that you won't receive it. The very same thoughts you construct and entertain to garner some sort of mercy, pity, or kindness, from God, are the thoughts that will keep you from believing that your prayer has already been answered. These are the thoughts you must mindfully banish if you wish to fill your life with divine abundance. There is no room in the light for darkness of any kind – self-pity and self-loathing included. **Calling yourself a sinner is – by definition – a sin.** You are judging God's creation as less than perfect and this demonstrates only fear and a lack of true understanding – a lack of gratitude and appreciation for what God has done and given you. In other words, you have clearly "missed the mark."

Mindfulness ultimately leads to what is really the most important component of effective prayer, and that is belief. When Jesus spoke of belief, He was trying to impress on His followers the importance of belief – belief in the process, and the very effective systems He used to perform what His followers saw as miracles. It is really quite simple; things are the way they are believed to be. This works in every possible direction. You will recall an event the way you believe that it occurred, whether you are accurate, or not. By the same token, if you believe you will die of cancer in three months, you will unless you replace that belief with a belief that you will survive.

Later, we will look at the use of prayer for healing, and why this was perhaps the most important part of Jesus' ministry. He basically taught people how they could, if they only believed, convert the power of their thought and belief into a physical reality. Where could this power possibly be more important than in the restoration or management of one's health and quality of life?

Jesus, for this reason, used healing as a powerful inducement to convince others to at least give his methods a try. What better motivation? If we refuse to hear Jesus' message for what it truly was, then we are doomed to a life of misery (hell) and lack; and our assuming this human form for this time we are here may very well have been a wasted endeavor. If we are meek (fearful), instead of courageous and faithful, then all we get is earth – the earth we clothe ourselves in and the earth we return to.

Our true inheritance is the power and the kingdom; but we must believe to achieve. If we are meek, or timid and unsure, this reflects an obvious doubt, or lack of faith and belief, and all we will inherit is the earth and those worldly things we find laying around us. We are here to be and do – to live and learn – not to have and hold onto temporal things. Confusion on this point leads to a great deal of suffering as people replace *health and happiness* with *money and possessions* as their primary focus in life. Money isn't bad; in fact, it can do tremendous good in this world. The focus on money, rather than on joy and bliss, however, is a tremendous distraction which can undermine us in a big way! This is obvious if we simply look around and observe human nature.

Effective prayer can be arrived at accidentally, naturally, or with diligent practice. An *accidentally*-effective prayer action – one that seemed to produce results, just when you needed them most, despite the fact that your prayers seem to never produce the results you want – is great when it brings you desirable results. These events usually result from a more stressful than usual situation leading to more intense than usual prayer action. In other words, you did something different than usual and got different results – or, at least this time, you recognized the results as such.

Mindfulness may help you remember, observe, and recreate, in future situations, the mechanism that led to your success. If you diligently practice the methods and techniques that do produce effective results, then you can achieve your desires all the time – not just in times of crisis. This is where mindfulness and belief come in. Of course, you may have been raised by very aware parents who taught you, without fear and judgment, how to successfully create the outcomes you desire. In this case, you already have an awareness of mindfulness and mechanisms for creating effective prayer actions; and you certainly believe in these things.

We are focusing on developing an effective prayer practice, however, so we must place emphasis on mindful adherence to positive thought and a real belief that the process of prayer works. There are many who would say, at this point, "I believe some of these things, but not all of them. I'm going to just keep doing it the way I was taught in church." That's great and I always advise people to keep doing those things which are working for them – that is, as long as those things are indeed working. The efficacy of prayer is the whole point. If it isn't working, you are either not doing it right, or you are doing other things that are having an even stronger impact on your physical reality. Why continue practices that bear no fruit?

Given a mindful approach to life, and a belief in the process of prayer and manifestation, the only other thing needed to complete an effective prayer action is a technique. Remember, every thought is essentially a prayer and each thought is acted on. Mindfulness in maintaining a backdrop of positive thought, so to speak, will create a life that *is* a backdrop of positive events. On top of this backdrop which we call life, we can use prayer to actively create the scenery we desire.

We do this with prayer actions; that is, by actually praying, or asking, for what it is that we desire. These positive things do sometimes come against a negative backdrop; but "randomly-effective" prayer is more of a survival mechanism than a reliable vehicle to carry you to a life of fulfillment. When you maintain a positive outlook and, therefore, rich and enjoyable surroundings, effective prayer actions only add to the wonder and beauty of your creation. "Asked-for" miracles painted on a canvas of positive experience define a life of fullness and fulfillment. This is worth striving for. If you don't believe it, it is only because you have never experienced it. And this is true of all beliefs.

There are many important pieces to a truly effective prayer action. There must be a desire, even if the desire is to give thanks. The desire is your prayer – the thought that inspires contemplative communication with God, or whatever you believe you are created of and from. Belief is the next critical factor. As we have seen, it is best developed through mindful observation of creation. You must believe that you are presenting a request to the creator and that it will indeed be acted on. You must believe, in other words, in the process of prayer.

The Secret to Life and the Universe isn't really a Secret...

But it is a Formula.

When we speak of the Great Secret of Life, we are speaking of what some call the Law of Attraction; but others simply quote Jesus, or the prophets of the Old Testament, and say that the Secret to Life is: "As a man thinketh, so is he." Regardless of what you call it, we create our experience in our minds – with our thoughts, or prayers. And then, we reap in our bodies and lives what we have sown in our minds. This is simple ancient wisdom and truth. All great religions and philosophies speak of thought and emotions; all great governments have "think-tanks" full of scientist and "idea people" who think-up new technologies and strategies – to use thought-energy to create realities which never before existed. Prayer is concentrated thought; and prayer works – concentrated thought *always* produces results.

Yet, for some, knowing the Secret of Life is not enough; it doesn't seem to work for them. If a person who is of "little faith" thinks they have money problems, and then sets about thinking even more about money than they already do, then it is likely that they will see their money problems getting worse – because they will probably be thinking about money in the same way they were when they acquired the debt, or imbalance, in their financial lives. Now that they know "the Secret," however, things seem to be getting worse.

Thinking only of your intended goal is a big key to success. Some people spend too much time thinking about the "how" and not enough time thinking positively about the goal. But the most important component in true success is the emotion of heartfelt belief. Belief in anything will do; it is the emotion, or feeling, that matters. Once you find that feeling, you need only apply it to any dream or goal in order to create success. Unfortunately, many people never figure out how to think positively; so they just think MORE of the same OLD thoughts – and get more of the same old things. How you think is as important as what you think. The Secret to happiness, in other words, is thinking happy thoughts.

If you find this difficult at first, that's not unusual; try simply surrendering any doubt, even if only for a moment, for the sake of a brief experiment. The next component is the thought pattern (prayer) that is intended to convey the essence and nature of your desire to the appropriate department for processing or, in other words, to the creative force, or creator. This is essentially an equation for manifestation. To manifest a particular desire, you observe the thought which alerts you of your desire, and then your Answer will be created by multiplying your Thought of the realization of this desire by the power of your belief. We might express this as, $A=PxB$, where (A) is the answer to your prayer which is arrived at by multiplying that prayer (P) by your belief (B).

Imagine that (A) would represent 100, as in 100% fulfillment of your desire or wish. This would mean that to receive the desired answer (A), PxB will have to equal 100%. Consider the prayer (P) for a moment. If you prayed, or thought, about the answer to your desire every moment of every day, you would be devoting 100% of your time to praying for this thing. Or, if you didn't pray 100% of the time, but your intentions were perfectly conveyed to the creator most of the time – without any negative or counterproductive thoughts – this could represent 100% effectiveness of prayer. In this scenario, a little belief will go a long way – even if it be only as big as "a mustard seed." You will ultimately experience that in which you immerse your mind. This would look like: $A = 100 \times 1$.

Or, on the other hand, if you had perfect belief in the process of manifestation, you need only think of a thing briefly and it finds its way into your life. This would look like: $A = 1 \times 100$. These are just arbitrary numbers; but the point is: There must be some degree of belief and a predominating thought pattern to produce a specific result. The product of the combined energies (thought and belief) would need to be sufficient to produce the desired result, or energy would need to be added to at least one part of the system, or equation. Remember, wanting something very badly is not the same as believing very strongly that you have it. It may actually be compounding the reality of your lack of the thing you want. There are many methods, or systems, for working with prayer that will help you achieve some degree of mastery over the variables of this function.

We can look at prayer objectively and see that when we pray, we are creating a thought pattern inside our mind and *thinking it* to God. We do not use any of our physical abilities to broadcast this thought or prayer into the physical world, we simply give it a mental "push" into someplace within us, someplace inside our mind that either answers this prayer, or knows where to find God in order to forward our request for us. Either way, if we pray silently, we must realize that the secret ingredient to prayer is somewhere inside our mind. There are some things science knows about the mind that support several ancient prayer practices, as well as similar activities such as hypnosis and meditation. Basically, there are techniques you can use to achieve the optimum brain function for prayer to be most effective. To understand this better, let's look at hypnosis, self-hypnosis, and affirmation-type prayer, to see how some very interesting parallels between these practices hold keys to enhancing every part of your life.

When using hypnosis, therapist will utilize various methods to relax the client to a point of conscious relaxation somewhere above the sleep threshold. Typically, this is when the brain is in an *alpha* state of brainwave activity. There are varying degrees of relaxation, and different people go into hypnosis differently and achieve results in various levels of trance; but the point is, the relaxation is an attempt to lull the conscious mind into a state of passivity so the beneficial suggestions offered by the therapist can filter into the subconscious mind and help the client experience positive changes or situations. There are other ways of achieving success with hypnosis that don't really involve relaxation, but instead simply bypass the critical factor, or so-called, left-brain cognitive functioning, so the suggestions of the therapist can go, unchallenged, into the subconscious.

In fact, we experience continuous, waking hypnosis when we are children and do not yet possess enough conscious intellect to protect our subconscious mind; so we accept as truth everything we hear from parents, teachers, clergy, or any trusted figure. These suggestions become part of our internal, subconscious programming and, as such, a part of us – our core beliefs. Until a child has reached the age of about 14-years, they remain in a state of high receptivity, or a hypnogogic state, as identified by slightly slower brainwave function than a busy, alert, adult mind. It is in this state that the child's identity and beliefs are uploaded – creating the set of ideas the child will retain as their identity and knowledge about what the world is and how it works. This is why these years are called the "Formative years." Stresses occur later in life when the child finds exceptions to this early programming, but can not adapt to this new information because they were also programmed with fear or inflexibility – both of which are learned behaviors.

Remember, it is our subconscious mind that is the trusting, but fearful, inner child that isn't very mature but does its best to keep us alive. This is who we are talking to during hypnosis – the "son." We are trying to give this inner child a task to accomplish for us. Have you ever told yourself that you would wake up at 6:00 a.m., and then went to bed without setting an alarm and woke up at the time you had stated? That was your subconscious mind doing its thing. That was self-hypnosis; and that was the way prayers are answered in a very simple demonstration of ask-and-receive.

In fact, my point about hypnosis is that people go into a hypnotherapy session with a request, like wishing to lose weight or stop smoking, and the hypnotherapist bypasses the critical "Father" who may, because of past experience, not believe that it is possible to quit smoking. In this case of a lack of faith, the therapist can utilize a more effective thought pattern (P) to achieve the desire (A) of being a non-smoker. If you believed (B) strongly enough, then you wouldn't need the elaborate prayer, or technique (P), the hypnotherapist provides; you could simply thank God for making you a non-smoker, and then enjoy your new reality as a non-smoker.

Make no mistake, hypnotherapy works; and it works in a very similar manner to prayer. People who believe they can't achieve their desires for themselves – usually out of lack of faith or will-power – can tell their desire to the hypnotherapist, who then bypasses the "thinker" and delivers the request (prayer) directly to the same part of the mind (the "Knower") that receives your inner thoughts when you build up your prayers in your mind and then release them into an even deeper part of your mind. That is the subconscious mind.

Now, whether the subconscious then takes the necessary steps, or forwards this prayer to someplace that we have no conscious access to, is of no consequence to us. We don't have to know how it works in order to benefit from it. God works in mysterious ways, but we know this works. In fact, people have been doing hypnosis for thousands of years; and over 140 years ago, a Scottish physician wrote a book describing hundreds of surgical operations he had performed while using only hypnosis for anesthesia. There were no complications, and recovery time was much quicker than with traditional methods. Also, there were fewer post-operative complications.

The fact that a hypnotist can also induce practically every negative medical symptom known to man by simply suggesting it, gives testament to the fact that we can generate negative realities with negative thought patterns. Hypnotists don't actually *cause* the negative symptoms in these demonstrations; they simply suggest a symptom to a part of your "thinker" which takes advice literally and acts on it immediately. This is the basis of "being careful of what you ask for because you just might get it!" Being careful of what you ask for is the same as being mindful of your thoughts; and as thoughts are prayers, this is clearly a warning that prayers for bad things are answered in the same manner as prayers for good things. As a hypnotherapist, I have always viewed hypnosis essentially as assisted prayer – helping people pray for things they can't figure out how to pray for on their own.

As for the religious implications of hypnosis – there are none. Hypnosis, like people, prayer, and God, was around long before any religion or religious practices were created by man. In fact, hypnosis and other trance-work were very likely what led to the visions that inspired us to think we needed organized religions. Hypnosis, in other words, was very likely one of the precursors to religious practices that has been all but lost to most people.

In Numbers 12:6, the author writes, "And He said, hear now my words: If there be a prophet among you, I the Lord will make myself known unto him in a vision, and will speak unto him in a dream." Also, in Job 33:14-16, "For God speaketh once, yea twice, yet man perceiveth it not, in a dream, in a vision of the night, when deep sleep falleth upon men, in slumberings upon the bed; then He openeth the ears of men, and sealeth their instruction." Throughout the Bible, the messages that we are responding to are simply the dreams of men. The constant war in the Middle East can be traced back to a dream in which one man was "told" that his people were entitled to a particular piece of land. We understand the dream state better now; and can confirm the absolute ability to contact higher intelligence in these various states and levels of consciousness.

Just because we have lost touch with our guidance over the centuries, replaced by the continuous onslaught of high-energy media and entertainment distractions to our central nervous system and peace of mind, there's no reason we shouldn't be seeking to reclaim that connection. Indeed, it is that connection which is our birthright and the source of our life and power. Why should we allow ourselves to live at the mercy of several-thousand-year-old dreams when the nature of this guidance is forever changing, and when we have been given instruction as to where and how to find this guidance? We can have our own dreams; and they will be more appropriate and helpful in our own circumstances. These gifts are a part of our humanity.

All of the prophecies in the Old Testament were dreams and visualizations of men – not gods. Joel 2:28 reads, "And it shall come to pass afterward, that I will pour out my spirit upon ALL flesh; and your sons and your daughters shall prophesy, your old men shall dream dreams, your young men shall see visions." If we do not avail ourselves of the various forms of sensory input we are capable of receiving, then how are we to know God? From the stories of men whose own beliefs have long since shut them off from this source of all knowing? These scriptures are not simply meant to confuse us or to instruct us to take a goat to work and sacrifice it to our boss when we want a raise or promotion; they are intended to reveal the nature of receiving communication from God. This happens in very specific states of mind and consciousness, as is reflected throughout all ancient writings – including the Old and New Testaments of the Holy Bible.

The simple truth is that nothing happens in hypnosis that doesn't happen in prayer – except the definite, measurable, and often immediate, results hypnosis produces. Again, if your style of prayer is doing this for you; keep up the good work. If it is not, however, and you want it to, you need only look into your own mind and observe how it seems to operate. The answers all lie within, just as the Kingdom of Heaven does.

When you do self-hypnosis, there is no therapist with you. Instead of having someone else "stick their head in your closet" for you, you go into your own closet (subconscious mind). As Jesus said, "…what you ask for privately (in your subconscious mind) will be given unto you openly (in your physical reality). Self-hypnosis is, in my opinion, no different than prayer except for the fact that the word *prayer* holds religious connotations.

If I said that I were going to go in my room, close the door, and sit quietly for a while and relax, and that I would then proceed to issue forth, in thought form or verbally, such statements as, "God, thank you for restoring my health; thank you for making every cell in my body perfect and whole according to divine order," etc, and I would repeat such things for a time before I stopped; would you say I was describing the act of praying, or self-hypnosis for the purpose of achieving health and wellness? How can you tell the difference?

If I were giving a client instruction to continue self-hypnosis for such a thing, the only thing I would add would be instructions on how to relax or get in the best possible state for opening your subconscious mind to accept these suggestions at a level that will see them become a reality. This would most likely achieve exactly the effect that they hoped for, too.

Hypnotherapists are usually paid quite well because hypnosis works very effectively – no matter what you call it. Basically, I am suggesting that there are techniques that can enhance the way your prayers are processed; you can at least make them work as well as self-hypnosis. I believe that when you come to an awareness that you really are already in possession of tremendous power which, in a variety of ways, can produce all of your desires and create a life of fulfillment, you will stop limiting yourself and start realizing your true potential.

The word "Hypnosis" simply and literally means: Hyper (heightened) – Gnosis (knowing, or awareness). Hypnosis is simply a state of relaxation all humans pass through naturally several times each day – such as when going to sleep, and just after waking up. Your brain speeds up and slows down just like a car. Hypnosis is essentially like driving your car somewhere between 7 and 14 miles-per-hour.

You don't do that very often – unless you are being very careful or very conscious and specifically looking for something. But you can not start and stop your car without passing through that speed range; just like you can not go to sleep, or wake-up without your brain passing through a hypnogogic state. This is why people say prayers as they go to sleep. *"Now I lay me down to sleep..."* "Sweet dreams," and "Good night," are also prayers (or hypnotic suggestions, if offered by an *outside* voice...) meant to induce a peaceful state of mind.

When you have a child, you direct and instruct the child so that, upon growing up, the child has at least your capabilities and awareness of the world in which they live. That is the nature of evolution – each generation reaches a little further than the one before. Children aren't playthings created for the amusement and entertainment of the parent; they are parents-in-training. When Jesus taught that we were children of God, either He meant that in a literal sense (in which case the above logic would apply and we need only learn how to use our powers so we too can become efficient creators); or He used it as a metaphor to get the same point across and to perhaps add the awareness that we are safe and secure with our "Father" watching over us. In either case, it is obvious that we have incredible powers that we have hardly begun to explore. Also, I don't believe we are very far at all from unleashing the true potential of prayer, and similar practices.

Pray at Bedtime

Practically anyone can conjure up the image of a child saying their prayers before going to sleep at night. "Now I lay me down to sleep," were the first words of prayer I can remember using. Thinking about your day before getting out of bed is a variation of the same principle.

We can now measure with machines what people have always understood about the brain and the unconscious mind. Brain activity, which we measure in cycles-per-second, or Hertz (Hz), offers a measurable reflection of sleep and mental activity; as we become fatigued, our brain activity slows and we gradually lose consciousness. Likewise, using only thought, or meditative techniques, we can slow the brain to the level of activity we naturally experience as we wake in the morning and drift off to sleep in the evening. Scientifically, this is known as the Alpha-Theta threshold, and is measured in the area of 7-Hertz (7Hz).

This "sleep threshold," or "sleep-gateway," is a state of being neither completely awake – in the classical sense – nor completely asleep. This is the realm where we can easily deliver our conscious desires to the unconscious part of our brains where they will be acted on – even in our sleep. This is the state of consciousness spoken of by the great masters when they spoke of being "still," or "quiet," or of going "into your closet" when you pray; this is also the state of consciousness used for hypnosis and self-hypnosis. And, this is a state you naturally pass in and out of several times each day – most notably while waking and drifting off to sleep.

So, take advantage of the two best opportunities for prayer, or *natural hypnosis*: Morning affirmations and Bedtime prayers. Shape your life with your bedtime prayers; and script your day with your affirmations. "What you ask for in private will be given to you openly."

Affirmations are another way to achieve things in life and they also give us another example of a minor procedural observation that could make all the difference in the world if you incorporate it into your prayers. Earlier, I alluded to a problem with verb-tense that may be neutralizing your prayers. In hypnosis, and especially in using affirmations, it is important to let the subconscious mind know that the thing you wish to see has already occurred. This may be confusing to some people, but instead of asking for God to give you some thing – which highlights the absence of that thing in your life – thank Him for that same thing as if He has already given it to you.

The latter approach, shifting from future-tense to past-tense, or present-tense, impresses with gratitude the reality that the thing exists. A thing must exist in order for you to experience its presence; reinforcing the reality of your desires existing in this moment is very important to actually seeing them in this moment. Another teaching of Jesus says, "Declare a thing and it is so." This statement is not ambiguous. *See Appendix Three for more information on Affirmations.*

Remember, it is always now, and at any time you are experiencing a thing, it will be *now*. It will never be *the future*; so if you mentally place a thing there, the same mechanism that turns your prayers into reality will keep that thing where you mentally placed it – in the future. If you are still confused, don't worry about it; just do it. Write it down and read it to yourself if you don't think you can keep the tense straight in your mind. Just stop thinking about it and try it – it works. You don't have to convert your religion, or even keep doing it if you don't want to; but the accounts of people who use this strategy diligently are more than compelling.

Let's review what we have so far in the way of effective prayer techniques. Of course, the whole reason for prayer is attainment of something, so the first step would be to become aware of a particular desire. Mindful discernment will help you determine which thoughts are worthy of your attention and energy, and which thoughts are not. One way of determining if a thing, or desire, is worthy of your time and energy is to see how many people will be served, or will benefit, from the manifestation of this desire in the physical realm. Ask yourself, "How much love and gratitude does this prayer contain for all of creation?" Then, you must believe; you must believe in the prayer process and believe that you can indeed realize that for which you pray. Why waste your time praying if you don't believe?

Finally, you must put your prayer into action. This involves formulating a thought pattern that best represents that which you would like to see in your life, and phrasing it as if it is a reality in this moment – now. There are many methods of delivering your prayer action, or new thought form, so try as many as you would like until you find one or more that you like, and that works for you. We will look at several examples in the following chapters.

Basically, you will want to use a method that puts you in a calm, centered, relaxed state, and allows you to pray from a peaceful, thankful spot in your heart; and acknowledge that God has already put into motion that which you desire. Remember, "Whatsoever you ask for in prayer, believing, will be given unto you." The words need not rhyme, or form any sort of verse, they need only convey your deepest desire – that which is in your heart.

The methods in the following chapters will help you get started with some very effective prayer forms. These methods have all proven very effective for those who use them, but are by no means exhaustive. Any method you use will work, provided you believe in the method. However, you must remember that things formed in the physical world operate within certain systems of natural laws. And if you diligently apply these laws in practice, you need only a "mustard seed" worth of belief.

The prayer methods in the following chapters are each structured according to these observable laws, and have worked reliably and predictably for people of all faiths, religious affiliations, backgrounds, and beliefs. It is up to you to apply these principles. It doesn't have to be difficult; you can pray for answers to come easily. You must go to the right place to pray, however. You can pull up to a drive-through car-wash and try as hard as you want to order a cheeseburger, but you are not likely to get it because you are not in the right place. Getting what you want in life is simply a matter of priorities; and priorities are based on beliefs about what is important and what is not. Things got the way they are *now* because you didn't take the time to do these things *then*. I can not set your priorities for you; I can only show you what has worked for so many. The rest is up to you; the time is now. It is always now.

Chapter Nine Key Points and Afterthoughts

- All things are the result, or product, of a union of other things. The answer to a prayer is the result of a desire being expressed in thought – with some degree of faith, or energy from the heart.

- If you think a thing is possible, and you want to experience that thing, then you need only think about it creatively and allow yourself to receive ideas and inspiration which will lead you there. If you follow your heart, you will realize your dream.

- "Bad" things happen to "Good" people when someone thinks of such a thing. We assume that the "good" person must have asked for his own misfortune; but this isn't necessarily the case. Being robbed may feed a hungry person when you otherwise may not have had the opportunity.

- Engaging in a case-by-case study of why bad things happen is a perfect way to keep your attention on bad things. If you don't know better than to dwell on negatives, then what makes you think you are sophisticated enough to figure out the why's and how's of all the negative events in the Universe? Let go of the morbid need to know and you will be a happy, healthy person.

- There really is no "Good" and "Bad;" there is only what you want to experience and that which you do not want to experience. Think only on those things you wish to experience in some way. "Good" thoughts are those thoughts which lead to what we consider to be good outcomes; "Bad" thoughts are those thoughts which lead to uncomfortable or unpleasant outcomes.

- If you believe prayer works, or hypnosis, or meditation, or any other proven method of creating change in the world, then you must believe that thoughts in the mind have creative power. If you believe this, you must realize that there is no logical reason for entertaining negative thoughts.

- At some point, you must charge your prayer with the energy of belief; you must act on your plan and see if it works. Then, if you do not succeed at first, you must continue to execute your plan, or a modified version of your plan, until you have reached your goal, or learned something of value. All outcomes are valuable gifts of experience and wisdom; accept them, bless them, and release them.

Chapter Ten

God and the A-Bomb

lbert Einstein was one of the greatest minds of all time. He was certainly well ahead of his own time. Albert Einstein was very passionate about humanity and cared deeply for his species. He wasn't necessarily known to be all that social, but he did indeed care for humans in general. Einstein spent the better part of his life asking questions and then wrestling with the answers which always came, but proved very difficult to translate into words. Like many people, Einstein figured out that if you posed a question to your inner mind, you would indeed receive an explanation. The problem, in Einstein's case, was that he asked much larger questions, with much more profound answers, than we humans were ready to handle.

When Einstein received one answer, it may have come as one *burst* of information that then took him weeks or months to sift through and translate into something he could share with the rest of us. This is how all great thinking, or creative, processes work; this is what the process of inspired (infused with the spirit) thinking looks like. Then, having information he didn't possess before, Einstein was able to ask even bigger questions.

Soon, the answers he received began to be of such tremendous scale that they could be interpreted in many ways – ways that would lead us to the brink of self-destruction while simultaneously propelling us forward in our technological evolution. Einstein asked questions of himself that were of such tremendous gravity that the answers were both too simple to believe, but so complex that no person will ever truly understand all of the implications.

One such inspiration received in the mind of Albert Einstein was the famous formula which defined the convertibility of mass into energy: $E = mc^2$, or, Energy = mass multiplied by the speed of light, squared. This simple little formula, which partially explained what happens during nuclear fission, was given to Einstein through inspiration; but he first had to ask for it in order to receive it. Einstein wasn't likely to have prayed for a way to incinerate thousands of humans, but this answer was evolved into an atomic bomb that did just that. Einstein knew where this would lead, but also knew there were forces in the world that would surely use such inspiration for evil. So, he basically gave this insight to what he saw as the lesser of two evils, and encouraged President Roosevelt to begin work on the atomic weapon in hopes of beating Germany to the acquisition of this technology.

What Einstein was searching for was a better understanding of God, and of the workings of nature and the universe. What he received were formulas that gave some idea of the relative nature of existence as well as the incredible amount of power we have at our fingertips. By using simple principles of physics, we were able to unleash a tremendous amount of energy – from a *rock*, no less! To get a similar energy release through traditional means would have required moving tons of explosive material, and imparting a lot of energy to make that material detonate. Instead, we got one bomb that could do all of this. Of course, this was a virtual Pandora's Box that we can never close.

Einstein's work was meant for good, not evil; but the problem was that his work fell into the hands of men. We haven't exactly proven to be good stewards of anything we have been given thus far; and true to our nature, some of Einstein's work was used in the development of a tool of mass murder and destruction. Of course, the "trigger man" would make justifications about saving lives – and we were in a war where this may have actually been the case – but this formula held much greater implications than a new, more expedient means of killing human beings.

Proponents of nuclear power will also point to all the good done with nuclear power (it's not just for killing, anymore), but at what price? This is a threat that, having been loosed on the planet, will always be among us. And so we have a lesson of what the mind of man would choose to do with the creative forces of God. If this were a test, we would have failed. Actually, it was and we did. God, the source of all inspired thought, gave Einstein (an inspired thinker), the simple answer to his quest – a formula for the trinity in terms a mathematician could sink his teeth into and work with. I believe God gave Einstein a mathematical formula for creation and existence – a mathematical formula for prayer and how it works. He asked the right question, got the right answer, and then watched it used in the wrong way. There always seems to be another side to every coin.

Einstein demonstrated that he was aware of the nature of inspired thought. He was obviously aware that the information he was given did not come from him, nor did it belong to him; and any person is capable of receiving such insight. The thoughts that emerged in the mind of Einstein would essentially prove useless for anyone without a physics background with which to understand such insight and inspiration.

Einstein understood that there were likely many physicists asking questions similar to those he was asking, and that the mere act of asking the right question in the right way would surely bring an answer. When he received this insight, in other words, he knew it was only a matter of time before other, like-minded scientists "tuned-in" to the right frequency of thought and received the same "transmission." Einstein's letter to President Roosevelt, urging him to pursue a nuclear weapon, clearly demonstrated that he knew it was possible that someone already had. The nature of quantum physics, and the hundredth monkey principle, point to just such a probability of simultaneous discovery.

Einstein didn't invent the atomic bomb; in fact $E = mc^2$, and his letter to Roosevelt, were really his only two contributions to the Manhattan Project (the atomic bomb project). But it was indeed Einstein whose inspired thinking pushed the evolution of nuclear physics. Einstein, like Galileo, Newton, and other inspired thinkers, both before his time and after, understood that entering into a prayer-like state of thought, or mindful contemplation of an idea, would ultimately result in the emergence of gifts of knowledge that would push human evolution ever forward. Unfortunately, humans are rarely ready for such leaps in awareness when they come, and rather than simply evolve, we throw ourselves into various levels of turmoil – sometimes even persecuting the visionaries who bring us these gifts.

After writing the previous chapter, it occurred to me that my simple attempt to point out the nature of the interaction between necessary components of prayer wasn't so simple. The formula, $A = P$ x B, is really no different than $E = mc^2$. In fact, nature is full of such three-part equations; I=v/r (Ohm's Law), A+B=C, $A^2+B^2=C^2$, and other simple expressions point to the importance of unity, balance, and equality in nature.

One thing is made up of other things; and all things can be divided into constituent parts. Our minds work this way, and observe things in this way, because they are a product of the same God that produces all nature. Just because we stumbled onto ways of expressing, in our own language, things we find in nature, doesn't mean we invented the nature we "discovered;" nor does it mean that we invented the laws we use to reduce nature to the stories and equations we use to explain nature's manifestation around us.

What Einstein was looking for was answers to nature's secrets. Manipulating energy seems to be of prime interest because all things are made of energy. If you can reliably manipulate energy, you can manipulate the universe. The danger that often goes overlooked with such discoveries is that control is an illusion – there is no human who can control this kind of power (though there have been many who thought they could). Even under the best conditions, this "genie" is always trying to escape. The only safe way to utilize this great secret is in thought form, or prayer, and even then we must be ever mindful of our tremendous power. Our thoughts which are unseen give rise to that which is seen; by the time we are able to see our thoughts, those thoughts have already had a real influence on our experience – and on our future thoughts.

This simplified expression of this part of Einstein's work has three variables; energy, mass, and the speed of light. Einstein's work was oriented in the physical world and wasn't based on something accelerating past the speed of light, so the variable that seemed to be most easily manipulated was the atomic mass. By experimenting with various elements, each having substantial atomic mass, and using controlled explosives to accelerate the material to very high speeds – very quickly – the amount of energy that was released from the subsequent fusion, or fission, of the nuclear material being used was hardly imaginable at the time.

Nonetheless, someone imagined it; and it did in fact happen. A thought became a thing that can not be undone. "A" became manifest, or became the reality that represented the *answer* to our prayer; and we don't like the answer. Actually, we simply misinterpreted and misused the answer that we asked for, and were given.

We used this secret to unleash great misery on mankind instead of reconciling this new information with old wisdom for the betterment of all men. The merging of two forces of nature to create a third, much more significant entity is the nature of nature – this is the nature of trinity. It shouldn't, at this point, be of any surprise that the atomic bomb project leader, Robert Oppenheimer, named the first atomic bomb test, and the site, *Trinity*. Oppenheimer was inspired by a John Donne poem he had been reading, in which Donne made reference to the "three-person'd God." These writings on the nature of existence, and of the trinity, were inspirational to many who sought to unlock the secrets of nature.

When these physicists saw what they had wrought, however, they all realized what they had done, and that they could do nothing to stop it. The joy of their success was followed by an expanded awareness with which they could clearly see the horror of what was to come. Einstein learned that by joining mass together at tremendous speed, a critical mass was exceeded, and something greater was formed. By crudely manipulating the physical aspects of this formula, you can vary the results slightly, but by working with the other variables, this same formula can be used to create anything imaginable, as well as the unimaginable. On hearing of the news of the atomic blast unleashed on Japan, Einstein is reported to have exclaimed, "Oh, horrible!"

Einstein was able to receive and understand the insight that he was given because he spent much of his life reading and studying this type of information. He loaded his mind with the "bricks and mortar" of physics concepts, just like our minds have been programmed with whatever we have been feeding them. This was Einstein's (m). He accelerated this mass to the speed of thought, or to the level of complete belief in the reality of this concept (which may very well be represented by the speed of light times the speed of light), and released it to that part of his subconscious mind that answers such questions, builds such concepts, and creates our reality.

The answer received was his (E) – a configuration of energy that matched the requirements he established as a suitable answer. He was then able to recognize (know again) that this was what he had asked for. You see; perhaps the most critical part of prayer is recognizing what the answer looks like when it comes. He was able to recognize it because it came to him in the language of mathematics & physics, which is the language he used to ask the question. The answer he received was indeed the nature of physical existence – the trinity. The answer Einstein received was also the method by which he received it; $A = P \times B$, or $E = mc^2$.

The nature of such equations is that if $A = P \times B$, then $P = A \div B$ and $B = A \div P$. Each part is critical to the whole, and each part can be manipulated to change the final answer to the equation, or prayer. If you want to manifest a particular thing in your life, there is an energy exchange that must take place. The answer to your desire will become a reality when the method (P) you use to achieve it, multiplied by the power of your belief (B), supply sufficient energy to balance the equation and give you your answer (A).

The power of our belief is the easiest variable to work with, but the most often overlooked because we can't really quantify it scientifically. I think this is basically what Einstein did. Our methods of achieving our desires (P) are also variable and practically unlimited; but the most powerful force known to man is his belief. Reality is as you believe it is. Your belief creates reality. This is the most powerful force involved in the unification of the trinity. Einstein expressed this factor as the (speed of light) ^{2}, but we can simply believe; the math is so much easier that way. Believe; and it is so.

Our prayers are answered with energy; that's all there is. Whether it is a thought that pops into our heads, or a person showing up on our doorstep, these things are all simply configurations of atoms – they are energy. So our answer (A) to any prayer is going to come simply as an arrangement of energy (E). Our "A" and Einstein's "E" are essentially the same variable; they each represent the manifestation of the fulfillment of our original request. Whether the energy is in the form of so much heat that an entire city is incinerated, or in the form of a healing, energy is energy and all energy follows thought. This Belief Formula, when applied by a warring nation who wishes to win a war by defeating an enemy, may manifest as massive destructive force. It became a reflection of the fearful thoughts of those who wielded this tool – multiplied by the speed and power of belief.

War, essentially, and the desire to destroy the enemy (which we viewed as the Japanese people), were the "bricks and mortar" that were fed into this formula and a huge explosion and subsequent victory was the answered prayer. This absolutely demonstrates the importance of being careful what you ask for. All prayers are answered – even the ones we see as bad. If you think it with enough energy, it will come to pass.

118

Men hoped (prayed) for a method to kill many people, and received one. Even if you argue that they weren't hoping to kill people, they were simply building a new kind of bomb; they still had a vision of a device that had one designed purpose – the wholesale annihilation of humans. This prayer, as history has recorded, was indeed answered. All prayers are not necessarily good; but they are all thoughts. And as thoughts, will be acted on by the creative Force according to basic principles that are observable but beyond any true understanding within the conscious mind of most human beings.

That this power produces outcomes that are beyond our understanding is evidenced by Oppenheimer's reaction to the Trinity test; he was originally relieved that the bomb wasn't a dud. He almost immediately realized the paradox of experiencing relief at the reality that thousands of souls would soon have the opportunity to experience annihilation at the hands of this "idol" to the power of man.

People are often consumed, or driven, by a goal, destination, or an outcome. This is the proverbial finish line many are trying to reach. Unfortunately, when life becomes centered on a destination, thing, or an accomplishment, it ceases to be life – at least in any meaningful sense. We are often so focused on a particular outcome that we are blinded to all else – especially repercussions of that outcome. A small child focuses on bouncing a ball off the outside of a house to the exclusion of any thoughts of a broken window, or any consequences that may follow, for instance.

Likewise, scientists strive to complete a project that will produce a new weapon, or some other potentially lethal device, with little thought given to the day after their project is complete. They focus on a "successful" outcome, or on an arbitrary completion date, but spend little time considering life on a planet where such horrible devices exist! This lust for knowledge, despite what the acquisition of such knowledge might bring, is at the heart of the story of the Garden of Eden, and is truly a tragedy that has befallen mankind.

There is more than enough Biblical literature for a "God-fearing" nation to realize that whatsoever you do unto another, you also do to yourself. "Judge not, that ye be not judged," "Do unto others as you would have them do unto you," and "He that lives by the sword shall also die by the sword," (or bomb, as the case may be…), are but a few of the excerpts from the Bible that warn of the reciprocal nature of the universe. What is so frightening about this is that the same hearts and minds that stand on biblical reference to judge their neighbors for various affronts to God – like drinking, cursing, or being homosexual, for instance – will turn right around and demonstrate that another man-made paradigm is even stronger than religion.

That overriding philosophy, in a time of fear, is patriotism, or nationalism. Patriotism gives us justification to over-ride God's law when it suits the powers that be. "Thou shalt not kill…" becomes, "Thou shalt not kill unless you are the church (Jesus, the Inquisition, Holy Wars, witch burning, etc…), or the government (state sponsored execution, assassination, terrorism, wars, etc…)." You get what you ask for ("ask and ye shall receive"), and if you are thinking about it, you are asking for it.

Just because we can't easily see our thoughts and desires, doesn't mean they aren't real and they aren't there. Energy has always been converted to mass and mass has always been converted to energy. $E=mc^2$ works in all directions – that is how you check the results of such an equation. It doesn't just work this way because some physicist came up with an equation that told the story of manifestation in mathematical or scientific terminology; it works this way simply because it always has. Each is created of the other.

Mass is easy; but obviously it isn't the only part of Einstein's equation that is real, or the formula wouldn't have worked and we wouldn't have "Godzilla" movies to remind us of the "monster" we unleashed on the Japanese people, and indeed on all of humanity – including ourselves. Let's replace the form of energy that the atomic bomb brought us with a form of energy that is beneficial to all men.

In other words, let's replace the heat and explosive force of what the (E) in Einstein's equation became, with a manifestation that supports the highest good and divine order – like peace, or health, for instance. Now, let's replace the mass, in Einstein's formula, with prayer, or a thought form, that aptly conveys our desire – one born of love and gratitude. Finally, instead of using explosives to accelerate nuclear material to great speeds, let's use our belief to accelerate our thoughts to *beyond the speed of mere light*, so that they might break free and become that which we desire – a world free of mass murder by any name.

Einstein's formula is a way to explain the nature of the relationship between energy, matter, and light, thought, or intelligence. It is a formula for the convertibility of one to the other – in other words, the recipe for changing one into another. We used it to convert matter into a lot of energy – several different types of energy, to be precise.

Thought produces various types of measurable energy which, through this equation (working backward from the classic form) are converted to matter. This does not apply only to prayer, but to emotions, habits, patterning, programming, thoughts, feelings, and sensations of all types, which are all combined to shape each moment of our lives – precisely according to the law. This relationship, like Einstein's $E=mc^2$ (in any configuration), is cyclical and always exists. It was not invented by Einstein; it was revealed, observed, and described by Einstein through a process of asking and receiving. This relationship that Einstein describes has always existed, and it always exists – not just when we choose to bang rocks together to make sparks, or "bang" heavier rocks together to make nuclear explosions – but always, in all forms, and in all possible ways. It is nature even when we aren't experimenting with the variables. It simply is.

The atomic bomb is proof that this is a viable concept, and an icon of the tremendous power that man can wield. Prayer, too, is proof of the interaction between these forces. Einstein didn't invent $E=mc^2$, he observed it to be an explanation of an interaction that had always existed in nature. What he did, however, is ask (in thought, or prayer), in his mind, a question no man had yet written the answer to. His question was answered through this same medium and, when acted on, produced very real results.

Einstein shed light on the mechanism through which all discoveries come to light – the mechanism of thought, or prayer. Unfortunately, the light from the atomic blast all but obscured the truth and reality of what actually happened. The fear created by this misuse of power affected the entire planet and ultimately led to years of war, fear, McCarthyism, terrorism, escalating nuclear threat, cold-war, and other derivative by-products that are somewhat less glamorous than the "ultimate victory" we sought and so naively thought we had found.

History has shown us that "ultimate victory" doesn't last, and therefore is an illusion that never did exist. It is a dream chased by mad-men who often convince the multitudes to follow. Every empire ever built has collapsed, or will collapse, because the citizens of that empire revel in their false-pride, grandeur, and over-blown egos, instead of learning about their past. It is this course which dooms all who steer it to repeat their past.

Man is only sophisticated enough, so far, to blow his whole planet up; he's not quite sophisticated enough, yet, to quantify prayer to a degree that will allow him to truly, completely, and finally believe in it. When that time comes, and it will, then belief will be achieved and the trinity will be complete – prayers will be answered instantaneously and manifestation of all desires will be assured. It was perhaps this way before the intellect became such an adversary, perhaps this is the true meaning of the story of the Garden of Eden. Before we convinced ourselves that we possessed some kind of knowledge, our every desire was instantly made manifest.

Our knowledge is not complete, so it is not reliable. When we place our faith in the unreliable, we train ourselves to be faithless. We come to believe, in fact, that failure and disappointment are natural parts of our existence, so we accept them and then we expect them to show up in our lives. We can not always make our desires real with sheer force and effort, so we lose the ability to believe in those desires. It is our desires that comprise our prayers; and a belief in prayer is the only way to make prayer work effectively. You must believe in your desires in order to achieve them. To do this, you must turn to methods that allow you to believe in the reality that you wish to create. You must believe.

This chapter is not intended to be a lesson on physics, or on the history of the nuclear program, but simply a story about how thoughts become things. Even if the thought was born of good intentions, it can be painted, or colored by the filters of our beliefs, to become practically anything. Good thoughts become good things and bad thoughts become bad things. It seems there is always someone in this world that can think a good thing into something bad. Let's strive to think bad things into something good.

If we instead choose to dwell on how tough life is, we continue to live a tough life. Living a tough life doesn't offer much inspiration to think good thoughts, so we continue thinking about what we continue to see in our lives – thereby creating more of the same in a continuous cycle. If you don't take charge of your thoughts, the cycle continues. If you really need a good reason to change your mind, or thought patterns, look around you. It is your mind and your thoughts that has led you here and created all you see. If you find anything you are not happy with, you need only find and change the thought that created it.

The world around us, and our history as a species, supports the fact that we are great creators. Our free will, however, enables us to create misery and destruction as readily as beauty and love. We have the choice to believe in either; the formula, however, is the same. Our intention, in this case, is the only thing that changes and, along with belief, sets the stage and colors the backdrop for all creation. Free will is a gift, but it is also a responsibility. What we do to another, we do unto ourselves and these things can not be undone. Let us be mindful, faithful, and let us all strive to be diligent with our thought and word, for it is with these tools that our tomorrows are built.

Prayer is Choice

Our gift is free-will. This simply means that we can choose our thoughts; for you can not choose a feeling, or an action, without thinking first – or without choosing to think. Our only decision from one moment to the next is what thought to place our attention on. Focused, concentrated attention to our fondest wishes defines any prayer – and we all have the power to choose when and where to focus our attention.

Consider that when you pray, all you are doing is concentrating your thoughts for a brief period of time – usually to give thanks, and ask for help for yourself or someone else. What if you concentrated for more than a few moments? What if you *chose* to spend time thinking about what you wanted instead of the problems in your life? What if you could learn to not worry about things you can not change or control? Choose better thoughts and your life will change for the better. All thought is prayer; all prayers are answered – so choose your thoughts wisely!

"When I do good, I feel good. When I do bad, I feel bad.
And that is my religion."
— Abraham Lincoln

Chapter Ten Key Points and Afterthoughts

- Thought is Energy which we can measure with machines built from human imagination (the same Energy measured by the machines).

- Energy is the same as matter ($E=mc^2$); thoughts are things.

- Certainly thoughts ultimately become things, or cause the creation of things. Good ideas often lead to great creations and even fortunes.

- Thoughts are things; good thoughts are good things, and bad thoughts are bad things.

- If you are thinking a thought, you are asking for a physical expression, or experience, of that thought. "Be careful what you ask for, because you'll probably get it – maybe sooner than you think!"

- Thoughts are energy – all thoughts. Energy is energy; but will travel and manifest along the lines of force, or thought, produced to generate a specific result.

- We often focus on a goal without giving thought to the consequences of creating something; there is always a dual nature to every creation. "Be careful what you wish for; because you'll probably get it!" Goals and wishes are thoughts about desires – prayers are thoughts about desires. Thinking is creative.

- Albert Einstein once said that he just wanted to know *how* God thought; "all the rest," he said, were "just details." When you ask big questions, and remain focused, you receive big answers.

- There's more to the story of the "Genie in the Bottle" than just getting wishes; there is always a balance which often shows up as the "unseen downside."

- We are always thinking and creating with our thought. It seems necessary to first realize that we are doing this, and then learn to consciously create those things we have come to desire, before we learn the ultimate lesson – how to create peace in our outer world by creating peace of mind. This can only be done with prayers (thoughts) of peace, love, and acceptance of what is.

- You must learn WHAT to create, and HOW to create effectively; both are learned through experience.

Chapter Eleven

Methods of Achieving Effective Prayer

here are many different ways in which people pray. The methods of prayer are perhaps as diverse as the people doing the praying. Regardless of the method, however, prayer does have a definite affect on our experience of life in a very real and physical sense. Though science hasn't figured out a way to measure and calculate prayer, and its effectiveness, there are people who have learned how to operate the prayer "mechanism" effectively and reliably. These people use a variety of methods, but all of these methods seem to share some common elements.

We won't waste much time looking at prayers that don't seem to work, but there are also some common traits among these ineffective prayers that could be detrimental to your life and to your prayers. There are many ways to pray, and many of them are very effective. Regardless of the words or methods you use, belief is the key ingredient in any prayer. "Whatsoever ye shall ask in prayer, *believing*, ye shall receive." *Matthew 21:22*

The most effective prayer forms that I have encountered all make use of the workings of the subconscious mind and the various levels of mind and self. Each aspect of you, each level of mind, and each level of consciousness, has its own job to do. When they are all doing their own things, everything is fine and things always work out for the best.

Trouble starts when your subconscious mind starts doing things that your conscious mind usually does, or vice versa. Also, conflict will manifest in the physical realm in response to inner turmoil. When the conscious aspect of you is in some disagreement with your subconscious mind, you will experience real difficulty in the physical realm. You

125

will also find that your prayers do not render the same kinds of results when you are stressed, or experiencing inner conflict, as they do when you are in a state of peace and harmony. Imagine the different aspects of mind as we discussed them earlier and it will help you develop a smooth, working relationship with all the parts of you that must cooperate to get things done. Bring your "selves" together, and your prayers will be answered quickly, surely, and in ways you can hardly imagine.

There are many reliable methods for establishing favorable prayer conditions and outcomes. The most favorable conditions involve placing your subconscious mind – the inner child – in a state of harmony. The subconscious mind is the part of you that is going to deliver your prayer, or get your prayer answered. You must get your prayer to the subconscious mind in the most effective way possible. The ideal state for prayer, therefore, is the state where your subconscious mind is most receptive to beneficial suggestions. This is an "alpha state," or a state where your brain is producing alpha waves, or brainwaves cycling at a rate between 7 Hz and 14 Hz, or cycles per second.

It is in this alpha-state where your conscious mind is relaxed and receptive, and your subconscious mind is open to receive your desires without any conflict from the conscious mind. There are audiotapes, that will produce this state of brainwave activity for you while listening and wearing headphones; but there are many other ways to do this without such devices.

Hypnosis uses many techniques to bypass the conscious mind and help the subconscious accept positive thought patterns, but many of these require the assistance of a hypnotist. Self-hypnosis, on the other hand, is quite easy; and though you can not use some of the same techniques as in hypnotherapy, you can easily achieve an alpha-state and get amazing benefits from any thoughts or prayers you take into that place within, or part of, your mind. Whether you are praying, meditating, or saying affirmations, this relaxed alpha-state is where you want to be.

Before praying, or doing affirmations, set aside a time where you will not be interrupted and go someplace quiet and peaceful. Go someplace where you will not be bothered by any outside distractions, and just relax. If you have soft music you would like to listen to, that's fine; just be sure that the music doesn't have lyrics that will engage your conscious mind, or possibly program your subconscious mind. Music commonly used by massage therapists is usually quite relaxing, and always instrumental (without lyrics or vocal parts). When you are ready

126

to pray, make sure that you have no physical distractions, like having to go to the bathroom, or being thirsty. Get in a comfortable position with your hands by your side and your legs and feet uncrossed. Now, take a few deeper-than-normal breaths and you are ready to begin.

Spend a few moments relaxing your self from head-to-toe. You can visualize a wave of light, or water, or relaxation, flowing over your body relaxing each muscle it covers as you allow the wave to travel from your head to your feet. Or, you can simply relax your muscles one-at-a-time, systematically covering your entire body. In the back of this book, you will find Appendix 1 has specific instructions for doing progressive relaxation, so we won't elaborate on these techniques here. Appendix 1 provides you with a real hypnotic induction commonly used by hypnotherapist all over the world, so you can learn how to relax yourself, and also see what kind of language causes your conscious and subconscious minds to respond in a desired way. Once you have completed your progressive relaxation, you can begin your prayer actions.

Kris Attard, a Senior Mindscape™ Instructor with the International BodyTalk System™ Association, introduced us to a couple of deepening techniques that I often teach to clients to enhance their alpha-state. A deepening technique is a technique that induces a deeper state of relaxation when used in conjunction with any relaxation procedure. The technique involves, after a progressive relaxation, visualizing the colors of the rainbow from red-to-violet. First, visualize the color *red*. If you can not see red with your eyes closed and relaxed, visualize or think of an object that is red, or simply think the word *red*.

When I began using this technique, I thought of a fire truck, then an orange, a lemon, a grassy meadow, the blue sky, there was a particular shade of purple that I could visualize because of a kayak I owned at the time, and then I would visualize violet as having a bit more pink mixed in with the purple. This was my way of visualizing Red, Orange, Yellow, Green, Blue, Purple, and Violet, in this order.

When I went to teach my son this technique, he said, "Oh yeah, Roy G. Biv.!" I hadn't heard this before, but this was the mnemonic he was taught to remember the order of the colors in the rainbow – Red, Orange, Yellow (Roy), Green (G.), Blue, Indigo, Violet (Biv). He had no problem remembering the technique. This color sequence, Kris told me, has some interesting effects on the brain. I find it easy to use, useful, effective, and it does seem to have a perfect deepening effect for this application. It seems to help bridge the gap between physical relaxation and mental relaxation.

Another meditation-type technique used in self-hypnosis, which is also used in Mindscape™, is to visualize your self in a special, quiet place. Make this scene as vivid as you can by involving all of your senses. Choose a place that makes you feel relaxed when you think of it; choose a favorite place, or a place where there is no stress, and put yourself in the picture. My place is a campsite alongside a river. Utilize all of your senses in your imagination. I would pick up a leaf, or a rock, and feel it in my hand. I would hear the water rushing by, and even smell the water and the trees. I would reach down into the river and feel and taste the cool water. I can even visualize a trout in an eddy by my campsite. I see myself sitting on a boulder at the water's edge; and this is where I pray.

This state used to take me anywhere from three, to five, minutes to achieve. Now, I can simply relax my eyelids and my eyes to the point where, if I just casually tried, I couldn't open them. I then spread this feeling over my entire body and walk under a rainbow caused by spray from a waterfall on my river. I closely notice each color as I pass under the rainbow and walk through my quiet scene – touching, smelling, hearing, and tasting along the way – to my "prayer boulder."

This process now takes only a few seconds before I am in a state where I know what I see will come to pass. This will be somewhat different for each person, but the process works if you just do it. The most difficult part of this whole thing for me was coming to realize how real this process actually is, and that it is worth spending time practicing. It is a vehicle that can carry you to the fulfillment of your desires. Believe me when I say that the most successful, healthy, and happy people on the planet all do something similar in order to create their future experiences and realize their goals and desires. You are worth the time it takes to create a great life for yourself with your mind!

Once you have achieved the proper mind-state for prayer, you can begin your thoughtful dialogue with your creative force. By "thoughtful," I mean that you want to be very careful of the words and thoughts that you issue forth from this state. You want to be certain that you only ask for things you actually want to see, or want to happen. It is important here to not focus on things in your current experience that you are not happy with, or are trying to replace; think only about what you want – and do so with love and gratitude.

Relax for Health, Happiness, and Success!

Relaxation is the key to health, happiness, and successful prayer actions. Just imagine trying to communicate with someone who was distracted and chaotic; clear communication is not likely. When you are stressed out, you are not in the most ideal state for communicating, or organizing your thoughts. Stressful thoughts manifest as additional stresses in life; so relax before you pray. Just remember the ancient advice to "be still and know I am God," and to "go into your closet" when you pray.

In order to relax, simply sit in a comfortable position and close your eyes. Spend a few moments thinking about the various parts of your body – telling them to relax. Allow the muscles around your eyes to relax, and the muscles of your face and jaws to loosen, as well; then allow that feeling to spread as you relax the muscles of your scalp and neck, and then shoulders, chest, back, and abdomen. Relax your fingers and hands by consciously telling them to "let go;" and then allow the relaxation to spread to the rest of your arms. You can do the same with your feet and legs – relaxing your feet and then allowing your calves, knees, and thighs to relax. You may want to spend more time on the lower back, shoulders, or any other part which may tend to hold on to stress. A progressive relaxation induction is included in Appendix One of this book; it can be recorded if you would like to use it as a type of self-hypnosis tape to assist you with your relaxation.

Do not enter this state with negative thoughts or emotions, and do not make requests that you will regret later; because you just might! Have the answer to your prayer firmly in mind – write it down, if you have to – before you begin. Visualizing the fulfillment of the desire that inspired the prayer is the most effective means of achieving your answer. Thanking God, or your Creator, for having already made this thing a reality is the next step. Finally, and most important, you must believe in this process and in your desire. You must believe that the answer to your prayer, in other words, has *already* been received. This is confusing, but very important.

Prayers for something to happen *someday in the future* will happen some day in the future; unfortunately for you, you will never be in *the future*. It is critical that you visualize the realization of your desire – the answer to your prayer. Visualize this as if it has already happened and you will, if you believe, see your answer. Notice that in the prayer forms we will look at, the requests are more like gratitude for something that has already occurred than they are like wishes for something to happen. Visualize your fulfillment, visualize your joy at receiving what you asked for, ask *believing*, be grateful for having already received it, and then release your prayer with faith that it has come to pass.

Don't worry about it or try to make it happen. You must simply allow the process to bring you what you want. It works. Try it. Trust it. You have nothing to lose and everything to gain. Remember to be specific and understand you are going to see, or receive, this thing to the extent you focus on it.

"She kept saying to herself..."

In the book of Mark, in the New Testament, there is a story of a woman who suffered a bleeding disorder for 12-years. She had visited many physicians and tried many things; but none of them worked and she only got worse. When she heard that a great healer was coming to her town, she kept telling herself, "If only I could touch his garment, I will be healed." Despite the crowds, and her weakened condition, she made her way to Jesus and touched his garment as he passed by; and she was healed of her condition.

We cannot overlook the obvious facts in this story. The first fact is that she had a *desire* to be made well (A). The next fact is that she developed a *plan* (P); and continued to affirm this plan to herself – as is the case with any affirmation, or affirmative prayer action. Finally, she found the energy within herself, the *Belief* (B) in her plan, to boldly execute her plan – and she did. In the moment she made her plan "real" by putting it into action, her condition was healed. Jesus didn't charge her a fee, or say to her, "You are lucky that I'm 'magic;'" but rather, "Go and be well; your FAITH has healed you." He was telling her that her desire to be well (which she had for 12-years) was not enough to heal her; nor was her plan. Her BELIEF was the **active** factor which **moved** her and brought her desire into physical reality.

To review, the components of effective prayer are: A desire that you believe in and that is not detrimental to you, or anyone, in any way; an effectively formatted request, thought form, affirmation, or prayer, that adequately expresses your desire to the Creator; and Belief in the process and that your desired outcome is already assured. Now, you have to have an effective delivery method, which includes: A quiet, peaceful place; a state of mental relaxation (alpha-state); visualization of your desired outcome; and the delivery of your properly formatted prayer action or thought pattern in a way that leaves no doubt in your subconscious mind as to the reality of the outcome. When you combine these elements, you change your world.

Keep in mind that these are simply suggestions for building effective prayer techniques – not absolute requirements. These things do indeed work; but this mechanism is always at work, whether you go through these motions, or not. These steps simply help build mindfulness and bring together elements that put you in control of what you are manifesting; they put you in the "driver's seat." But rest assured, if you are not doing these things, your thoughts are still becoming manifest in your life! You just aren't taking a consciously active role in shaping what you see in your life.

The only thing left for you to do now is believe. That has always been all you have ever had to do to have your every desire manifest in your life; we have just had our ability to believe trained out of us to an alarming degree. You also have to learn to form your prayers in such a way that they contain no ambiguous, contradictory, or negative connotations, and they do not trigger any prior programming that will neutralize your prayer's effectiveness.

In the following chapter there will be several examples of prayers that will give you an idea of what some effective prayer forms look like. You can use any of them, or you can build your own. I would suggest building your own because the words in these prayers mean certain things to the people who constructed them, but they may contain different messages for your subconscious mind. Also, the chapter on "Healing with Prayer" contains some prayers (methods of creating and receiving change) that have been used effectively in addressing a variety of medical conditions. Any of these examples will suffice to guide you in creating effective prayer actions for yourself.

Whole-Brain Prayer

There are a number of ways to pray, and a number of body and hand positions one may employ during prayer. Some of these positions are born of convenience or necessity; but most common prayer traditions, such as kneeling, or folding one's hands together, are not only innate to us, but have a logical basis and practical purpose.

The most peaceful, productive, and creative states of mind are those which cause brain activity to be smooth and coherent – when both hemispheres are working together properly. Stress and distractions cause a disruption in the flow of information between the cerebral hemispheres; whereas mental and physical relaxation restores effective cerebral communication. There are also mechanical methods of restoring "whole-brain" communication and disengaging the stress response while enhancing the efficiency of the mind with which you pray and create your experience.

If you can imagine a business executive leaning back in a padded, leather chair with his legs crossed and his hands held up in front of him with fingertips touching – looking very thoughtful – you would have an image of one of the ways to mechanically induce a whole-brain state. By touching the fingertips together, crossing your legs, arms, or touching any part of one side of your body with any part of the other side, you create neural connections from one side of your brain to the other; the more cross-contact points, the more nerve signals and connections. By kneeling and folding hands together during prayer, there is a quieting of the nervous system which is conducive to effective prayer. The health benefits of sitting in these "prayer positions" are undeniable and are greatly magnified if thoughts are focused on a happy, healthy way of being in the world.

Educational Kinesiology (Edu-K®) and Brain Gym® are both methods of using whole brain postures, or positions, to calm the nervous system, eliminate stress, and enhance learning rate, retention, and comprehension with children. When people are very happy, they clap their hands; try clapping your hands and see if it makes you smile. If it does, then it turned off your stress response, which means your brain is getting more nutrients and oxygen because it's getting more blood flow. You are actually smarter and more creative when you are happy; that's because your whole brain is working properly and getting good blood supply. So put your hands together; and get your head together.

Chapter 11 Key Points and Afterthoughts

- Any method of prayer can produce results; but the method must be faithfully applied in order to produce any result.

- Even faith "as small as a mustard seed" can move mountains – if focused on the task.

- All ancient wisdom teachings emphasize thought processes or states-of-mind. Teachings on prayer, and how to pray, use phrases such as, "Be still," "Be quiet," "Go inside," "The Kingdom of Heaven is inside you," "Go in your closet," "Seek in private," and "Seek first in the Kingdom (inside)," to describe where prayer happens, and where the energy is focused.

- When in your quiet, still place visualize only what you want to experience; but do it as if the best possible version of that experience had already happened. Pretend you are looking at a memory; focus on feelings of joy and gratitude. "As a man thinketh, so it is done unto him," simply means that if you want something, you have to think about it; and if you want a happy version of it, you have to be happy when you are thinking about it.

- The great teachers of prayer entered into these highly productive mental states and tried to guide us into these states with descriptions and metaphors. There are many ways to interpret these teachings; if you are not producing good fruit, try another interpretation.

- Focusing on your breathing, and controlling it, is one form of relaxation that is easy to learn and practice – and it will keep your lungs healthy.

- Relaxation is the physical state which accompanies a calm, still mind.

- A joyful state of mind makes prayer more effective, and creates healthy physiology within the body. Joy is worth cultivating. Remember, "Be of good cheer," and you will be made whole.

- See your prayer as having already been accomplished. See your prayer in your mind's eye; visual prayers are the most effective. If you don't think you are a "visual" person, begin now affirming that you are: "I see clearly," etc...

- "If you're happy and you know it, clap your hands!" Putting your hands together is an age-old way of achieving a balanced, whole-brain state; consider some of the hand positions used in prayer.

133

"Nothing happens unless first we dream."

— *Carl Sandburg*

"If you believe you can, you probably can. If you believe you can't, you most assuredly won't. Belief is the ignition switch that gets you off the launching pad."

— *Denis Waitley*

Chapter Twelve

A Look at some Effective Prayer Forms

s I hope you have realized, by this point, the style of prayer you use is only a small part of the formula of reliably effective prayer. The state of consciousness you are in at the time, and the degree to which you are able to believe in prayer – and in your prayer being a reality – are the truly vital factors.

Having said that, there are some prayer-forms (thought forms, etc.) which seem to work quite well and thus warrant a closer look. The elements of each prayer, the intent, and the verb-tense used in the prayer, all seem to hold some significance in determining how well a prayer will work. Keep in mind, each of your thoughts becomes something; mindful, thoughtful living is the best way to ensure that all of your thoughts, that are indeed being responded to, produce pleasant fruit.

Prayer, however, is usually more focused on the fulfillment of a specific desire and therefore is typically approached with more energy than most common, everyday thoughts. Consequently, effective prayer will produce some result; and that result will likely be more profound to you than the typical manifestations that you observe every other moment of your life. If we understand the importance of right living and right thinking, our lives will reflect this in many ways and we will benefit from the situations that appear in our paths. Understanding how to use prayer effectively will take care of those situations where life got away from us and we need to fix something, or change where we are and what we see.

There are many styles of prayer, but many share common elements, such as: Thanks or gratitude; a request for something; praise or adoration; forgiveness; an address; a closing; and maybe an acknowledgment of God's greatness. These are all great ingredients for inclusion when building a prayer. Each element has a specific purpose; and like tools, you should choose the right elements, or components, of prayer in order to create a successful prayer. Belief is the ultimate power tool! With enough belief, you won't need much else. But since we are building a prayer, let's look at the various components of a prayer and see why they are there and why these elements, if misplaced or misdirected, could have a negative affect on our prayer and its outcome.

Jesus gave his disciples instruction on prayer. He told them to pray a certain way. Why do you think He would do such a thing? Maybe Jesus knew that there was more to prayer than simply reciting pious poetry to an unseen God that is believed to be up in the sky separate from us. Perhaps Jesus was telling his disciples, and each of us, that prayer is a mechanism for attainment and achievement. Every mechanism has working parts and a certain manner in which it should be used to obtain the best results and not cause unwanted problems. Jesus was very specific when he said, "And when thou prayest, thou shalt not be as the hypocrites are: for they love to pray standing in the synagogues and in the corners of the streets, that they may be seen of men." Matt. 6:5. Jesus also said, "But when ye pray, use not vain repetitions, as the heathen do: for they think that they shall be heard for their much speaking." Clearly, there is a reason for this admonition. Jesus then went on to say, "…when thou prayest, enter into thy closet, and when thou hast shut the door, pray to thy Father which is in secret; and thy Father which seeth in secret shall reward thee openly." Matt. 6:6. Obviously, Jesus was teaching that there were many ways to pray, but there was perhaps one way that works best of all.

"Be Still and Know I Am God."

Suffering comes from thinking about the future, the past, or the self – or from the attachment to ideas about how these things should be. We can worry about the future and ask our God to protect us; or we can resent the past and seek comfort or compensation from God – or we can be quiet and still and listen. We spend most of our mental energy thinking up ways to change our lives or to avoid some uncomfortable experience, such as hunger, pain, loneliness, embarrassment, etc. Most prayers are actually offerings of words to a God who – supposedly – already knows what you are going to say. Some say, "God doesn't answer prayers because he can't get a word in edge-wise!" Try this: "Go in your closet," close your eyes, remove any external distractions, be quiet, be still, and listen. You'll be amazed at what you can hear when you aren't thinking and talking!

Prayer is thought of as the active state of communication between a person and their God; while *a prayer* is what is said or thought by the person during that communication. It is important to realize that most *prayers* are simply poems, or verses, which are remembered and repeated without the original emotions of the author of the prayer. Though it is quite impressive to memorize long, flowery tributes; the repetition of that which you have memorized is a different kind of mental activity than that which is entered into by monks, and others, when they actively Pray, or meditate. The prayer effort, if from memory rather than the heart, may very well be "in vain," as it is unlikely to produce the same effect as free-flowing, heart-felt sentiment and desire. All thoughts are indeed creative; some ways of thinking, however, are much more effective than other ways of thinking. Think whatever you wish; reap as you sow.

It is the method, rather than the words, that is most important. For when one prays to be "seen of men," whether it is in church, in a coliseum, or on a street corner, there is an underlying distraction that limits access to that part of us that *can* pray effectively. Only through quiet, meditative, contemplation of our desires will we achieve them through prayer. Jesus is simply saying that if we are busy putting on a show, as so many do these days in the various forums we have built for our multitudinous religions; we are not focused on what is important to us. Effective prayer requires going into "your closet" (subconscious mind), and stating what you want to be. This can only be done when there are no distractions, or anything else, requiring any of your attention.

This isn't to say that it is wrong or bad, to pray in church congregations, or anywhere else you wish; it simply means that there may be more effective choices available to you when you pray. You have a choice of locations when you pray; and you have a choice of mental states you can enter into for prayer. You also have a choice of techniques, or prayers, you may use. Jesus was simply teaching that there are certain components that make a prayer effective, and if you pray in a certain manner, you will see your prayers answered the way you want them to be – "On Earth as it is in Heaven," or, in other words: In our physical reality the way we imagined/prayed in our mind.

Jesus clearly outlines the manner in which effective prayers can be offered. With the Lord's Prayer, Jesus highlights some very important characteristics of prayer. First of all, the Higher Self is addressed in order to bring together John Donne's "three person'd God" that represents a complete trinity. "Our Father which art in heaven…," therefore, is representative of our request to the higher authority that typically runs our life. Yet it also means something more. Our *Father* would be that which provided the *pattern* that forms and directs all things. All of the ancients from which we draw our religious beliefs, as well as knowledge of our connection with divinity, realized that the source of all light, energy, and life in this solar system is the Sun – the One in Heaven that sends us light. We must consider all related possibilities because we weren't there, and neither were any of the people who want us to believe their somewhat limited perspective of events.

Though this may seem strange, keep in mind that people don't go along with beliefs because they make sense; they go along with group beliefs to fit in with a group. If you can find a perspective that works for you – I mean really produces a great life for you – then you have found **your way** and no longer need to tread the much wider path Jesus referred to. Consider the context and frequency of biblical references to Light. Also consider that it is believed that the Lord's Prayer was in existence – in a variety of forms and languages – long before Jesus arrived here.

Clearly, we want things; and it requires a cooperative effort within ourselves to realize our goals. The statement, "Thy kingdom come." represents the closing of the trinity. To come, in this sense, means a drawing near, or a closing of the sides of the trinity; to experience the kingdom of God is to experience a whole, or holy, union of those invisible, spiritual aspects of God within ourselves. In other words, if you wish to ask something of God, simply ask it and be willing and ready to receive it. But, before asking, you must center yourself by seeking out a quiet place where you will not be distracted and then going in the closet (your inner self) and bringing together all the parts of you – unify the spiritual realm with the physical and mental.

"Thy will be done in earth, as it is in heaven." is a reference to the fact that what happens in your mind (heaven) will happen in the physical (earth) realm. This is a common theme throughout life, and the Bible.

138

Hermes Trismegistus, a great and powerful magus, was supposedly buried with the greatest secret of the ages. When his tomb was eventually opened, the secret was revealed: "As above, so below; as below, so above." Proverbs 23:7 says, "For as a man thinketh in his heart, so is he." These are but a few of the hints, given to us throughout history, as to where to find the answers to our prayers.

Later, Jesus reminds us to "...seek ye first the kingdom of God, and His righteousness; and all these things shall be added to you. Take therefore no thought for the morrow: for the morrow shall take thought for the things of itself. Sufficient to the day is the evil thereof." Essentially, seeking this unified state, giving no thought to the past or future (being centered in the moment), is the attainment of the kingdom; and it is in this state that all things you ask will be given unto you. There is plenty to worry about today without adding the troubles of another day, so get in the moment, get centered, get in "the zone," and ask for what you want. "Whatsoever ye shall ask in prayer, *believing*, ye shall receive." Matt. 21:22.

Relax and Have Faith

Faith is the calm energy of positive expectancy and knowing that you are "okay." Many people must see a thing before they are assured of its arrival; others can simply ask for a thing, and have faith that it is accomplished. Many people become impatient and anxious when they can not see what they want, or can not see how it could possibly come to pass. This feeling of impatience and anxiety, or maybe even fear or worry, is the opposite of faith; it is the opposite of the feeling you need in order to manifest positive experiences. You will still manifest experiences, however, with or without positive expectancy – all thought is creative. You will attract a reflection of the energy you are feeling. Relax; be happy; and have faith in your good coming to pass – regardless of circumstances. "Fear not; believe only."

"Give us this day our daily bread. And forgive us our debts, as we forgive our debtors. And lead us not into temptation, but deliver us from evil: For thine is the kingdom, and the power, and the glory, for ever." represents the rest of this manner of praying. There are several important components within these last lines. First of all, present tense is used throughout. This is a powerful piece of evidence that Jesus was indeed aware of the nature of the mind: that those things we imagine in the future tend to stay there, while those things we imagine as a reality that has already occurred, or is occurring, tend to manifest as reality. By saying, "Give us this day our daily bread," Jesus is demonstrating an awareness of the importance of staying in the moment, and that worrying about tomorrow takes away from today. He simply directs His subconscious mind to feed them this day; tomorrow, He will do the same.

Giving and receiving forgiveness is another critical point that is intended to free-up valuable energy that could be used to attain your goals. Forgiveness is about love, and it is about freedom – especially freedom from the past. Holding onto old hurts is very damaging to you and will gradually rob you of your ability to love, or to believe; these are both very important factors in effective prayer. Finally, "...lead us not into temptation, but deliver us from evil...," is a directive to stay on the high road of the High self where prayers are answered. This is essentially a wish to not be led into a mental state where nothing good happens, but to be delivered to a place where all things are possible.

Remember, the person Jesus is giving His prayer to, in order to have it delivered to God, is the subconscious mind. This is the basic self, inner child, id, or whatever term you wish to use for that part of us that uses our senses and transmits thoughts into the non-physical realm of God so that He can send His answer back to us in our own, physical realm. You must realize that this is the same aspect of your *self* which makes you give-up when things become difficult, eat when you are upset, run when you are afraid, or engage in any other reactionary behavior when "it" is not getting it's way, or when "it" is threatened. This is the part of us that "leads us into temptation." This part of us needs to be directed – not asked.

The last phrase, "For thine is the kingdom (spiritual realm), the power (ability, strength, or agency), and the glory (nobility, magnificence), for ever (continually)...," is an affirmation of our inner excellence and connection with the One mind, and One heart, and One body of God. It is a directive to our selves to live right and strive for these higher qualities of existence that bring with them great rewards of their own. It is Body (Soma), Mind (Psyche), and Spirit (Pneuma). It is the Trinity. Our goal: Unify the Trinity – forever.

This prayer is also understood to mean that each day we should honor our source and seek guidance in our actions here in the physical as to not be distracted from our human work by lower order distractions. "Our Father, who art in Heaven" we honor you and your name as that which gives us life and light. "Thy Kingdom come" represents the springing-forth into the material world ("come") of that which is in "thy Kingdom" – which is inside of us, yet not physical (our mind). This quite simply means let all good thoughts become things. And "thy will be done" further means that we wish to perform those actions in this realm that reflect the will of the One which sent us here. And furthermore, that these things come through, into the physical realm, as they are projected in our minds – "on Earth as it is in Heaven."

"Give us this day our daily bread" is an acknowledgment that our sustenance doth indeed come from the same source as we do. In asking that our debts, as well as the debts owed us, be forgiven, we are seeking assistance in releasing the past; by releasing the past, we allow abundance to flow freely again (There are very few people who worry about things such as debt and grudges and also live abundantly.).

"Lead us not into temptation, but deliver us from evil" simply means to guide us and keep us on our path. Sometimes our seeking physical pleasure distracts us from our purpose here. In biblical terms, the word *sin* was translated from the Greek word *Hamartia*, which means to "miss the mark, or 'bull's-eye.'" In this context, the word *evil* could essentially mean to "miss the entire target." In other words, our words *sin* and *evil* literally mean to either stray a little off your path, or to drive into a spiritual ditch. "Lead us not into temptation," is simply a request that our thoughts guide us down the middle of our life's path.

The rest of the Sermon on the Mount goes into great depth in discussing the triune nature of man and mind, and explains clearly the difference between the conscious and subconscious minds, and the way to best achieve unity between the various aspects of who we truly are. With this sermon, Jesus passed on the secrets to practically everything He ever did, or taught – though simplified, how-to stories are hardly the same as the application of those principles. With the Lord's Prayer, Jesus gave us a very effective prayer form that contains within its very own words, the directions for its use. If we focus on merely speaking the verse correctly, however, we miss the point; which is that there is a sequence of things you must do in order to create, within God, those things you desire. It is the method here that is so important.

Another interesting characteristic of this prayer is that Jesus doesn't ask for anything, He instead issues directives for those things He wishes to experience. He doesn't ask for food, or beg humbly of God; Jesus flatly states, "Give us this day our daily bread." He doesn't only command the delivery of our bread, but further specifies "this day" as the time frame in which this desire is to be met. Jesus is not praying to an all powerful being who doesn't take kindly to being ordered about; He is praying to an inner part of Himself that sees to it that those requests will come to pass. Some may argue that Jesus was a supernatural entity, and not a man; but this is simply a lack of study and an ignorance of what these words actually, and quite plainly, state.

The Romans would have loved for us to believe that they had the power to kill a living god. In fact, their message to the Jews was quite clear: "Here's your king! What do you think of him now?" Anyone can do what Jesus did, and more – if you believe the words of Jesus. Still, many deny their own power – the same power Jesus demonstrated and encouraged us to use – in order to maintain a hand-me-down position of inferiority to church and state, or any authority which could hurt, kill, imprison, or tax them.

This position, though, may make it easier to assume that Jesus could speak to God in this way; but Jesus wasn't simply speaking to God. He was directing *all* of us in the manner in which to pray. Was Jesus instructing each of us to issue demands, or commands, to some Higher Authority? Yes, He was. Is that Higher Authority God? Or is that Higher Authority within us that directs all parts of us and sees to it that what we desire, if we only believe, will come to us? Certainly, it is God that answers prayers, but it is not by way of a merit system – and not because we bully Him around. God answers prayers by way of the natural functioning of the Universe – or the Lord. We first ask our requests of our Higher Self, which in turn directs our subconscious mind to fulfill these requests through the Lord (which literally means, "male with authority"), or the natural operation of God, or All that Is. God is all things; and the Lord is the law of interaction – the authority of the masculine (paternal), or patterning, energy of all things.

It is our subconscious mind that interacts directly with the intelligence of the Universe to bring about what we want. It is through the Lord, or Power of Intention, that the unformed is made formed. Man is not the Law, but a product of it, and a creator of small-scale models of the Law created in order to make men feel important. When man sought to make himself "the Law," or "Lord," an important perspective was lost to many. Jesus was teaching the "Law of God, or the "God spell (Gospel)." This was the principle Jesus used to work within "All that Is" in order to perform what we considered miracles, but what Jesus considered small works which we would greatly exceed.

Today, people think of the Gospel as the first few books of the new testament; but they don't seem to pick-up on the reality that Jesus wasn't in His own stories, He didn't carry a Bible, and was at odds with religious convention because they enslaved people with their customs rather than empowering them with the New Wisdom He was teaching. Of course, the wisdom wasn't New, but it was new to most of the people who heard Jesus speak. Focusing on teachers, events, and stories, is to lose sight of the *lessons* of those teachers, and the reasons the events and stories have endured. No, the gospel that is taught and preached today is not the same Go'spel' Jesus taught.

The Lord's Prayer is just one prayer form. There are many others, but to be effective, they each have to address the same part of your mind; and they must be accompanied by belief in what is asked for – a current belief that what is desired already exists, even if you haven't seen it yet. There is no limit to the number of times you can pray, nor is there any limit to what you can ask for. Just remember to be careful what you ask – you will receive it. Whoever is responsible for the Lord's Prayer, it is obvious that it is an attempt to pass on a method of invoking Divine guidance and intercession. Jesus was certainly aware of this when He taught this prayer to His followers.

Huna, a very old, Hawaiian spiritual practice, also makes use of the various aspects of the *self*. Though Christian missionaries went to Hawaii with the intention of saving the people there from themselves, the Huna practices worked, still work, and have thus survived. The Christian missionaries preached all they knew, but learned nothing in return. We have a bad habit, in this country especially, of discounting anything that seems different than what we already know, or currently practice.

Clinging to old ways and ignoring information given to others simply because *they* appear to be different from *us* is a sure way to halt progress and spiritual growth or evolution. In most cases, the differences are only cultural and language-based. Observe with an open mind the similarities between various religious practices and you will find that most people basically believe the same things, but use different words to describe those things. It is indeed this failure to acknowledge God at work anywhere else in the world which has crippled our faith and severely limited our ability to grow as spiritual beings and access the kingdom of God in our own daily lives.

Huna views the person as a union of the High self (Amakua), the Basic self (Unihapili), and the conscious mind (Uhané), just like most religions. In Huna, a prayer action basically involves five-steps that first require you to bring together this triune of selves. Huna recognizes that thinking creates thought forms and that these thought forms are realities for the Basic self. Thought forms charged with the energy of belief become physical realities. As with any religion, or religious practice, a prayer action begins with a desire. The first step is to decide what you want to do, wish to obtain, or desire to see occur. In other words, you must decide on your prayer and know what the answer to that prayer looks, or feels, like.

The second step is to ask permission of your High self for this thing to transpire. It may not be a good time for you to ask for a particular thing. Your High self always knows what is going on, and when it is safe and acceptable to bring certain things into your life. The third step is to gather your energy which you will be using to send your prayer to the appropriate place. You do this simply by taking a few "deeper-than-normal" breaths.

The fourth step is to send your prayer to the Higher self. This is accomplished by creating a prayer that is more of an affirmation of a foregone conclusion – basically you are thanking your Higher self for already seeing to your request. You visualize the prayer action already completed or answered. Finally, you do your part and occasionally come back, as if you were watering a plant, and give your prayer a little more of your energy in the form of belief. All of these things are done in a relaxed state and require only a belief that what you wish to see is good, and already accomplished.

144

Huna is an island practice and is the product of a merger of people from various island groups in the Pacific Ocean. It is interesting, therefore, how similar these concepts and practices are to so many modern religions on a philosophical level. Huna also recognizes that those thoughts that you dwell on become part of life, and that disease springs from a lack of energy, or life force, in the Basic self. Before doing Huna, it is common practice to clear away any thought forms that may be hindering your progress, and any entities that may be affecting you adversely. This is akin to "casting out demons," or performing exorcisms, as is common practice in Christianity. Huna is a very interesting and effective practice for delivering prayers to that part of us that will provide us with our answer.

Affirmations are another common and effective method of prayer. Keep in mind that to pray is to ask for what you want. The most effective methods of doing this involve affirming that your desired reality has already come to pass. Affirmations do just this. An affirmation is the acknowledgement that the thing you desire is now a reality. As with more traditional forms of prayer, affirmations can be said in many ways, in many places, and at any time. There are, however, some things that you can do to enhance the effectiveness of any affirmation.

First, you must decide what it is that you wish to affirm; this should be a truth about a situation you desire to see manifest. For instance, if you are sick, you probably wish to be healthy and whole again. In this case, you would affirm your good health, not wish for your bad health to go away. Affirming your good health will create good health as a reality in your life, while focusing on the bad, in any way, will cause it to linger. Affirmations should always be positive and focused on the desired outcome, not on the problem.

After deciding on an affirmation, you should get yourself in a quiet, comfortable place where you will not be disturbed. Then, you should relax yourself to attain the optimum mental state for saying affirmations. This is the alpha-state and it can be achieved in many ways, such as through the use of special music, or self-hypnosis techniques. **(A progressive relaxation exercise is provided in Appendix 1 to help you learn to effectively achieve more productive states of mind.)** Simply being in a calm, relaxed state, however, is sufficient for praying and saying affirmations. The point is that you don't really have to worry about any of these things too much, but you should make an honest effort to achieve optimum conditions if it is optimum results you intend to receive.

Finally, repeat to yourself for several minutes, whatever you wish to affirm. It helps if you say the affirmations out loud, as with all prayer forms. Your subconscious, or unconscious mind, utilizes your physical senses (which is why we have smoke detectors and alarm clocks...); so saying affirmations aloud dramatically increases the absorption of the affirmation into the subconscious mind.

It is best to keep the affirmations, and prayers, short and simple. This is not to say that you can only do one affirmation at a time, nor is it to suggest that you can only pray for one thing at a time. Ask for as many things as you want – as often as you want. Keep the individual affirmation statements short and simple, however.

It also helps if you say the affirmations in the third-person context. For example, if Jennifer wishes to be healthier, then Jennifer might say, "Jennifer enjoys her excellent health!" Some people name their subconscious in order to develop a better understanding of, and relationship with, this aspect of themselves.

Of course, "I AM" statements are perhaps the most powerful words in the Universe; so spend plenty of time affirming that "I am receiving, experiencing, enjoying, etc..." whatever it is you wish to receive, experience, or enjoy. Using both first-person and third-person provides agreement between two aspects of your self; and "what any two agree on in prayer" will indeed come to pass.

Remember, with affirmations, as with prayer, the more belief you possess, the quicker you will realize your goal. It is also helpful to remember, at all times when dealing with the subconscious mind, that it is really an immature intelligence that thinks like a child. Do not get too sophisticated with your prayers or affirmations; and refrain from using any negative or limiting language in your affirmations – children take you literally whether you mean it that way or not. Be creative, but also be direct, specific, positive, and confident that you have received your desire, when you are making your affirmations; and always use present-tense to create a present reality. The future never comes.

Joseph Murphy and Ian McMahan, in *The Power of Your Subconscious Mind*, describe several additional methods of "affirmative prayer." Among these methods is what is referred to as the "passing-over technique," in which you simply assign your desire to your subconscious mind. This method is very effective and can be used to achieve anything you can imagine.

The passing-over technique works in the same way as when you tell yourself what time you would like to wake-up in the morning, and you do – without an alarm clock. Likewise, this phenomenon is the reason so many people, before going to sleep, write down questions they would like answers to and keep a pad by the bedside for when they wake-up with the answer. Use it. Experiment with it. Play with it. Ask for whatever you want, but be sure you truly want what you ask for before you ask.

Other techniques for effective prayer, offered by Murphy and McMahan, include a method developed by Professor Charles Baudoin, which involves simply condensing the desire into a brief, definitive phrase that can be easily compounded into the memory by repeating it over and over. Short phrases that represent concepts, such as, "Success is mine," or "Abundant health," when repeated several times daily, set up thoughts and experiences that lead to the manifestation of these concepts in your life.

Again, this technique can be even more effective when used at bedtime. Giving thanks for the realization of this desire, or desired state of being enhances any method you use, and works alone, as well. Of course, thanks should be given as if you have already received your wish.

Self-hypnosis is another type of prayer-action that produces amazing results; and it does so by using the same principles of mind that prayer utilizes. There are many good books on self-hypnosis, but the best way to learn is to go to a professional hypnotherapist. Learning from a professional is not necessary, however, in order to achieve success through hypnosis.

The principles are the same as the other forms of prayer we have discussed. First, you need a quiet place where you will not be disturbed. You will then achieve a desirable level of relaxation through one of many available techniques, and then you will give yourself suggestions designed to create a specific outcome – just like prayer. It is helpful if you write yourself a script to use so you can do as little conscious thinking as possible while doing self-hypnosis. Dim lights and soft music may add to the relaxation while doing any of these prayer actions. The only secret to self-hypnosis is that you must do it to get the results. This, coincidentally, applies to all the forms discussed here.

Visualization of the desired outcome is a key component that will dramatically improve the success of any method of prayer that you use. Simply visualizing your desired outcome, over and over, while in a relaxed state, will often produce exactly the result you pictured in your mind. Seeing, or imagining, yourself smiling as you realize your dream is a technique that enhances the efficacy of visualization, and can help insure against that "big reward" coming at the expense of someone else.

Visualization, combined with breathing or focused breathing exercises, is even more effective. Imagining that you are watching a video or movie of your *realized* desire is another excellent method of visualization that will lead to a successful outcome. Always remember to be specific and include happiness as a part of your visualized outcome.

Tapas Flemming, an acupuncturist and healer, developed a system called The Tapas Acupressure Technique (TAT), in which specific acupuncture points are held with one hand while the other hand simply covers the back of the head at the base of the skull. To learn about the specific hand positions for doing TAT, you can contact TAT International online at www.TatLife.com.

I highly recommend contacting TAT International and learning as much as you can about this amazing system, as I have seen it help many, many people. This system is quick and easy to learn and to use. I mention it here because the hand positions accompany a series of statements that apparently produce almost instantaneous results. The nature of these statements, however, is very similar to many prayer forms, including the Lord's Prayer.

The steps of TAT begin by identifying a problem that you wish to see resolved. Usually, these problems are of an emotional nature, but any problem that you see as such has its roots in the way you are thinking about something. The next step with TAT is to place your focus on the opposite condition, or to affirm that the situation has no control over you. Then, in the present-tense, you give thanks for the healing of all the origins of this particular problem; then express gratitude that all the places in your mind, body, and life that have been affected by this problem are healed.

Additional steps include affirming that all parts of you that got something out of having this problem are healed, and then forgiving yourself, God, and anyone else that may be involved in any way – whether you hurt them because of this problem, or you see them as responsible for your having experienced this problem. When you are finished doing TAT, it is recommended that you thank God, the Lord, or whatever, or whoever, you believe has healed you.

TAT is an energy technique which utilizes meridian and nervous system energy to achieve certain results. As such, it is recommended that you limit the use of TAT to ten-minutes each day, unless you have some method of testing for bio-energetic feedback, such as kinesiology-type muscle-testing, or some similar testing method. Before beginning, as with Huna, it is important to check and see if it is alright to proceed with working on a particular problem. When I say that it is important to check to see if it is alright to work on a problem, I am suggesting that you check with your Higher self, or your inner authority. You can use a testing method, as mentioned above; or you can ask and trust your intuition. It is also recommended that you drink plenty of water on days you do TAT. I would say that it is a good idea to drink lots of water every day, but especially on those days when you are actively doing some sort of meridian work or prayer action for specific problems.

3-Steps of T.A.T.

Short-Version

*There are several versions used in applying the TAT procedure; this is a short, three-step version which is very quick and incredibly effective. While holding one hand over the back of the head, and the other hand in the TAT pose, put your attention on a problem and take a few minutes going through this process. More information on TAT is available at www.TATlife.com.

Step One: While holding the T.A.T. pose, say, "I forgive anyone who ever hurt me like this before."

"What Happened?"

Step Two: While holding the T.A.T. pose, say, "I ask forgiveness of anyone I ever hurt like this before."

"What Happened?"

Step Three: While holding the T.A.T. pose, "dialogue" with the problem... Simply sit and 'be with' the issue at hand and "listen" for any insight or guidance which may be forthcoming.

"What Happened?"

In another healthcare modality I have studied, one of the techniques sometimes used to help the client achieve healing is to simply have the client give their self permission to get better, or to accept help or healing. In many cases, the client will have to actually write a contract with their self setting out the agreement as an accepted reality. Making a contract, pact, or formal agreement with your self, or decreeing the reality of your desire is also effective. Job 22:28 reads: "Thou shalt decree a thing, and it shall be established unto thee..."

The title of a popular book on the subject of creating success also encourages us to "Write it down and make it happen." In business, and throughout our lives, we establish contracts to ensure we receive what we ask for. It works. Use it faithfully and see for yourself. And always remember to honor your contracts; you do not want the baggage that naturally comes with breaking a contract.

Write it down; Make it real.

We have all heard of the idea of writing things down in order to have them come to pass. Grocery lists, to-do lists, memos, wish lists, gift registries, letters to Santa, and other reminders make sure we follow through with our desires, or that our desires are communicated to others – sort of "written prayers." Plans, blueprints, recipes, and driving directions, likewise, offer guidance to others as an unseen idea is transformed from thought to thing. Besides the obvious fact that just any old ingredients, combined in just any old way, won't necessarily produce the results you seek; writing down your desires allows others to participate in ways that, ideally, will compliment, or speed the manifestation of, your desire. Writing a thing down turns an invisible, non-physical thing into a physical thing others can see and act on.

Journaling is another form of making things happen by writing them down. By keeping up with the inspirations you are given during prayer or meditation, you may just find a "million-dollar idea" scribbled down on a page of your journal. Certainly, you will begin to notice a pattern as you write down your dreams and inspirations. You can also practice creating new realities by writing stories about things you wish to experience. Remember to write as if you are excited and grateful that this wonderful experience has already come to pass.

It may seem strange to talk about hypnosis and acupressure alongside the Lord's Prayer in a discussion of effective prayer techniques, but remember the original purpose behind your prayer – the fulfillment of a desire. These techniques, like all effective prayer forms, utilize principles of the mind that have been clinically demonstrated over time to be highly effective. If you wish to see a desire fulfilled, it doesn't make sense to not use whatever methods you have available to achieve your desired outcome. These methods do not replace God, prayer, religion, or anything, but were ultimately derived from the same sources as all religious practices. I simply mention these other practices to demonstrate the inescapable similarities between various actions that are all intended to do the same thing – to change the future. Or, more precisely, they are all intended to *create* a desired future situation. We are all creators and these are simply a few of our very useful and effective tools. Use them, or not; the choice is up to you.

The similarities between these methods point to the most important components of prayer: Peace, gratitude, faith, trust, courage, and love. Any method that encompasses all of these principles will be effective. In each of the methods mentioned here, it is essential to be peaceful and calm when praying; and it is equally important to be simple and direct with your desires. Belief is the key ingredient; it powers your prayer.

Fashioning your prayers as if they have already become reality, and believing they have, is the secret to successful prayer actions. Visualization of happy outcomes will also prove to be a big benefit for you. Essentially, however, anything you do is perfect; because you are a child of God. Ask for whatever you want, whenever you want, and however you want; just do so with belief and you will experience the reality of your creation.

"A man is but a product of his thoughts; what he thinks, he becomes."

— Mahatma Gandhi

Chapter 12 Key Points and Afterthoughts

- Prayer is simply a thinking process.

- Prayer consists of at least three important parts: The desire, which will become manifest as the physical answer to your prayer; the plan, or ritual, you plan on using to create your answer; and the faithful application of your plan. Your Answer will be the result of your Prayer as it is empowered, or multiplied, by your Belief, or faith.

- If it is thought, it is prayer; if it is prayer, it will produce some effect in the physical world – according to your belief.

- An effective prayer is like a contract; if a certain thing is done, a certain result will be experienced. Also, like a contract, a prayer is more likely to produce good results if executed with trust and in good faith.

- The Tapas Acupressure Technique (TAT) was a doctor's answer to a prayer to relieve the suffering of her allergy patients. True to its essence, TAT works a lot like a prayer with an "antennae" to amplify the energy and focus of the prayer.

- There are several "healing" techniques in use by doctors, psychiatrists, and other therapists and coaches, which utilize a prayer-like dialogue, or affirmations, along with a focusing-tool, or a whole-brain posture, designed to induce a relaxed state, or a whole-brain state. The effects can be instant and miraculous. Among these techniques are: The Z-Point Process (Z-Point), The Emotional Freedom Techniques (EFT), Psychological Kinesiology (Psych-K), and Neural-Emotional Technique (NET).

- An effective prayer method is to relax and remove yourself from any distractions, and then visualize yourself experiencing the reality you are praying for. Remember to imagine your prayer as already having been accomplished; and imagine yourself smiling as a result.

- When adequate planning, or mental preparation, has taken place, action will be inspired. It is important to take steps toward your own goals when they present themselves. For example, if you have prayed to meet new friends, you must accept invitations to go new places.

- Your part, in any effective prayer, is simply to ask, and then receive. Ask by imagining having, doing, or being, whatever it is you are praying for.

This is the Lord's Prayer as most of us have seen, or heard, it:

The Lord's Prayer

"Our Father, who art in heaven,

Hallowed be thy name.

Thy kingdom come; thy will be done,

On Earth as it is in heaven.

Give us this day our daily bread;

And forgive us our debts (trespasses),

As we forgive our debtors (those who trespass against us),

And lead us not into temptation; but deliver us from evil.

For thine is the kingdom and the power and the glory, forever, Amen."

This is the Lord's Prayer as it appeared in first century writings
– prior to "Roman" Christianity:

The Lord's Prayer

"Our Father, who art in heaven, hallowed be thy name.

Thy kingdom come; thy will be done on Earth, as it is in heaven.

Give us this day our daily bread;

and forgive us our debts as we forgive our debtors.

And lead us not into temptation, but deliver us from evil;

For thine is the kingdom, the power, and the glory – forever.

Our Mother, who art upon the Earth, hallowed be thy name.

Thy kingdom come; thy will be done in us as it is in thee.

As thou sendest every day your angels, send them also unto us.

Forgive us our sins as we atone all our sins against thee.

And lead us not into sickness, but deliver us from all evil;

For thine is the Earth, the Body, and the Health. Amen."

There are many ways to "Honor thy Father and thy Mother;" and they are all important to your health and well-being. There is a feminine aspect in all things; in thought (prayer), creativity is the feminine, or "right-brain," aspect and inference and planning is masculine, or "left-brain." Since the beginning of time, all cultures, or empires, which have disenfranchised the feminine aspect of life, thought, and nature (usually for the gods of war and money), have fallen to their own greed and violence. There can be no Father, or Son, without a Mother.

"There are only two ways to live your life. One is as if nothing is a miracle, and the other is as if everything is a miracle."
— Albert Einstein

Chapter Thirteen

Healing With Prayer

t the beginning of this book, there was a chapter entitled, "Why Pray?" The answer, of course, was: "Why not pray?" The basic premise of this entire book, in fact, is that there is no practical reason not to pray and every conceivable reason to pray. Furthermore, prayer is the most powerful, yet least understood, of our innate gifts.

Prayer is the power we use to shape creation. As we become more aware of our true nature, it becomes clearer and clearer that mindful thought and faithfully asking for what you need are the keys to creating the kind of life you dream of experiencing. You are not likely to experience a situation you do not somehow believe is possible.

You may, of course, witness some pretty unbelievable things, but perhaps amazing, or astonishing, would be better choices of terms in those cases. Humans have such limited scopes of understanding that unbelievable in one culture is absolutely commonplace in another. Belief underlies experience. We pray because, at some level, we do believe all things are possible.

Belief underlies experience. Prayer is an experience. Prayer is simply thought; and if you have a thought that you believe in, you will soon experience that thought as a reality of some sort. You will see an answered prayer. When we see so many things in life fall into categories that could just as easily be explained as prayers being answered, as anything else, why not pray for everything you could ever want? You can certainly take whatever other practical steps you intended to take, but why not pray if it could bring you the answer you seek, and maybe even save you some time and energy?

Sure, we stand in church and pray, and may even say a prayer at dinner; but if we really believed in prayer, and understood what prayer truly is, we would spend a lot more time doing it, and have much more peaceful and fulfilling lives as a result. We are apparently missing an important part of the picture, however. Are we so unwilling to believe that our thoughts create our reality, that we aren't even willing to experiment with some committed, positive thought for a change?

If God told you today, "You can have anything you want, my child; just ask for it...," would you bother to ask for what you want, then? Incidentally, that is exactly how it works. "Ask and ye shall receive." I know this to be true, I use it, and I truly feel compassion for those who, without even trying something, can be convinced that it won't work, or that it isn't valid. Prayer works. And in case you can not hear it, you are indeed being asked to make a wish.

If you were extremely ill, would you spend five minutes, three times each day, saying affirmations simply because you read in a book that thousands of people have created their own cures in this way? Or, would you just go to the doctor and let your health ride on his faith and know-how alone? So many people will allow their skepticism to stand between them and their desires, or the answers to their prayers.

Why not try it now? If you have some chronic pain or illness, or if there is something that you truly want out of life, create an affirmation and start saying it for several minutes when you wake-up, while taking a break in the middle of the day, and before going to sleep at night. You probably wouldn't be surprised at how many people don't even have faith enough to "waste" fifteen minutes of their day asking God for what they want.

Don't just try to do it one day and then give up; that is not faith. Keep saying your affirmation until you receive what you asked for. I believe that if your expectation is strong enough, you need only think a thing once in order to experience it. I imagine that, in practice, this would look a lot like Jesus kneeling beside a sick man and "knowing" him into a state of better health. Jesus knew the man was no longer ill; and the man was no longer ill. Jesus had absolutely no doubt within Him.

Certainly Jesus faced His own worries; but His resolve was solid and trepidation was always overcome by faith. He knew everything that He would ever do — and then it would happen. But, let's assume that your faith is somewhat less than Christ-like; you may need to do a little more of the work – like praying for five-minutes, instead of five-seconds. If one person has used this method and ended up receiving what they were asking for, why not try it if there is the possibility it could mean letting go of an illness? Are you really that attached to your pain?

Many people don't pray because they equate prayer with religion; and most people have more than enough reason to run the other way when encountering anything religious. Still others simply don't take the time to pray because they simply don't believe in it, and there are those who are religious but have abandoned real, faithful, expectant prayer out of impatience. Basically, their prayers weren't answered quickly enough, so they gave up.

Each of these cases is the result of unfortunate events that led to the acceptance or formation of belief systems that unnecessarily limit your access to the power of prayer. Prayers are always answered; we just don't always recognize the answer when we see it.

We have also been trained to pray in ways that focus more on our unworthiness than on our wishes. If it is your belief that you are unworthy to receive, then your prayer will be answered accordingly; you will get what you believe an unworthy person should receive. Yes, it is as simple as that. You see, skepticism is yet another reason people have abandoned prayer. You are not serving yourself, however, if you are not even taking the simplest steps toward fulfilling your desires. The simplest step is to faithfully contemplate the joy of receiving what you want.

Jesus used healing as an incentive to pray. He demonstrated, quite effectively, that with prayer and faith (thought, and belief in that thought) anything can be accomplished – even healing yourself and others. You simply have to expect that, as a child of God, you will receive anything you wish. Then, your prayer has already been answered.

If you gathered together a hundred people, who suffered from an assortment of chronic medical problems, and asked them who among them prayed several times a day for relief, how many do you think would raise their hands? The fact is most people are chronically ill because they either believe they deserve to be ill or punished for something, or they do not believe they deserve to be healed – or that healing is even possible. Chronic illness begins deep within, long before any physical symptoms manifest. If you want to heal, you must decide that it is possible to heal, you deserve to be better, and that you are ready to heal. This is truly all there is to it.

The only problem with this is that there is a difference between saying these things, and truly knowing or believing these things. Many people think that proclaiming, "I believe!" is the same as *believing* simply because that's all they've been taught or shown. Then, when they proclaim their belief, and ask for God to heal their sinning soul, they act disappointed in the lack of immediate results. What they fail to realize is that their belief in the "fact" they are sinners, and sinners are undeserving, ensures that they will receive what they believe a sinner should receive – which is probably not healing and mercy. Visualize what you want; and know it is yours. Dream about the things you want to see; and know that they are real.

If you say that dreams don't come true, I would have to ask you at what point you stopped dreaming and started doubting, and what made you choose that particular time frame as a completion date for your prayer? What might happen if you continued to expect you prayer to be answered instead of proclaiming it a failure? What if your answer was to arrive the day after you hit the "cancel" button on you request?

Unfortunately, you may never know. Why sit around thinking about how you were ignored by God when you could be thinking of all the different ways your prayer could be answered, and how grateful you are that God does such things for you? Why view yourself as a victim when you could just as easily view yourself as the recipient of great gifts – even if some of those gifts are lessons that you asked for in some way, but would rather not learn?

You have free will to entertain any of these thoughts. Some of them will produce positive outcomes, and some of them will produce negative outcomes. You can certainly assume a negative outcome and then you will not be surprised when your prayer goes unanswered. Or, you could hope for a positive outcome, but doubt that you deserve or could ever have such luck, and so feel justified in your doubt when you failed to receive your answer (that you *believed* you would *not* receive).

Either of these choices has the additional side-effect of producing negative emotions, complete with the stress response that naturally accompanies such feelings, and the assurance that even if your prayer is answered, you have mentally reduced a gift from God to a mere fluke that will surely never happen again. More likely, though, your prayer is answered according to your faith and what you asked for; you just failed to see and acknowledge it. These things, consequently, reduce the effectiveness of each subsequent prayer action.

Compounding belief systems, that suggest poor use of your natural abilities (like prayer and manifestation), or a poor relationship with the Creative Force of the Universe, is a sure-fire way to create a miserable experience here on Earth. If you want things, but then follow that desire with a conviction that your desires are probably unattainable, or that such good fortune is for one more worthy than you, then you are creating a new prayer that will replace the initial desire with a perceived failure.

If two wishes can not coexist, I believe you will see the manifestation of the one that requires less energy, or less "movement of the Universe," to accomplish. If you would naturally follow the path of least resistance, do you not think God would have also figured out the value of such a concept? Where do you think you got this idea, anyway? It is a natural law. "That could never happen to me," is a very easy prayer for the Universe to answer – especially since the person who made it is not likely to take steps in the direction of making their prayer a reality.

If, on the other hand, you choose to know that if you didn't see the answer to your prayer, it just wasn't here yet, you would always be in a state of expectation and fulfillment. You would always either be receiving the answer to your prayer, or expecting it to happen; both of which are good places for your body and mind to be. The emotions which accompany this state are conducive to positive thought patterns, and therefore, positive manifestation.

You can choose whether or not to believe this; but not believing is not seeing, so make sure you choose wisely. Positive thoughts lead to positive emotions which are proven to reduce stress. Reduced stress allows your body to function more efficiently and helps strengthen your immune system. Although there are many other physiological benefits, these things alone will make your body considerably healthier. You are serving your body well to think positively. Your positive thoughts, or prayers, create positive health conditions. Positive prayer leads to good health.

To heal would be to replace a condition of what you might consider *poor health* with one of *good health*. A common misconception is that something is done to the illness which causes it to go away. Rest assured, directing energy into any illness will make it worse, not better. Seriously consider the kind of energy that typically surrounds terminally ill patients, for instance. These individuals often receive – to compliment their condition – a lot of fear, worry, grief, and doubt from the people around them. The results of this type of thinking are very predictable and have a demonstrable worsening effect on the spirits and health of any patient.

Your time and energy would be better used improving your own health and life. As we so often say, "You must be able to see yourself out of your present condition in order to get out of your present condition." If you are sick, for instance, dwelling on that will keep you in that place. Do you realize that people – thousands and thousands of people – die each year from the flu, from colds, from pneumonia, and a long list of other illnesses that can only breach your natural defenses if you weaken those defenses in some way?

Do you realize that, once you get sick, you are either dying, or recovering? What is the difference between someone who dies from the flu and someone who merely misses a few days of work? The person who died simply failed to reverse their condition.

The reasons for this are numerous, but the outcome is the same. If you allow an illness to progress, unchecked, and do not change any of the factors that led to the illness in the first place, your condition will only get worse. True, you may get a cold, and recover – all the while being the same "miserable you" who got you sick in the first place. But failing to learn, and failing to change, will result in further illness that will likely increase in severity until you die. There is no telling how long this process will take, but we all succumb to it eventually.

Think about your medicine cabinet, and then think about your life. Do not do this from a standpoint of judgment, simply observe what you find. The more issues that you refuse to let go of, the more containers (pill bottles, for instance) you will need in order to store them. Now think of the most chronically-ill person you know of, and then think about what you observe in their life. In fact, start observing life, people, and their behaviors; start listening to the things people say. You will be amazed at what you notice. Then, compare the various attitudes you find with the health conditions that accompany them.

Do you see the similarities among certain people with certain chronic illnesses? Can you see that people with similar personalities will often develop similar physical appearances and health conditions? It is actually quite easy to see when you become aware, and it is quite interesting, too. Realize that these things apply to everyone; so look at yourself honestly and understand that you created what you see – maybe accidentally – and you can just as certainly reverse anything you choose. Focus on the bad, see yourself as a victim, and wallow in misery if you wish; but remember it is your free will keeping your focus, attention, energy, and life, in disarray. Shift your focus and you will change what you see in your life. Free will simply means that you *can* choose to not be a victim of your own negativity, or other people's emotions and attitudes.

It is surprising how easy it is to become so self-involved and so wrapped-up in negativity. Negativity is insidious and contagious. It takes strong defenses to not succumb to the negativity of others, but you must resist the urge to join-in if you expect to protect your health and well-being. This understanding is the first step to healing. Understanding that illness is not something which attacks you, but something invited by you in order to shift your focus, is an essential step in removing yourself from the victim role. This is the first step to healing.

When we talk about healing with prayer, many think they can simply say a few magic words and be relieved of their symptoms so they can return to living as they were before. You can, actually; but if you are not willing to see the pattern that brought you to illness, and you are not willing to change your approach to life, you most likely do not have adequate command of the faith needed to manifest healing so quickly and effectively.

There are essentially sick people and well people. The vast majority of people in this world fall into the category of "the sick and poor" who Jesus said would "always be among us" for this very reason. If you observe closely, you will find that the two do not have a whole lot in common. If you are in poor health, it is a result of choices that you made, or failed to make. Remember, "If you choose not to choose, you still have made a choice." You must choose wellness; for if you stay where you are, illness will choose you. Prayer is thought, and it is the thought of choosing wellness that begins the journey toward health.

As we discussed earlier, mindfulness of right thinking is the key to right living. Right living brings with it health and happiness. When you are thinking on good things, you are praying for, and will receive, those things. Maintaining a positive view of your health is the key to maintaining good health. Your positive expectation of health is your prayer for health; trust that it will be answered and it will be.

Make an effort to hold a positive image of your health in your mind at all times and you will be rewarded with what you seek. Trust me when I say that there are many people who do not get sick. I can assure you that these people do not spend their time seeing themselves as being sick, or worrying that they might become ill. Pray for health and you will receive health. If you are already ill, the same principles apply; don't focus on where you are, focus on what you want or where you wish to be – a state of wellness. And be happy that it is now yours.

When Jesus, or His disciples, performed an act of healing, they didn't take action against the symptom or disease; they understood that we are created anew each moment and that creation is colored by our expectations. They simply assumed a positive outcome and expected to see it. They decided what they wanted, and they commanded it. Healing can happen just that quickly – one moment you are ill and the next moment, you are recreated anew. "According to your faith, it is done unto you."

The best advice I have ever received regarding healing is to simply tell God what you want, or expect, and then know in your heart that it is so. If this is your focus, and your faith is strong, practically anyone you set your sights on will be healed.

This is not to encourage anyone to go around living other people's lives for them, or taking away their lessons, or opportunities to learn and grow; but to assure you that if someone asks for your help, it is absolutely within the scope of your power and ability to know that they are well and to witness that reality "on earth as it is in heaven," or, in your physical reality as it is in your mind. You can indeed help a person heal their body, mind, and life.

The prayer methods outlined in the previous chapter will all work if you insert the opposite of your particular illness, symptom, dis-ease, or pain as the focus of the prayer. For instance, if you suffer with Fibromyalgia (a stress-related, chronic illness which can be very painful), you shouldn't make Fibromyalgia the focus of your thoughts or prayers if what you really want is **good health** – a life free from Fibromyalgia.

Anything you say, however, and anything you ask for, is fine. As long as you are clear in your mind as to the nature of your thoughts, you will receive what you ask for. Being clear and specific is of great value here as you will soon find should you neglect this advice. Praying for what you don't want, instead of what you do want, is an example of a misguided prayer.

162

For instance, if you wear glasses and you pray for God to "take away my vision problems…," you may learn that one way of losing vision problems is to lose your eyesight completely – blind people are neither near-sighted, nor far-sighted. There are no such hidden traps in affirmative prayer. "God, thank you for my perfect vision…," leaves little room for surprises. There are numerous examples of prayers that have been used to restore health, and they all share common elements.

Gratitude, desire, and expectation, along with faith, are all components of any effective prayer. I could tell you that if you say, "God thank you for restoring perfect health to all parts of my body, mind, and life…," that you will be restored to wholeness. If you did this faithfully, you would indeed achieve the results you desire, but you will probably find that choosing words that hold meaning for you will be all the more effective.

Also, there are some potentially "tricky" words that most people would naturally assume would be good "prayer words," like "God," for instance. Unfortunately, years of religious wars, persecution, demonizing of women, abuses, and other hypocrisies have turned many against the church, and even God in some cases. This doesn't mean that these individuals aren't allowed to pray, or even that prayer won't work for them. Everyone who thinks prays; and all of those thoughts are acted on. You don't even have to believe in God to pray. Prayer was around – and working – long before men decided they needed religions and gods to worship.

Even people, who are religious, go to church, worship God, and love Jesus, could still have negative belief systems or triggers associated with any of these words. They may not even be aware of a subconscious grudge against God (perhaps over the death of a pet during early childhood, etc…), or an unconscious negative association that will undermine not only prayer, but maybe even the *will to be well* or to live. The point is you could have been praying to God for years with no apparent results simply because the word "God" triggers unfavorable subconscious connotations that basically negate your prayer actions.

Anyone alive today is descended from someone who either experienced, or witnessed, some atrocity that would lead to such negative associations. Our DNA ensures that the cells in our body remember these things so that we might keep ourselves from experiencing them in our own lives.

Healing with Prayer

In the bible, there are dozens of accounts of healing – from all manner of illness. The cures never involve surgery or prescription drugs; they always involve changes in the way a sick person is thinking. "Be of good cheer," and "Fear not," are two of the more common prescriptions offered for restoring health where illness has taken hold. A great healer was oft quoted as saying, "Your FAITH has healed you." Faith is a feeling inside which is generated by the way you think about certain thoughts; we usually call these thoughts "beliefs," but they are nonetheless thoughts in the mind.

Because the thoughts which could have caused the imbalance are myriad, and these correlations are largely unknown to the average person, it isn't recommended that one scan their thoughts for afflictions – there are far too many of those to worry about. Looking for problems guarantees you will find problems; "Seek and ye shall find." Rather, the best course is to think positively, and optimistically – to have faith in your healing. You can not think a negative thought while simultaneously entertaining a positive thought; it is easiest to simply replace, or displace, all negative thought habits with repetitive positive thought, or affirmations. After doing this for some period of time – perhaps a very short time – you will notice the negative thoughts as they arise; and you will see the correlations between your thoughts and behaviors, and the way you feel. When you become aware of these things, you can face them and avert them with reason or love; until then, you will continue to feel as if you are a victim of some unseen and unknown foe. While it is true that your foe is unseen – because thoughts are invisible – your foe is not unknown. You are the monster in your closet!

From this moment forward, think only positive thoughts about your health; be patient and have faith that your health has already been restored. This means no longer thinking of illness and symptoms – no matter how "real" they seem. If you die, you would have died anyway; positive thought will not speed your demise, but it could slow or prevent its untimely arrival by creating healthier physiology – this is a scientifically proven reality. There is no need or benefit in reporting on unfavorable conditions; these reports are prayers for more of the same. Remove unhealthy, or negative, influences from your life; think positively; visualize yourself doing an activity requiring good health (one you love); and do it. Do not entertain "What-ifs." Be of good cheer and be well.

However, these genetic memories will replay themselves unless we transcend them and find more vital and dynamic ways to live and love life. This is indeed evident to anyone who: A.) knows a little about human history, and B.) watches the news or the people around them.

The world we live in seems to be in a perpetual state of reliving the past. True, the names, faces, and costumes have changed, but we dwell on those things that have happened, and we recreate the past by doing so – and most people will never even realize this is happening.

Jesus and His disciples had very simple methods and very basic prayers. They simply took an ill person, who proclaimed their desire to heal, and told that person that it was so – that their healing was an accomplished fact. There are at least twenty-seven examples of this type of healing in what little bit of the Gospels actually made Emperor Constantine's final cut of the Bible. The end of the book of *Acts of Disciples* suggests that there would not be enough books in the world to list all such miracles that were witnessed of Jesus and His disciples, and were undoubtedly documented by other followers, witnesses, and disciples. Jesus found a way to effectively teach others how to heal using only a small degree of the faith He seemed to possess – perhaps only as much as a "mustard seed."

Why were these lessons all but lost to us over the following years? I am sure that those who killed Jesus, as well as those who spent the next few-hundred years transforming the ministry and teachings of Jesus into what we now call "Christianity," would know the answer to such a question; but *we* may never know. It is up to us to continue to seek the truth that Jesus, and other great healers and teachers, tried to give us all – the truth of who we truly are. It is time to reclaim our birthright – our inheritance – and begin to live a life of fullness. It is time to rediscover our true power and nature as children of a God that playfully swings planets around stars, and in which all things are possible. It is time to remember that we have always held the power of healing, manifestation, and divine wisdom. It is time to heal.

"To wish to be well is part of becoming well."
– Lucius Annaeus Seneca

Chapter 13 Key Points and Afterthoughts

- Praying is thinking; as you think, so you are. If you think healthy thoughts, you will be healthy; if you cling to a belief in illness, or negative thinking, then you will be ill. This isn't to cast blame; there is no blame. Your symptoms are a sign of imbalance; all imbalance starts in the mind – with a thought.

- I have never met a positive, happy, healthy person who doubted that their thoughts shaped their experience – including the state of their health. Though I have met many skeptics who think they are healthy – having learned to live with what they call "mild," or "chronic," discomforts, and unhappiness. Pay attention to your body; it is telling you about your unconscious thought patterns.

- Release the idea that health and happiness are fleeting; there is no need to fear disease or death – perhaps your fear has kept you from seeing this. Never claim anything you do not wish to experience. Remember, "Decree a thing; and it shall be so."

- Those who speak most of ill health and troubles always seem to have something to talk about; those who habitually see themselves in their minds as being a model of Divine health tend to become that which they behold in their mind's eye.

- You have the power of health inside you. You have the power to dissolve any harmful thought, and heal any illness. You must only believe it is so and accept it. Circumstances and life-long beliefs may make this difficult; but a true belief in health and goodness is the only way to lasting health. Happiness is the best medicine; and belief is the only true cure.

- There is no prescribed time-limit for generating belief or manifesting the answers to prayers. Be patient and unattached to outcomes. Illness doesn't "go away;" health returns when healthy thinking resumes.

- Health is a reflection of wisdom, not intellect, and of balance, not the imbalance caused by desire and attachment. As long as illness is present, there is learning to be done. You are on a journey of experience; you will learn what you must regardless of how long you pause to play the "victim" of your life. Healing begins with a decision to create better for your self, and continues as long as focus doesn't shift back to negative thinking.

Chapter Fourteen

Unmasking "This Little Light of Mine"

We are born of pure light, a miracle of creation. We are perfect in our own separate ways. We do only what we are shown, and that which came with us to this place as our essential nature. So we do exactly as we were designed by our creator to do, and make our best attempts, given our individual abilities and circumstances, to repeat the behaviors we witness after we arrive here on the planet.

We try to do things we are shown by others; we are programmed by example. We see; and we do that which we see. We experience various things; and then we experience various feedback which should indicate which things will prolong our existence, and which things will shorten it. We make future choices based on the feedback we receive from our environment. Our essential nature is life-ward, or God-ward. Onward and upward we go, unless we are directed in another direction. This is the nature of life.

We experience our journey into, through, and out of this world, with innate guidance toward the path of least resistance. Sometimes we choose that option; sometimes we choose one of the infinite varieties of what some well-meaning, but misinformed, people call "wrong" choices. All choices are actually right choices if we truly have free will. Each choice will ultimately lead to the same place ("All paths lead to me…") but will all have slightly different scenery. The essence of that statement, and of free will, is that you can not mess anything up; you can only experience and learn.

We can do anything we choose and, regardless of the feedback our actions bring us, we always end up at "me." It is always now, I am always me, and I am always here – no matter where I go. Even when I die, no matter how it happens, I will still end up in the same place – whenever and wherever I AM. All paths, it seems, really do lead to me. We can't change that, but practically everything else is a matter of free choice and free will.

We allow the things we see in our minds to happen in our reality and we accept the results they produce. These events fill the time between here and there; but these events are not *us*. We often identify so closely with the experiences we have that we often come to believe we *are* our experience.

For example, if you are married, you may identify yourself as a wife. But you are not that; that is something that you are experiencing. You were not always a wife; and there are many ways you could find this experience coming to an end. Being a wife, or identifying with that role or ego, is a temporal experience. But you are always you. Even if your path leads you into, or even through, a marriage, or any number of events, you are always the "*me*" who thinks she's a wife. You are always the "*I am*" as It is experiencing what you have come to call *your experience* – no matter what that experience is. We are always the "little light" which was born into this world.

We are each born into this world with generations of genetic programming already in our system. If we are born with a particular disability, that information, or condition, was given to us by our parents, who either received it from theirs or picked it up during their own lives. When I say, "picked it up…," I mean, for instance, that a baby born with a respiratory disorder, whose mother smoked several packs of cigarettes per day, most likely received the genetic code for the respiratory condition from the mother. This code is a product of emotional experiences in the mother's life which led her to become a heavy smoker, and then compelled her to continue that habit to the detriment of her child. Science now knows that emotional events change the DNA in a person's cells, thereby allowing the person to pass along genetic information which will prepare their offspring for life in the same environment that caused the mother to be stressed-out in the first place.

This condition is one of the first "masks" that this parent will place on this child. The mother now has another reason to feel sorry for herself, and someone to share in her grief – the child. This is not the mother's fault, either. She too was programmed, by events in her life, to respond a certain way to certain situations. It is not the "light" that smokes three-packs-a-day, but one of the masks she was programmed to wear. If the baby were to die from this condition, it would only be the body carrying the dis-ease which would cease to be – not the Light which gave rise to that body.

The light is eternal and doesn't require a vessel; it only uses one for this brief experience on Earth. There are times when the masks we are driven to wear become too heavy and we are forced to shed them. If we are too heavily invested in, or believe we are one, or any number of the masks we wear, then the body may have to die with the mask, or masks. This is why people who strongly identify themselves with their careers will often die shortly after they retire and their identity ceases to exist. Or, why it is so common for spouses, after thirty, forty, fifty or more years of marriage, to die within weeks or months of each other. If we identify with a mask too strongly, we may be programming ourselves for sudden death should our mask ever die, or become obsolete.

The light, however, lives on. The light animates us and any mask we wear. The light shines through our masks and enhances the illusion, or allows the truth to be seen; it depends on how many masks one has and how attached to them they have become. I see it kind of like clouds in the sky. All clouds are made of the same stuff and no cloud lasts for very long. Light pours through the clouds when they are light, and there is only an image of beauty and wonder. But, when the clouds are *heavy*, they hide the light. When the light has trouble shining through, the clouds take on an ominous presence – one of darkness and impending bad weather.

By the same token, when our masks become heavy, our appearance begins to change. This change manifests as dis-ease and illness, a change in affect or temperament, or as life situations not going as well as we think they could. All because of a dark cloud (mask) blocking our light! Of course, just like a cloud after it rains, or a wave after it has broken on the beach, all masks are ultimately abandoned, or shed, ending our illusion of individual expression and returning us to the ocean of light from which we seem to have emerged. Shedding emotions through tears is no different that the clouds shedding some of their weight in the form of rain. Clouds, emotions, and disease come and go; it is the joy and sunlight which is always there whether we cover it with sad stories, or uncover it with a good cry and a new plan. Your essence is pure light in a very literal sense. Hide it under a bushel? NO! Let your light shine!

There is a toy, a particular kind of flashlight, which I use to illustrate this point. This flashlight has a bundle of fiber-optics extending from the lens so that there in no single beam of light, but the light is divided into maybe a hundred, or so, smaller lights shining out of the ends of each of these small little tubes. I think this is a great metaphor for what we truly are. We are each one of these lights; we appear to be separate, but only through our own individualization of the One light from which "I" came. We are all "I;" we are all the "I am." We are all light – a part of the same light.

We each come from the same source, but we each follow a slightly different path. All paths have common elements, but no two paths are the same, nor do any two paths have the same view. Each path has an apparent beginning and an apparent end – and a journey in between. Each path represents the journey of one ray of an infinite source of light traveling through a unique segment of time and space. Each little light has its own unique experience. True, there may be other strands close-by with a similar view – but no two have an identical view, or perspective.

For starters, you are not in your view of the outer world, though various parts of your body seem to be at certain times. You are the only one that does absolutely everything you do, exactly when and where you do it. Consequently, you are the only one who sees absolutely everything you ever see. Therefore, your thoughts and feelings, which are products of beliefs and attitudes that you formed based on the above series of sensory inputs which were unique to you, are uniquely your own. No one else, therefore, could think or feel everything you do, because they couldn't possibly believe all the things that you do. They haven't seen all the things you have seen; and it is these things that program your belief systems and attitudes.

There will be general agreements based on our proximity to one another. For example, all the branches of a tree know they are branches, but some of them are branches pointed toward the north and some are branches pointed toward the south. These branches would have an awareness of each other because of an underlying sense of the Oneness that obviously comes from the One tree they are all connected to, and therefore *connected by*. They would have many branches between them to act as barriers that keep familiarity from developing, and to keep conflicts from ensuing.

The branches to the north may never see much of the sun and may be tempered by a cold wind, while the branches to the south sees much of the sun and is sheltered from the wind. Everyone understands the effect weather has on your attitude. This is common throughout nature; all living things respond to the energy created by changing weather: Sun = happy, cold rain = gloomy.

If I am a branch facing south, the branch to my left, or east, would be able to see a little further over the east horizon, or around the left side of the tree. That branch and I would have many agreements about the weather, and the view, and our position above the ground, and our distance from the Tree, or God, or the sky, or whatever, but we would not have exactly the same view. I may know more about the branches to the west, while my neighbor would naturally know more about our other neighbors further to the east. We could learn from each other those things that were passed around from far reaches of the Tree, or we could harden ourselves to any understanding of the Tree as a whole. Even trees have a choice; they simply choose more wisely than humans.

Any one of the strands of light of our "light tree" can see many other strands, but can not see all the strands; nor can any of the other points of view be seen, either. We are aware of their presence, but do not know enough about their viewpoint to see any common bond. So we put a mask on ourselves and label those lights in close proximity to our own, "Us." We also put a mask on the lights we can not see thereby naming, or labeling, "Them." We do not realize that *they* came from God via one of the many paths we didn't see. They know something about God that we don't know, just as we know something about God that they don't know. And it is the same thing for both of us — neither of us knows the path of the other.

That person, or "those people," is one part (or many parts, depending on the size of your fear or hatred) of God that we simply judge unworthy of our love. When we judge others, we judge God; and if we judge God, we judge ourselves which were created by God. This is the essence of "Judge not, lest ye judge yourself…" We must remember as we cast judgment upon that singular strand of light that we find so different from our selves, that we too are only a singular strand of light and we too are different from them. It is only the masks, with which we cover our light, that hide the truth of who we are. It is only through uncovering, or unmasking, the light that the truth of the light can be fully seen.

We must realize that when we put on a mask, regardless of how many others have agreed to wear the same mask, we are covering the light and truth of who we are. Just because others do this thing, you are not required to mimic their behavior; you are just programmed to. It is this programming that is responsible for all of your dis-ease in life. We are programmed, largely by fear, to seek acceptance from others. We do this by wearing various masks – the clothes we wear in order to fit in at school, the suit and tie we wear to work, the religion we choose, the job we choose, the house we live in, the words we use around different groups of people, and so on.

We run these programs continuously, and have from the day we were given them. We adhere to the beliefs and attitudes of the programming out of fear of judgments from others who may know what, or whom, it is we are supposed to be *pretending* to be. We fear condemnation for falling short of our cultural responsibilities. It is fear which is primarily responsible for our hiding behind masks – why else would we hide? People wear masks to pretend to be something different, or to not be seen for who they are.

In other words, we wear masks to hide our true essence or identity out of shame, fear, or to gain some type of reward such as adoration, acceptance, or recognition. Verily, we have our reward; for these people (practically every one of us on this planet) have become what they saw themselves to be, and have hidden who they truly are. I don't know where she got this, but my wife often says, "Everyone is hypnotized; who hypnotizes you?" Indeed, you might want to consider where you acquired the various masks you wear – especially if your programming isn't working for you the way you would like. You aren't stuck; you can always change your mind about anything you wish.

Keep in mind that the things in your reality are all things you believe. They are not just things that you think, although they start that way; they are things that you really think a lot! They are things that you not only think are real, but things you truly believe are real. If you don't believe something is real, it is clearly because you haven't seen one, or convincing evidence of one, in your reality. If you have seen a particular thing, you would then, presumably, believe it. So, regardless of whether

172

those things in your reality were created by you or not, if they are in your reality, you believe in them. And if you do not believe in them, they are not in your reality. Regardless of cause and effect, there is a relationship between belief and reality.

Things that are not in your reality, you would have no awareness of, and therefore they would not exist as thoughts; whereas if you have a thought of a thing, it exists in some form. All form is energy, and the more solid the form – the more dense the energy. So, it seems, the more energy you put into something, the more *real* it becomes. Energy is energy, so it doesn't really matter if it is in the form of physical exertion or thought, except that some forms of energy travel faster than other forms – thought is faster than light, light is faster than sound, etc. As energy slows down, it creates a log-jam, or blockage of sorts, and becomes denser – more physical. Your thoughts have tremendous potential energy just waiting to be ignited with belief.

If you are wearing a mask, you created it; and you did this for a reason. A mask, just as any other creation, is made of energy. You once made a decision, or a movement, in the direction of this new identity. You had to put energy into acquiring the new mask. You had to attend medical school, in other words, to put on the mask of a doctor. You must get married and devote a certain amount of your energy to maintain the mask of a wife. Different masks have different weights; the denser, or heavier, the mask, the more energy it requires maintaining. You must choose how much energy you are willing to invest in any particular mask, or you will set up an imbalance that will ultimately result in stress and dis-ease as your body naturally goes about restoring balance.

Imagine, for instance, that you are a "soccer-mom." In this culture, a soccer-mom is a dutiful mother who is always busy taking the children to school, and soccer practice, and PTA meetings, etc. The soccer-mom is always shopping, cooking, driving, cleaning, washing clothes, making sure everyone is where they need to be – and that they are there on time. The job of a soccer-mom is not always easy; and it is often a tiring and thankless position.

If you are a soccer-mom, you do this for a reason – maybe even many reasons. It doesn't matter what those reasons really are; but let's just say that you want your kids to get the most out of their childhood, and sports, or whatever, so you do what it takes to give them that. So your reason for donning your "soccer-mom mask" would be self-sacrifice, kindness, generosity, the desire to be a good mom, or something along these lines. There is an underlying reason you want to be the kind of mom who does these things. "Soccer-mom" is the mask; the reasons listed above may be the straps that hold the mask on, but there is an even deeper, underlying reason that is attached to a belief someone taught you, or that you assembled on your own.

It takes a lot of energy to be a soccer-mom. Whatever the reason is that you wear the mask of "soccer-mom," it must be pretty important to make you want to spend your time and energy maintaining that identity. The point is, in fact, if you say, "Oh, it is! I really love watching the kids grow up!" then you definitely have a balanced equation and are actually improving your life by doing that which you truly love doing. If you really feel like the whole thing is more of a burden than a pleasure, then you are not getting enough out of this mask to justify wearing it. You may keep it on out of guilt, but you aren't doing anyone any favors. If you take a child to ballet or soccer practice with love and joy, that's a gift. When you take a child to practice because you'd feel guilty for not being a good mother if you didn't, then you are giving resentment, and not love, to that child.

The child feels the energy; and because the energy they feel doesn't match the mask you are wearing, a paradox is set up where the child must decide which of you – the *you* the child feels, or the *you* the child sees and hears – they should please. The child is now choosing masks of their own, instead of simply being themselves. Even if they are true to themselves, there will be an undercurrent of energy that will make them feel separate. If you are not doing the things that you are doing out of love, don't do them; the resentment caused by doing those things hurts you and all those around you.

If any of the masks you are wearing are not giving you the joy you think they should be, and most of them will not, then you have to choose whether you are going to continue spending energy maintaining that which is doing you no good, or invest that energy into something that brings you joy. If it's not working for you, it's working against you; and if it covers the light and truth, it's probably not working for you – even if you think it is.

When I compare religion with spiritualism, it is only to illustrate the difference in the perspectives each mask offers. None of this is to say that religious people are not spiritual, or that you have to either choose to be religious, or choose to be spiritual. Religion is a great vehicle to get you nearer to where you wish to go. It will not get you all the way there, however, unless where you wish to go is pretty close to home. There will be a point where you have to decide to seek your own way, or go the way of the many. With religion, large groups of people are brought together with a commonly taught belief. These groups believe, among other things, that they share the same beliefs.

Since no two people see exactly the same things, however, no two people could share exactly the same view, or the same belief, for that matter. We can say that we basically see things in a similar light, and that our view is radically different than what can be seen from over there; so *we* are more alike than different, and *they* are more different than alike –

So we come to an agreement to wear the same masks so we can separate ourselves from those with different views, instead of trying to see what the rest of God's creatures are looking at. There is nothing wrong with this; but it should illustrate that, if you are joining together with some people, there are many more that you are not joining with. Since all light has the same source, you are choosing sides based on some difference between you that you see only on the surface – a superficial belief. The only difference between you and them is the masks you wear, for underneath all masks there is only light. Religion, therefore, seems to be more focused on wearing the right mask, and wearing the same mask that everyone else is wearing.

Religion is a spiritual pursuit, and any form of spiritual pursuit can be rewarding. But to spread any particular doctrine, far and wide, even at the price of human life, is an attempt to force others to wear the same mask so we can all pretend to be, and believe, the same. Originally, beliefs are spread by those with the power to do so in order to have and to hold even more power. Fear is the weapon used to spread beliefs; but what happened to the courage to stand firm on your own beliefs?

It seems as if the instinct to "clump-together" is an overriding factor in the wholesale acceptance of group beliefs. Coupled with a little misinformation, the need to be among others of your own kind, and the fear of going against their established order, has a way of almost shaming us into compliance. This is as if you can not accept yourself the way God made you, so you seek acceptance from others based on whatever surface, or superficial, observations you can make and assume. You seem to find yourself separate from God, and you cover yourself in shame as if it were something you did wrong that caused your light to be cast out from your union with God.

This, in fact, is one of the plot lines of the creation story (perhaps all creation stories). You mask yourself to hide among others – this is really no different than antelope, or zebra, staying in closely knit groups in order to bolster their individual odds of survival should something bad happen. This herd behavior is born of fear and guilt, and it is maintained that way. If your mask is not only keeping you safe, but giving you all the joy you think it should be, continue wearing it until it no longer does so. If your mask is a burden, lay it down without delay.

When I refer to spiritualism, in this sense, I am really speaking of an almost reverse approach to the pursuit of knowledge of the spirit than that offered by group approaches; a singular path using the individual heart as the only guidance along the path, so as not to be swayed by the fears of others – which are so often cloaked as "good advice," or "reason." In this context, it is almost as if religion and spiritualism are polar opposites. I do not mean to imply that if one is good, the other is bad, or if one is right, the other is wrong; they both address the same part of your existence – just from different viewpoints.

Spiritualism seems to be more of an un-masking process. As opposed to a quest for religious propriety, spiritualism seems to require one to wear the mask of the "un-masker." When one puts on the mask of spiritualism, it is to become a person who seeks to remove all masks – to uncover as much of your light as possible. The quest for Spirit is basically the process of self-realization. We attempt to see who it is that put *us* on in the first place – our original mask, so to speak – because we believe that if we can pull away enough layers, or masks, we may be able to pull away whatever that very first mask was that made us appear to be separate from our very essence.

This journey inward is much more frightening than surrounding yourself with a herd; for this journey is one that is taken alone, "Because strait is the gate, and narrow is the way, which leadeth unto life, and few there be that find it." Whereas religion seems to unify people under a common, man-made belief system, spiritualism empowers individual unmasking. Fear and the subsequent desire for security will keep you with other like-minded people – your own herd, so to speak. The problem with following the herd is that they must stick to the wide path, and "...wide is the gate, and broad is the way that leadeth to destruction and many there be which go in thereat..." When following the herd, you must be careful not to "step in something;" and you must be ever vigilant for those who make their way in life by preying on herds.

It may seem like a waste of time to strive to see beneath the masks of our lives. We will die one day and then we will know what we really are, so why not just live life? Well, there is living life, and then there is *living life*. The more masks you pull off, the closer to the truth you get; the more burdens you shed, the brighter the light gets. As you get closer to your original light, you get closer to your true power. Your true power is the power of creation. The mechanism we use to create is prayer, or mindful thought. As we shed our masks, we are able to access more and more of our abilities, courage, and all of the powers and gifts that are our birthright. We all have this power as our inheritance, and this power gives us the ability to experience anything we believe in.

As you get closer to the truth, your belief and faith become stronger and more reliable. As you will come to understand, it is belief which fuels your thoughts and prayers; it is belief which leads to experience. You would never have done a single thing had you not believed, at some level, that you could do it. You made the decision, fueled by the belief in the outcome, and then you experienced the reality you created. As you live your life in greater and greater light, your life becomes fuller and richer. True, one day you will die, and only then will you know the truth you sought, but it is the life you experience in the meantime that your thoughts and prayers affect.

The journey to truth, as you could perhaps call life, is much smoother and more fulfilling if you are pointed in the direction of truth. If you aren't, you are basically going through life backwards, with only the past in your view. You will have your day of truth, but it will come quickly and all you will know of it is where you have been. Even then you will only know it after you are no longer there. Only after life has passed you by did you get a chance to see it. Face forward! Life moves fast – at the speed of thought, you might say! By facing forward you always know where you are, and you are always in the moment. And it is in the moment that we experience creation – not tomorrow, not yesterday, but right now.

Just as you wouldn't want to go to the beach with several layers of winter clothing on, you don't really need to go through life with all of the extra masks you carry. Maintaining any mask requires an expenditure of energy that could be better used elsewhere in creating a fulfilling life for your self. True, when you start shedding these layers, you will stop at some point out of some practical necessity (like not getting arrested for public indecency!), but you will get to an appropriate level of masks (just your swimsuit, perhaps) for where you are in life. You will feel more comfortable, lighter, and appropriately equipped for the moment without being overburdened with excess layering. There are times when a mask will lead you to a more comfortable outcome, but keep in mind; you are always making a judgment and a trade-off. A mask is ultimately a lie, and lies ultimately do you harm. Granted, I will keep my swimsuit on at the beach in observance of the law, but the price for "letting your light shine," in some instances, is just too high.

We are often required to produce a certain mask, in order to gain passage through a certain part of life. If you are traveling abroad, you need the mask of your citizenry, for instance, in the form of a passport. There are many times when you might find that you have to put on a mask simply to negotiate your life. That's just the way life is. Just be aware of how necessary your masks are, and how much enjoyment they bring you as compared to the energy they require. And be aware of why you wear them.

If you are wearing a sheep-mask, ask yourself if it was a "false prophet…in sheep's clothing" that asked you to put it on only to expose himself as a "ravening wolf" and devour you as a sheep. Some people wear masks in order to get us to wear one. Do you want to hide your light under a bushel just because someone else can't find theirs? Jesus said that, "Ye are the light of the world." "Let your light shine before men that they may see your good works…" said Jesus, encouraging people to be themselves, and be all that they could be. This can not be done by devoting a large portion of your energy to holding onto masks, or monitoring the masks of others. As you read, understand that you should be seeking to unlock your inner power. The key to this lock lies under the masks – deep inside you.

Losing Weight with Prayer

The weight we accumulate on our bodies is the result of stress, which is caused by negative thinking. By "negative thinking," I simply mean those thoughts which cause our body to experience the feelings of fear, worry, grief, anger, guilt, shame, embarrassment, and so on. These emotions are all the result of stress, or the stress response; and, as such, are all indicators that you are in a state of stress. Any thoughts – conscious or unconscious – which put you in stress trigger your body's protective stress-mechanisms.

When the body's stress response is active, digestion slows down, the immune system is weakened, and the stress hormone Cortisol is released. Cortisol helps your body convert that undigested food into fat and then store it in case you need it later. Fat is produced by the body in order to protect us during times of stress. Fat offers protection from starvation, from the elements, and from unwanted attention; fat also pads our bones and organs – protecting us from impacts – and makes us appear larger to our enemies. Fat is our friend; and as a creation which does serve us in many ways, we should give thanks for our fat – and then release it by releasing the negative emotions causing our bodies to hold onto the past (including the food we have eaten).

Prayer helps us lose weight in a number of ways. First, when in the proper state of mind for prayer, you are not in stress – or your stress response is in the process of turning itself off. When you relax and pray, your body is in a healing state and is releasing excess. Another way to lose weight with prayer is to visualize and affirm a healthier you – smiling and having fun being healthy and fit. Don't stare in the mirror and hate what you see; love what you see in the mirror and it will gradually become that which you wish it to be. This will not happen if you are on "bad terms" with your body because of years of negative self-talk. Change the image of yourself in your mind into the "ideal you;" and then, stay positive and do what you are inspired to do. A happy person, with health and fitness on their mind, will soon be inspired to do something fun and healthy.

Chapter 14 Key Points and Afterthoughts

- We can only do what our DNA is programmed to do, and what we learn to do; so go easy on yourself. The good news is that you can "re-program" your DNA; you do it all the time, anyway, so you might as well put a little conscious thought (prayer) into the conditions you wish to create.

- In the middle of "you," there is pure light, expressing itself through your DNA and the layers of programming through which it must flow to reach the surface. Like the raw energy flowing from the wall outlet into a computer, your Spirit is pure energy; only when programming begins "bending and shaping" the energy, does the contrast and diversity of life emerge.

- You are not what you think; your thoughts are things that come to you. You are not the events which have happened to you; those experiences are things you went through — and they are in the past. You are not what you do; you are the doer — not the work. Yet, you are your own creation — a creation of your continuous thoughts about yourself and what you are. If you do not change these thoughts, you will not seem to change much. Stagnant thought is the key to a mediocre existence.

- The more programming in a computer, the more resistance to the flow of energy through the computer — the processing slows down. The more beliefs and masks (egos) you have, the more resistance your Spirit has as it moves through you and animates you. The more resistance, the less animated you will be.

- We all know what we know. Or do we? The truth is that we each only know what we have been told. When that information serves us — great! Most of the time, however, what we have been taught only leads to lives filled with pain, suffering, and misfortune; it is a sad fact that most people are simply not happy and healthy because they were taught WHAT to think rather than WHAT thinking IS. If your life isn't working for you, try learning some new things; try asking yourself what kinds of things interest you — we tend to think differently when we are interested in a thing. We tend to think about the things we are interested in the way we should be thinking all the time — positively and creatively.

- It is often comforting to find others who seem to share our beliefs; but beliefs are subject to change, and this is tantamount to a foundation of sand. What you really share, with any large group, is at least one similar life experience and several common judgments.

Since God is All in All

"Since God is All in All to me
There is no hate or fear,
For love is all there is to see
And God as love is near.
If God is really all I know,
And all that fills my life,
In truth there is no evil thing –
No pain, no fear, no strife.

Since God is All in All to me
There is no lack of health,
For He supplies my life with good
And manifests as wealth.
If God is really all I know,
I give no thought to sin;
No impure thought, unholy deed,
Can touch the Christ within.

Since God is All in All to me
There is no time, no past,
No vain regret of days gone by,
No joy that did not last.
If God is really all I know,
With Him I'm satisfied,
And in His love I rest secure
And in His peace abide."

– a poem taken from the book: Be of Good Courage
by: Frank B. Whitney

"For those who believe, no proof is necessary.
For those who don't believe, no proof is possible."
— Stuart Chase

"Man often becomes what he believes himself to be. If I
keep on saying to myself that I cannot do a certain thing, it
is possible that I may end by really becoming incapable of
doing it. On the contrary, if I shall have the belief that I
can do it, I shall surely acquire the capacity to do it, even if
I may not have it at the beginning."
— Mahatma Gandhi

Chapter Fifteen

Acknowledging the Actions of God

here is no limit to the miracles we can experience in life. The fact is we have gotten so used to miracles that it takes amazing spectacles of universal movement to impress us. What I mean, for example, is that each breath we take is an unexplainable miracle of unimaginable significance. Medicine and science may be able to observe, describe, and even affect to some degree, the physical activity that accompanies the process of respiration; but we may never know, however, how or why that particular miracle occurs.

Childbirth, trees, and where art and music come from, are just a few of the everyday miracles we simply can not explain. But we take these things for granted, or simply ignore them, because we don't understand them. We integrate these things into our lives without fully appreciating their significance. Then, we expect "real" miracles to be performed on command before we accept the existence of a higher power – or before we truly believe in one. The adage, "If you can't take care of what you have, what makes you think you need more?" comes to mind. If we can't even acknowledge the miracles that surround us in plain sight, what makes us think we'd recognize a miracle in an unfamiliar setting, or scenario?

The observation that a magician can make the statue of liberty disappear, or a woman levitate, predictably leads us to the assumption that any such miraculous occurrence would probably be nothing more than an elaborate illusion or hoax of some kind. We can not fathom the workings of nature, and we have trained ourselves to believe that miracles must resemble magic tricks, so we quickly dismiss true miracles as coincidence, or luck. Or, for example, when we hear that someone has survived a terminal disease without medical intervention, we think that they simply beat the odds. If we looked deeper at such events, it would become clear to us that nature is constantly extending a helping hand in our direction. This is a miracle; but it is also simply nature's way.

Life is full of miracles, and if we could just acknowledge the ones we already have, we would surely be given more. Actually, we would just see more of what was already there. People change as they begin to notice things around them. It's as if they are waking up from a culturally-induced sleep, or trance. Our intellects are always ready to engage external stimulus; it's how we experience and learn from our world. The problem is that, today, most of our external stimulus is garbage that does us no good, and induces a form of cultural hypnosis, or "social hypnosis," in the words of Deepak Chopra.

Our brains are so busy with advertising, television, radio, work, the internet, and all sorts of useless, non-stop chatter that we spend hardly any of our waking hours listening to the forces within us through which we know God. This is perhaps the greatest tragedy that could befall a species that is obviously so capable of awareness. There is hope, however. We can awaken from our sleep and discover that the fear was indeed a dream – or a nightmare, as the case may be.

Our awakening can start with a simple acknowledgement of what it means to say that God is omnipotent, omnipresent, and omniscient. This leaves nothing out. God is all things. If you want Him to be a Him, for instance, then that's fine. He can certainly be that which you would like because it is not possible for you to imagine a single thing that falls outside the realm of omnipresence – He could be *anything* you choose to imagine Him as. God is all things to all people.

The only caveat to this is that you must realize when you imagine God as an old man, sitting on a throne of gold in the sky, or living on a cloud called Heaven, you have greatly limited the Omnipotent. Of course, no man has more power than the All-powerful (Omnipotent); so your limitation of God by a simple attempt to describe, or even imagine exactly what He might be, is clearly illusory – but nonetheless devastating to your ability to interact effectively with the ALL.

A volcanic eruption, or a hurricane, may be a very powerful expression of nature, but each is limited in its own way by geography, duration, etc. No man, however limited these expressions may be, is capable of stopping or controlling such phenomena. These are mere brush strokes made by the creative force on the canvas of creation. If there is no man-made force capable of controlling or limiting a mere expression of God, why then do we presume to subdue the entire concept of God with a single word?

We can't truly control any single aspect of God or creation, yet we continue to make our own attempts to control God by limiting God to a human's descriptive terminology. In other words, we have decided amongst ourselves that it is our place, or within our power, to decide who or what God is. Once you have agreed that God is all things, the discussion is over and so are any arguments or judgments about who is right or wrong about the *real* God. This type of imagery is primitive and was handed down to us from people living in an age of ignorance and superstition. If you assign God an identity, as such, you have created, for God, one *singular* thing that He is, while simultaneously creating an infinite list of things which He is not.

By warning against such limiting beliefs, I am not implying that you will anger God and bring His wrath upon yourself. My warning is that by pretending to be privy to some divine knowledge, like knowing the identity of God, you will surely miss many of the workings of God in your own life. In other words, you'll be looking for specific things in life and will probably miss the truly important things when they come around. You see, you are not going to be struck by lightning if you presume to know God's name; but you will know a much smaller God than you could know with an open heart and mind. It is out of fear (fear that we don't really know God, or that we are somehow separate from ALL that is) that we make up identities for Him — starting with the idea that *ALL* is gender-specific.

We can certainly know these pseudo-identities, however, because we created them. In fact, many of these identities were created by very fearful, and primitive, minds; most of which had agendas for doing so. Consequently, these are the easiest concepts to understand, as they are so simple. They do, however, represent a hand-me-down God who apparently acts with a great deal of inconsistency and violence. We are so busy trying to grasp someone else's ideas of God that we spend no time coming to know our own. This is truly a tragedy. For we, as humans, have come very far in the past two thousand years; but we have foolishly presumed to limit God to the parameters of ancient minds, as we thwart His evolution to the same extent that He allows ours!

Consider, with an open mind, the people of the Middle East. I am not judging these cultures; but turn-on any American news broadcast, or go into any barber shop or office building in the United States, and you will see what the general consensus is as to the sophistication of most Middle Easterners. Clearly, these judgments are based on stereotypes, but there is tremendous animosity and judgment directed at these cultures by many Americans – even by many devout Christians.

It seems as if Americans, in general, view the people from this area as being simple-minded or ignorant, unsophisticated, barbaric, unholy, or worse. Now consider what you would see if you were to rewind the clock, so to speak, and go back two thousand years, or even four thousand years. Regardless of what you believe about the current occupants of any part of this planet, two thousand years is a long time. If you think people are barbaric or ignorant now – and we are – just imagine the attitudes of that time.

Remember, we were burning witches in this country only three or four hundred years ago. Brother killed brother, in this country, only a hundred and forty, or so, years ago over the right to enslave human beings. We take the Bible, however, as if it were written by contemporary theologians, physicists, and philosophers, in our own time; but the image that you conjure up, as you imagine traveling back in time, is where these writings came from. We inherited our religion from primitive people responding to dreams, sacrificing humans and animals, and killing thousands because they blamed them for pestilence.

The same people who loathe or detest those from the Middle East cling tightly to the words of their primitive ancestors. We don't accept any other part of their culture – which is the closest anyone could come to an unadulterated continuation of Biblical society – but we limit our lives with their very narrow and fearful views of the creative forces of God. Remember, that period of time is marked by the complete confusion surrounding God, gods, Religion, Spiritualism, and Nationalism.

Also, fear and violence prevailed two-thousand years ago; one need only think of the crucifixion of Jesus if an example is truly necessary. Furthermore, the religions and political philosophies of the greatest military power are those handed-down over time. The victorious write history – after installing their own God – and the vanquished become history. The truth in those messages is based on that which is unchanging, not on temporary cultural paradigms. If a thing is no longer true, it never was true; our eyes have simply opened a bit wider allowing in a bit more light, or a clearer view of a greater truth.

I mention this only because our tendency is to hold God, and our realm of possibilities, to the limitations of ancient writings. Of course, we aren't open to ALL ancient writings, just a few ancient writings carefully selected by small groups of people with very big agendas – such as social order, or the unification of economic and political Empires.

If God were truly His own biographer, do you suppose He intended to be viewed differently by everyone who read "His book," so that we could fight about it for all time, killing millions in His name? Or do you prefer the idea that He just didn't do a very good job letting us know who He is and what He wants? Or perhaps you think that the All Knowing just didn't foresee what we would do with His words, or that He just didn't care? It is no secret what man has done with his various translations and interpretations of this book – all along remaining blameless because, after all, they're God's words, not ours.

Of course God is the Bible, just as He is everything else; that's what ALL means. But He isn't *just* the Bible, or *just* an old man in the sky, or *just* any one view – He is ALL. Think about it. How have you been limiting God in your own life? Forget the societal mechanisms of fear and control; and consider what an omnipotent, omnipresent God is capable of doing in your life. When you hear someone exclaim, "How is that possible?!" the obvious reply would be, "How is anything possible?" The answer is elementary. All things are possible in God. All things exist in God. If you believe that all things exist in a sort of energy matrix that we call the Universe, then that is God – for you.

The word God isn't a name; it is simply a word that we use to label – as we humans so enjoy doing – that creative force which is all things. God doesn't require us to come to any agreement with each other as to what He really is – we probably never will. If God knows all things, He certainly has observed this simple fact. It is humans who insist on forcing each other to acquiesce to the religious views of one person or organization lest they face man-made judgment. Jesus never said we were to spread religion at the tip of a sword. He instead instructed that the good news be spread wherever it was welcomed, and where it is not, then we are to "brush the dust of that place off as we leave."

God created all of us. The creation of everything is a pretty impressive miracle, if you ask me. God is also the stuff from which all creation emerges. God is everything there is and everything that happens. God is the reason for all we experience as duality; which is everything, by the way. When you see a tree, you see God; and it is no more or less spectacular than if you were to see a blind man regaining his sight or a crippled man stand and walk. It is only your beliefs that limit what you see and experience.

Have you ever noticed how many of the things you would like to see happen, actually do happen? How many times have you gone to call someone on the telephone and, before you could pick up the phone, it rang and the person you were going to call was calling you? Or how many times have you called someone and had them say, "I was just thinking about you!"? If this happened to one or two people once or twice, you could easily dismiss it. The fact is that this happens to practically everyone who uses a telephone. In fact, if you look closely at the frequency of these occurrences, you will likely find a correlation between these events and times in your life when you were feeling pretty good about things, or times during the day when you weren't particularly stressed about anything. This doesn't just apply to telephone calls; it applies to everything that happens – everything you have simply dismissed as coincidence, and every other moment you failed to recognize as such.

For many months, now, my wife and I have experimented with this phenomenon and found it to be astoundingly predictable and quite reliable. In fact, if we really need to speak with someone, we put that thought out there with love and, believe it or not, they usually call. Sometimes it is within a few minutes, sometimes it is within a day, but with very few exceptions, they call. If we aren't specific about how we speak to them, they will often knock on the door, or schedule an appointment, or just happen to "run into us" at the grocery store or some other place. This has happened with people we haven't seen for ages because they moved away. There is no limit to the ways things can work out.

These things happen to us all, but so many of us simply dismiss these events when they occur. This is unfortunate, because if you recognize these fortuitous moments as what they truly are, you will not only begin experiencing them more frequently, but you will experience them when you most need them. You will learn to command them through mindfulness and prayer. There is also a tremendous feeling of *oneness* that comes with activating, or becoming aware of, this aspect of your life.

This phenomenon works so effectively, as a matter of fact, that Jennifer and I have been forced into a heightened state of mindfulness because practically every thought we dwell on turns up in our lives in a relatively short period of time. For this reason, I have to say that it is absolutely foolish for anyone to dwell on any negative thought! These thoughts are prayers, of a very real sort, and will be addressed. This is the nature of St. Peter's admonition to "dwell on those things that are good." If you wish to experiment with this – and I highly recommend that you cultivate this power – be specific, be positive, and be mindful of your thoughts, because you will most likely see them again in some physical form.

Dwelling on the negative will produce a miracle in your life of a like nature. Trust me when I say that a downward spiral of depression is likely to result from dwelling on the negative. This is why it is so important to get outside, change your scenery, and find something positive to occupy your thoughts, when trying to get over a negative occurrence in your life. No matter how bad you think something is, it can always get worse. But it can get better, too. What's the difference? The difference is only the direction and nature of your thoughts; and that is all.

You see, the manifestation of negative events, following a period of negative thought and emotion, is no different than hoping and praying for good and then experiencing good. If you can recognize the thoughts that preceded any negative event in your life, it is the same as recognizing that you were thinking of the person on the other end of the phone just before it rang. You are acknowledging the actions of God. God is always giving us what we ask for. Ask and ye shall receive – you should be seeing a common pattern by now.

Open your eyes and look at the world around you with gratitude; it is all a gift from God. Even those parts of life you'd rather not see hold lessons or blessings for you. The traffic jam that you are stuck in, for instance, is keeping you from an accident that you would have otherwise experienced. The cold that you came down with brings you the day off you have needed, but have neglected to take. The relationship that ended abruptly opened the door for something bigger and better in your life.

Of course, if you see it as the end of your world, it just might be. People wallow in depression over such things and delay the good which awaits them. Mourn your losses, if you wish; it's only natural. But then get on with your life and your miracle. You have asked for something and God is trying to give it to you. If you don't like it, ask for something else. You have free will. That means if you want to see the world as a miserable place, you can. If you want to change it, you can – just do it! If you ask for it, it will be given unto you. This is a two way street. If it is given unto you, you asked for it, or it is one of the stepping stones on the path of manifestation.

If you get fired, for instance, you may not have asked for that; but you may have asked for a better job, more money, or nicer coworkers, and just haven't had the inspiration to go get it. Now you do. Clearly, I can't enumerate all the combinations of events that can form answers to prayers. No man can; and God does work in mysterious ways that are way beyond any knowing. In fact, you may never be able to see such connections with some events. But you will begin to notice; and if you work on it, you will see these connections most of the time. You will become one with this process and see your true place in it all. You are not a victim – you are a creator. Recognize this, acknowledge the works of God in your life, and you will truly experience a life of fullness.

Many people are aware of the importance of this step (acknowledging the actions of God) in the development of one's awareness. Some advise us to keep "spiritual journals" so we can look back at the markers along our life path and perhaps gain some practical advantage in future steps. These markers I am referring to are also called signs or guideposts by others, and coincidence or synchronicity by most. Squire Rushnell calls these events "God winks" and also suggests that you keep a journal. I believe that keeping a journal will certainly help you see that there is a definite pattern to these occurrences; and "seeing is believing."

Even the skeptics who write these things off as simple coincidence will come to see that there is nothing at all simple about coincidence. The entire universe has moved to give you a gift, a sign, a message, a lesson, or some other thing that you have surely asked for – whether you realize it or not. Your goal is to start realizing these things so you can stop haphazardly asking for physical lessons in life – many of which can be quite painful. If every time you pushed a red button, you heard a loud buzzing sound and a hammer struck you in the head, eventually you would stop pushing that button. Something else would likely happen, as well. You would probably develop a habit of covering your head every time you heard a loud buzzer! You would recognize an apparent causal relationship.

By the same token, if instead of a blow to the head, the same events produced some hoped-for benefit, you would most likely push the button any time you desired that benefit. The fact is, we get hit in the head an awful lot, but we also receive rewards. The button, however, is always the same; it is only our thoughts that change, and therefore different results are experienced. If we walk up to that button with positive thoughts in our head, pushing it will bring desirable results.

If, on the other hand, we are entertaining negativity in our minds when we push the button; watch out! Pavlov's dog is a lot smarter than Pavlov would have us think. I think the only difference between us and that dog is that the dog actually believes a reward naturally follows the ringing of the bell, and we believe rewards are a matter of chance. If we observe the synchronistic events in our lives carefully, we would see the pattern and perhaps we too would believe. Maybe then we would ring the bell more often and, *believing*, we would have our rewards.

It is not always easy to acknowledge the workings of God in our lives. A string of negative experiences will sometimes even turn people away from God. People just don't like accepting responsibility for the things in their lives. This is only natural considering that judgment is handed out so readily – pretty much anywhere you care to look. Observing and acknowledging this mechanism of prayer at work will change your outlook and your mind. You have seen it already. You only have to realize that the actions of God are for you, not against you. Only then will you be able to see the truth of who you are.

"Miracles are not contrary to nature, but only contrary to what we know about nature."
– Saint Augustine

Chapter 15 Key Points and Afterthoughts

- There are no limits; all things are possible to he who knows the law.

- If there are limitations in your life, there are limitations in your thinking. Limitations are simply "firewalls" between the operating programs, or beliefs, you use everyday and the new programs you would have to access in order to create a new reality.

- "Things" begin much earlier than we are able to perceive them; a thing is well on its way to being a physical reality long before it can be detected, in any sense, by any sensory perception. Yet the thing must exist in thought-form in order to guide the unfolding physical reality.

- All formed things are made of the same stuff, come from the same place, and are designed by the same creative force. If you can perceive it with your senses, it is an act of Creation much more complex than you can understand; though we tell ourselves simplified tales about the things we see.

- Everyone believes something; and no matter what you believe, it either serves you, or someone else – who may or may not have your best interest at heart.

- Even skeptics are creative; they create exactly what they expect – just like the rest of us. Skeptics simply lack imagination, and thus have never experienced the reality of prayer. "Though they have eyes; they can not see."

- Two consecutive experiences establish a trend. You can always create an upward trend by thinking and making your next thoughts and actions happier or more positive than your previous thoughts and actions. If this experience is better than the last experience, you are on an upward trend; if not, you need only make your next experience a positive one – and there is always something positive you can focus on.

- Until you are no longer here, creation is in a continuous state of change; you can edit your life as you go – to whatever extent you choose. Follow your heart and acknowledge the signs and gifts bestowed upon you along the way. Even in the most painful of experiences we find very valuable lessons, if not gifts.

- It does you no good if I am the only person who sees the good in your life; you are the one who must learn to see the good in your life if you wish to create more good in your life. Acknowledge this and begin seeing the good; as you perfect this, more good will be added.

Chapter Sixteen

What Does the Answer to a Prayer Look Like?

oes anyone really know what the answer to a prayer looks like? I believe we all do; though we may not realize we do. What I mean is that although we may expect that the answer should be in the form of what we asked for, it doesn't always turn out that way. For instance, if you pray for rain, the answer to this prayer should be easily identifiable. But exactly when should it start raining?

We know it will eventually rain and that the answer to our prayer is assured, but then we begin to doubt, become afraid, add our own criteria, and expect the answer to be forthcoming on our timetable because we embraced fear rather than faith. All prayers are answered; this relationship is all there is – ask and receive. The trouble is, however, that we humans have somehow decided that we know *how* a prayer should be answered, and how long that should take. It seems that most people tend to think that if it doesn't begin raining immediately after the prayer, they were either ignored by God, or prayer simply doesn't work.

Time is just a concept we created to quantify the distance between our actions, prayers, or thoughts (cause), and the answers or results (effect). The greater the distance between cause and effect, the more likely we are to give-up on our prayer being answered, or to begin to doubt the entire process. Doubt kills expectancy; and the death of expectancy leads to a feeling of failure.

When humans judge something as a failure, a new belief system is established that a particular thing simply doesn't work. This type of belief – a belief in failure – will render prayer practically useless because it will discourage the use of prayer ("This is a waste of time!") and, when prayer is consciously engaged in, it will not have the expectancy behind it that allows for the instant manifestation of the answer, in a form we recognize as an answer.

Also, you're going to get that which you believe in – your version of failure – which will further compound your error of understanding. You'll have what you believe to be evidence of your correctness, when all you'll really have is an excuse to stay unfulfilled and discontent. If we don't recognize the answer to our prayer, what is the point of praying in the first place? Learning and understanding what the answers to prayers look like is an essential part of the act of praying effectively.

The word *recognize*, as we mentioned before, basically means to know, or cognize, *again* – as indicated by the prefix *re-*. This is simply *remembering* what was asked for so that you will know it when you see it again. The first time you would *know* a thing is when you become aware of it as a desire and you *know* this desire in your heart. It is when we see our desire in our mind's eye that we are creating our prayer. Recognition happens when something comes into your life that you remember asking for – when you see the answer to your prayer. It is the process of recognition that allows you to find your car in a parking lot, although you may not believe it is lost.

You see, anytime you park your car and walk away from it, you have faith that you will find it when you return. You have experienced this act so many times that there is little doubt as to the outcome. The fact is that when you walk away from your car, it is lost unless you possess the ability to match an image in your mind with that of your car if you were to see it again. There are indeed people who experience this phenomenon, and in this world, it can be quite troublesome to not have the ability to recognize.

Finding the right car in a parking lot is indeed an answer to a prayer. You want to find your car, you expect to find your car, you look for your car, and you find your car in a series of thoughts and answers that guide your actions. If your car is not there, then your leaving it was part of a plan to separate you from your car to serve some other purpose or lesson.

You may not have asked, for instance, to have your car stolen, but if that happens it is the result of everything that led up to that event and a necessary part of the unfolding of future events. There will never be any way to exclude a past event as a part of the chain of events that led to the present. It can never be proven otherwise because it is always the case; the past leads to the present as it is created out of a field of future possibilities. You have been living within this framework your entire life. If you have figured out how this works, then you probably already spend your thoughts wisely as you are aware that they are what create and select our experiences out of that field of potential.

In other words, all things are possible; and we move toward, but no further than, the limits of our awareness. Someone must believe, or know, a thing is possible before that thing can be pulled out of the future and be experienced in the now. When you say, "I wouldn't have believed that was possible if I didn't see it with my own eyes..." you are defining the reason you haven't experienced that thing before. If there is anything that you believe is not possible, you are not alone; most people fall into this category.

You will not be faced with a reality that you aren't ready to see. You may not choose to accept the reality, but your exposure to it means you were ready to see it. You don't have to like it, but it was time for you to see it – because you did. You don't have to look very far to understand the concept that your awareness of, or belief in, a thing has no bearing on the existence of that thing. Most people have no idea how their television works, but that doesn't stop them from watching it. When you come up against new ideas that you haven't been exposed to before, instead of reacting with fear or anger, you could choose to realize that you are being faced with a new opportunity – something you can learn, or learn from, that will expand your awareness.

In the case of prayer, there seems to be an underlying belief that if the answer to a prayer doesn't come immediately after praying, happen exactly like we expect that it should, and look just like we imagined it would, then it must be something other than *our* answer. This way of thinking is very limiting. God, you see, works in "mysterious" ways – that is to say that the workings of God are beyond the knowing and understanding of the human mind. Why would we presume to be able to anticipate God's next move? Why would we want to limit our possibilities for experiencing God to those experiences we currently understand, or feel comfortable with? We can not know God in the sense that we know other humans, nor can we understand how God thinks; and it would be impossible, without this knowing, to predict the manner in which God would choose to orchestrate the delivery of our answer.

When we try to anticipate God's next move, in the context of verifying that our prayer is being answered or checking God's progress on our request, we only set ourselves up for what we have labeled as a failure. If you have a single guess at an infinite series of potential answers, you are most likely going to guess wrong. If you are in the habit of judging things, you will probably see this as a failure of sorts. With the judgments society has programmed into us, we see failure as something undesirable. No one likes to believe they have failed, and if you have judgments that you won't let go of, then you must let go of your ability to believe, in order to rid yourself of the burden of failure.

It is in this spirit that wise men encourage others to not believe a thing that they say. Consider these words and keep anything of benefit that you see in them. If you see no benefit, you are never under any obligation to accept anyone else's beliefs. Wisdom suggests trying everything and keeping those things that work for you. Keep in mind, however, that by the time you are reading the second chapter of a book, you are no longer the person that started reading the book. What doesn't work for you today, may work for you tomorrow, just as you have abandoned many old ways in favor of newer methods that serve you better – like microwave ovens, cars, and telephones. An open mind is an open heart, and it is through this doorway that we will experience a life of fullness.

Imagine, for a moment, that you prayed for rain. Now imagine that two days have passed since you prayed for rain and there has still been no rain. Of course, the reason you prayed for rain in the first place was because it hadn't rained in some time, so two more days represents "more of the same" for you. In the overall scheme, however, there is little difference between a 90-day drought and a 92-day drought, or even a hundred-day drought – unless at some point you developed an expectation, or belief, that the drought should end at a certain time. Imagine another couple days go by and you have forgotten that you prayed for rain.

Then, one morning, you go outside and see that you left your car windows open, perhaps believing now that it may never rain again, and it rained during the night – soaking the inside of your car. You respond like most people and experience anger, frustration, and possibly grief over the fact that your car's interior is soaked. You may even curse the rain. Is this any way to treat something you asked for? Well, it certainly is one of the choices people make, despite the fact that we can clearly see that rolling the windows up (or the thought which provokes that action...) is a prayer for a dry car, and the soaked seats is part of the answer to a prayer for rain. Obviously, we prayed for rain, and forgot to pray for a dry car.

A situation like the one above is not uncommon. In fact, whether it is rain in your car, an illness, or getting fired from a job, anything you receive is the answer to some prayer. The simple fact is that we do a lot of worrying, thinking, and focusing on the negative, so when those thoughts become things, we perceive the answers to our prayers in a negative context. It is our apparent inability to discern how we managed to ask for such things, which leads to our emotions and stress when things don't go our way. In fact, things always go our way. We have simply lost the ability to be clear about which way we want to be our way, or to clearly see the connecting links between cause and effect.

Things can go any way. All things are indeed possible. This is why people say, "Be careful what you ask for; you just might get it!" We need to be specific – and patient – if there is a specific thing we would like to see. Remember the *Genie in the bottle*? This is what that story is about. Just as they say that you can see what you want in life by looking around at what you have; your ability, or inability, to see creation is certainly no reflection on the creative Force that acts to fulfill your every desire. Just because you haven't seen it yet doesn't mean it doesn't exist; and just because you have judged an experience as negative, doesn't mean that you are under attack. God, or the Universe, or whatever force you believe placed you here, is for you – not against you. Get that straight in your head and you will have a much easier time seeing how quickly and precisely your prayers really are answered.

The Kabala advised us to blame no other person or external source for anything. The wisdom of Hermes Trismegistus reminds us that "As above, so below; as below, so above." The Bible tells us that if we ask, we will receive. It also tells us that we "have not because we ask not," and to "Judge not..." In fact, all ancient wisdom speaks pretty specifically on these points – "You asked for it, you got it..." Ernest Holmes wrote extensively on the subject of thoughts becoming things, and this perspective is not only evident in our everyday lives, but is shared by physicists, psychologists, metaphysicians, western medicine, eastern medicine, science, and religion.

Indeed, the most advanced and relevant sciences on the planet – such as Quantum Physics – can scientifically replicate and prove many of the points great teachers of the past have made about the nature of reality and thought. Many of the teachings of Jesus have been demonstrated in physics laboratories around the globe; and prayer studies are absolutely replicable and produce the results Jesus assured us they would produce, and hinted at when He said that we would do "these and even greater works."

Of course, the things you can produce with prayer are limited only by the limitations of your own mind and awareness. If you can conceive of a thing, Quantum Physics – like Jesus and many before and since – tells us that it is only a matter of time before someone is dealing with a physical reality which includes that thing we conceived. And as the thinker, you will be the one learning the biggest lesson of all. This, in fact, is one version of Karma; what goes around in the mind comes to fruition in the body. Think or *imagine* only good things and you will live only good experiences.

Einstein once said that imagination was more important than knowledge; sharing his own awareness of the fact that his knowledge was a collection of personal experiences colored by other people's thoughts, while it was his imagination that brought this world things none of us had seen before. This truth is all around us. Thinking on the things we desire brings them closer; worrying about things that cause us fear and stress only brings more of the same. In the Bible, Job said, "the thing I feared has come upon me." There is indeed "nothing to fear, but fear itself," according to Winston Churchill.

The monster in your closet is really in your head, as is every fear you hold onto. The closet the monster is hiding in is the same closet Jesus told you to go in and pray. It's no wonder people don't spend time praying; they've got monsters keeping them busy! Fear is a thought of "What if…," but it is still only a thought. What does the answer to a prayer look like? It looks like your thoughts, filtered through the screens of your belief systems, amplified by the amount of faith or love you put into that particular desire, and built out of the things you allow into your life – and in the context of the environment that you have created for yourself. These are not limitations to the ways prayers can happen; these simply seem to be among the obvious influences which color the answers you receive. Your thoughts are prayers – all of them. Your prayers are answered – all of them.

Whether you have a winning lottery ticket, a new car, a new job, an old house, or the flu, what you really have is the result, or product, of the things that have happened to you up to this point in space and time (here and now). Everything you have ever done is part of the process leading to everything that you will ever do, have, or experience. Your thoughts, or prayers, are behind all of those things. Believe me, if you hate your job, you will either quit, get fired, or make yourself sick. Why wait for the inevitable? Are we no longer smart enough to simply respond to our thoughts and feelings, and leave when we feel that it is time? Or have we come to honor our fear-based belief systems more than our inner guidance?

Why is it that so many people punish themselves by remaining in an uncomfortable situation past the point of realizing that they are not comfortable there? Take responsibility for your thoughts. You don't create your thoughts, but it is the thoughts you choose to dwell on that create your future – so what future are you looking at? Those thoughts you dwell on are usually the ones you illuminate with words to your family, friends, and anyone who will listen. When you give physical life to a thought by speaking it out loud, you have created a situation where others hear and begin thinking your thoughts. If you can see that thoughts are things, and you can see how telling others your problems and doubts only increases the number of people thinking (praying) that way, then you can surely see why your situation never seems to change. You are feeding it an awful lot of energy.

When I was younger, my father used to say, "If you ignore them, they'll leave you alone." At the time, he was referring to my siblings, disturbing my play – or me (when I was the one doing the *bothering*). But it is not really our siblings who bother us; it is our thoughts about what they are doing to us that create the discomfort inside.

I learned to ignore those things I couldn't control or change. At the time, I may have thought I was ignoring those who were disturbing my play; but I was actually ignoring my own thoughts that were trying to make me react to what I viewed as an intrusion. Ignoring thoughts really does allow them to dissipate. Giving them energy, especially by passing them around to others, is the best way to ensure that those thoughts enjoy a long life. Remember, if you don't have something nice to say, don't say anything at all.

Form follows thought. Thought is measurable energy. Energy possesses its own intelligence from which we draw ours. Energy is convertible into mass ($E=mc^2$); and all things are made of energy. Therefore, you can at least imagine how all things could be made of intelligence, or thought (prayer); though you may not understand the process by which that happens. The things we think about are the things we receive or experience. "Ask and ye shall receive." A prayer (thought) is the asking. The answer is the receiving of a physical manifestation of that thought.

All physical, or formed, things come from the unformed, or non-physical, realm. What brings that energy here and assembles it for us is the overarching principle of the Universe in which we live. Our essence is desire, or the desire to give and receive; our essence is love, attraction, and receptivity. We derive our essence from our Creator; the essence of that which created us appears to be that of love and of giving. You need only "Ask and ye shall receive." The great ones remind us, "You have not because you ask not."

We are here as the result of thought; and we receive all things as the result of thought. Some people call this prayer; but regardless of what you call it, it simply is. And it is simple. The answers to our prayers are the things we see and experience – all of them. If you are physically aware of it, it is the answer to a prayer. The answers to prayers are all we know. We just don't know that we know.

"We are formed and molded by our thoughts."
– Buddha

Chapter 16 Key Points and Afterthoughts

- Time gives us context for the events in our lives – time keeps everything from happening all at once.

- When we are waiting for something, our attention often goes to the wait, or waiting, and how difficult or uncomfortable that phase is for us; this makes time seem to slowly creep by and we begin to think that our ship will never come in. Now, you see, the focus has shifted – due to impatience – from our desire to the lack of that thing. Don't let time change what you are praying for (thinking about). This is the essential meaning of the saying, "A watched pot never boils."

- There are no true failures; incomplete thoughts, however, may lead to incomplete manifestations. Life is a continuously changing learning opportunity; view the fruits of your thought and effort and learn from them. Then, add thought where needed to edit your creations, or produce better fruit.

- Thinking is thinking; and it is all creative. Your body will walk around doing what it is programmed to do – all the while thinking what it has been programmed to think. It is your job, should you choose to accept it, to stay "awake," and aware of the fact that you are thinking and creating with those thoughts. You can begin to consciously choose which thoughts you will focus your energy and attention on; then, you will be able to practice and learn about the creative process so that you can take an active role in the creation of your own life – on your own terms – the way YOU want it to be.

- Your prayers are your thoughts; your thoughts are your prayers. Your life, experience, health, and environment, are simply reflections of your thought-life, or prayer-life. They say, "If you want to know what you want in life, take a look around at what you have – that's what you've been asking for."

- You are projecting your reality with your thoughts; and then filtering your perceptions of that reality with your beliefs. What you see is what you get; perception is reality. If you think your life stinks, then it will until you change that thought. Unfortunately, most people are waiting for their life to change before changing their thoughts about their life; this is not going to happen because this is simply not how life works.

- No wise man has ever been ambiguous on this point: Your thoughts are all that matters; they create your experience. When you are looking at your world, you are looking at the answers to your prayers and the results of your thoughts – even when you can not understand this.

"Remind yourself that God is with you
and nothing can defeat you.
Believe that you now receive power from him."
— *Norman Vincent Peale*

Conclusion

ow do you feel? Do you feel good? Do you want to feel better? Are you happy? Is there something that you would rather be doing than whatever you do now? Do you have everything you want? Are you enjoying the life you have? Do you ever even ask yourself these kinds of questions?

You are here for a reason and you have certain gifts and abilities that can help you make life anything you want it to be. If you are not aware that every moment of your life is an opportunity to live in a state of complete fulfillment, then you are doing it the hard way. I would say that I hope you're getting all you want in life, but I know you're not; because no one that was completely aware of their true capabilities would ever again have curiosity about things such as prayer.

You have read this far, and that should have at least taught you something important about yourself: Whether any of this makes sense to you or not, or whether or not you believe one single word written here, you know that you share a common curiosity to hear what someone else has discovered about manifesting their own existence.

You will have to face the fact that all along you have thought there was something more to life, in this realm, than you have been shown or taught. That knowing wasn't in your head in the form of hard evidence; it was deep in the middle of *you* where you *know* things. You also know that, whether you use any of these suggestions for your benefit or not, you are no different than many others in the sense that many people are looking for better answers to life's questions. You don't believe you could feel better; you know it. You wouldn't have read this far if you didn't have a *knowing* within you that you needed to be searching for something.

That knowing is a message to you – given to you as a thought. God is talking to you. He's trying to lead you out of the darkness and into the light. He's trying to show you the "Kingdom of Heaven." He's talking to us in the most efficient ways possible and we are allowing our bodies to distract us from the reality of the fact that we operate on a continuous flow of Divine guidance. We need only think of our next experience and it is given unto us. The only way to mess this up is to not truly believe it.

Even then, when we don't believe, the guidance is always there, and our experience always perfectly suits our beliefs. Blinded by our disbelief, however, we just don't recognize it as such. We can not, of our own accord, make anything happen. We wish things to happen and then we receive a series of thoughts, or messages, that lead us to the fulfillment of our desire. If a thing is not within your immediate grasp, it is easily sent to you. It is just as easy to create the thought of giving as it is to create the mindset of receiving. There is only one mind, and God communicates to each of us to fulfill the highest good. If you ask, you will receive, whether God sends you the thoughts to move you toward your desire, or sends someone else the thought to bring your desire to you, the order will be filled.

God works in mysterious ways; you will begin to see truth in clichés like this and in reminders of the simplicity of things. Where do you think the thoughts for catchy slogans and clichés come from, anyway? Where do you think recipes, or systems, for using the mind or building effective prayers, come from? How many things do you think happen outside of a God who is *all things*? People think, pray, and ask for answers to problems, like; "How can I convince someone to buy this thing I am selling?" Then they receive an inspiration: "Oh! I know! I can say that 4-out-of-5 experts recommend this product and people will accept the recommendation from our implied authorities because they are programmed to." Where do you think all of these thoughts come from?

$$A = p \times b$$

Making Prayer Work for You

- Prayer is thought; make all your thoughts positive and creative. This is a practical, useful, and beneficial pursuit.

- All things are created in accordance with a plan; you can help the process by making your own plan. Write it down; make it happen.

- Plans which are executed faithfully, or boldly, are bound to succeed; if at first you don't succeed, be bold and try again!

- All prayers begin with the awareness of a desire. If you have no desires, the work of prayer is very easy. Cultivate contentment.

- The manifestation of your desire will be the result of how you act and feel about (believe) the thoughts you receive about this desire.

- When the proper balance of plan, faith, and action is met, your prayer is answered; your goal is achieved. Be grateful and optimistic always; even "bad" plans can work with enough faith.

- When you think of your goal, think of it as if you are experiencing the joy of it already being here. This is the "magnetic," or "attractive," force which fuels your faith and inspires your actions.

- Learn to relax; and then do it! Your brain works better when you are relaxed; you're smarter and you pray better. You are also healthier when you are relaxed. Relaxation is the opposite of stress.

- Be patient. Impatience causes anxiety, which is stress – not relaxation. If you are praying for something to happen, your impatience emphasizes the reality that it hasn't happened. Stress repels, or slows the arrival of, our answers and demonstrations.

- Do little; and do it well. Do those things which you are inspired to do; they will lead you to the unfolding of the future you have created.

- Love all, and all you do. Love is the Creative/Attractive Force.

Coincidentally, this type of advertising is *straight-out-of-the-books* hypnosis. The people, who make millions of dollars designing advertisements to program a large group of people to all want the same thing, understand how the mind works and they use it. They understand how the mind turns desire into reality and they capitalize on that knowledge by using our minds against us to their own benefit. They have a wish, or desire, for a large number of people to buy a certain product, and they receive inspiration in the form of thoughts of which words to write in order to speak to the appropriate part of the mind. It doesn't matter that 4-out-of-5 experts are usually wrong. Their desire set in motion the prayer mechanism and the answer ultimately showed up, after a series of inspired events, in the form of increased product sales.

If you could understand what the people programming your mind know all to well, you could recognize it and not fall victim to this type of advertising, and you could also use these techniques to help you finally see your prayers being answered reliably and predictably. You need something accomplished, or you want something, and the desire sets the thought/prayer process in motion. We simply have to learn how to hear the answers when we receive them. Asking for what you want, while you are in a certain state of mind, bridges a critical gap in which the skeptical conscious mind can sabotage your prayer by creating a lack of faith.

There are many people studying the workings of the mind. You have to look, however, in order to see. In talks I give, I sometimes have people ask me why they have never heard some of these things about the mind and body before. The point is, of course, that you need not hear a thing twice. You heard it when you were ready to hear it. And everything you hear is new to you only once – the first time you hear it. If these people come to another lecture, they will no longer be able to ask, "Why haven't I heard this before?" This is an interesting habit we tend to develop after we decide to stop learning new things.

Can you imagine if every school child, when encountering information that was new to them, asked the teacher, "Why haven't we seen this before, if it's so important?" Hopefully, you will begin to see the paradox of many such beliefs and behaviors we develop or adopt over the course of our lives.

Where would we be as a species if new things were rejected simply because no one had heard of them before? Imagine if Wilbur Wright had said, "That airplane won't fly, Orville, I've never seen one before!" Thank goodness visionaries see past the limitations in other people's awareness. In 1899, for instance, the Director of the U.S. Patent Office suggested that they close the patent office because anything that could possibly be invented had already been invented. About four years later, the Wright brothers did something they "couldn't possibly do," because it "hadn't been done before." Yet they did it anyway. What were they thinking?! They certainly weren't thinking like *everyone* else!

What was the difference between this high-ranking government official and these two brothers? Awareness, and the way they thought about things, was probably the only difference between the Wright brothers and the bureaucrat – or anyone else for that matter. None of them had ever witnessed powered flight, so they would have been on common ground as far as contemporary knowledge, or "traditional wisdom," of powered flight was concerned. The Director of the Patent Office simply suffered from limited vision, or a lack of creativity, and it affected the way his mind translated how he saw the world – as a very small and limited place.

Are you beginning to see the way our minds tend to operate when we leave them to their own designs? I'll bet that you are. You see *"traditional wisdom"* is really a kind of ignorance created by, and based on, clinging to old, limited ideas and ways of thinking. It is the stuff of the common, collective mind. All great advances in human history were created by men who refused to limit themselves by the past thoughts of other men, and instead either built on those old ideas, or threw them out altogether and came up with something newer and better.

You get what you are able to see. "According to your faith, it is done unto you," even applies to flying. "No one has ever flown before, but I believe I can." The thing speaks for itself. We fly to and from space, now. Who was right? Jesus said, "You will know them by their fruits." You have seen yourself get sick and then get well without intervention, haven't you? Perhaps you had a headache, or a cold, that came and went on its own. So you have seen that the body has the intelligence and capacity to not only create and build itself, but to make itself sick, and to fix and maintain itself, too. So why is Jesus, or His disciples, healing someone such an unattainable, or unbelievable, miracle? Jesus didn't do anything people had not seen before in some form, or to some degree; nor was He the last to do many of the things He did.

Jesus, in fact, said that we would do this and much greater things. No one ever saw Jesus fly in a powered craft, did they? The Wright brothers had no real, physical reason or example to give them the faith that they weren't wasting their time – that faith came from within them. Again, the results of this are obvious. Each of the great achievements in history, and each of the mundane, everyday tasks we perform is an example of the essence of creation and manifestation; they are all miracles of and within God. This is how prayer works. You need only recognize the law that is in operation around you at all times, creating and managing your life, and start utilizing it, or working more effectively within it. Ask and ye shall receive.

Life is as easy as you allow it to be, or as difficult as you make it. Notice that we must *make* (create, or force them to be) things difficult. We must put extra energy into things in order to get resistance and stress in return. To simply relax and allow life to unfold for you is indeed the easiest, most natural thing to do. As this process runs its course, you can choose to get in the driver's seat and steer your own creation for a change. Just use your imagination; that is all prayer is, anyway – heartfelt imagination. See your life, in your mind's eye, the way you want it to be and feel this in your heart. Know in your heart that it is so; you deserve it, you want it, you believe it is possible, you know that it is so, and it is.

Imagination becomes reality through belief. You can refuse to believe this if you wish, but therein lies the answer to why you can not see the answers to all of your prayers. If there is struggle in your life, you created it, or you allowed it into your existence. Somehow, some way, you needed to have that particular experience. It doesn't have to be a bad thing; it is intended to be a learning experience, and those are good things. Take advantage of the opportunities to be thankful for such things – as ridiculous as this might sound.

Now, take the next step and express your gratitude for your lesson, accept responsibility for it, and then release it. You no longer need to hold onto struggle from the past. If you accept responsibility for your situation, you accept dominion over it. If you created it, you can create something to replace it. Remember, it's your life, it's your body, and you are the one driving. Whatever you want can be yours, be it health, wealth, wisdom, or whatever you can imagine. Make up your mind and make-up your life. The power is inside of you. Turn the key, unlock your true power, unlock the power of prayer, and get started on your path to a new life of peace, joy, health, and fulfillment. It is your choice. This is your gift. You have the Formula; now use it.

Appendix 1

Progressive Relaxation Exercise/Induction

*A progressive relaxation induction is a technique used by hypnotherapists to help the client achieve physical and mental relaxation. After talking the client through this induction, the hypnotherapist would most likely utilize some depth-testing techniques, to assess the depth of relaxation, and possibly deepening techniques, to deepen the level of relaxation.

After the client has become adequately relaxed, physically and mentally, the hypnotherapist will begin to speak or read from a specially-prepared script. At this point, the things spoken by the hypnotherapist, or written in the script to be read by the hypnotherapist, are specifically designed to assist the client in developing new thought patterns that will bring about the desired, positive changes in the client's life and/or health.

It is from this relaxed state of mind, ideally an alpha or theta state, that new concepts have the deepest influence. This induction will not create a state of unconsciousness, but will promote deep relaxation – making it an ideal exercise for stress reduction and a great way to achieve restful sleep at night. After reading through this induction a time or two, you will get the idea and no longer need to read this exercise. You will find yourself mentally going through the relaxation process anytime you wish to relax, de-stress, or meditate or pray.

Though this is technically called an "induction," I call it an exercise here because you will not be using this to induce hypnosis, but rather using it as an exercise to achieve certain goals in life, such as: relaxation, sleep, meditation, effective prayer, stress management, and improved performance in any area of life.

For optimum health benefits, I suggest using this exercise daily and incorporating visualizations and statements that affirm good health. After you have finished with your exercise, simply tell yourself that, "...at the count of five, I will open my eyes and be completely alert, energized, and feeling great!" unless, of course, you are using this as an aid to achieving a good night's sleep. In that case, you can simply allow yourself to drift off to sleep and you will awaken naturally, feeling well-rested, alert, and energized.

You may also record this induction on a tape or c.d. and then add any affirmations you would like on the end. I recommend repeating affirmations at least three-times each for best results.

Progressive Relaxation

Place yourself in a comfortable position, either sitting or reclined. Now, take a deeper-than-normal breath and release it like you are blowing out a candle. Now, take another deeper-than-normal breath and as you release it allow any stress or tension to melt away and allow your body to relax. Now, take one more deeper-than-normal breath and, this time, as you release your breath you can simply allow your eyelids to close (Obviously, you will not be able to do this while you read, but as this becomes second nature, you will no longer need to look at these words). Now, direct your attention to your eyelids...and the muscles around your eyes. These muscles are possibly the easiest to relax in your entire body. Allow these muscles to relax...you may feel as if your eyes are "sinking" back into your head. Allow your eyes, eyelids, and the muscles around your eyes to simply relax...relax them to the point where you know that, without taking away any of the relaxation, you would not be able to open them if you tried. When your eyes are relaxed to the point that you are sure that, no matter how hard you try, your eyes will not work unless you take away that relaxation. Good, now you can test your eyes to feel what that feels like, and then stop trying and allow yourself to relax even deeper. (Of course, you can open your eyes anytime you want; you will not become paralyzed from simply relaxing your eyes. If you open your eyes, however, it simply means that you removed some of the relaxation. Now try it without removing any of the relaxation you have

210

achieved.) Now we are going to spread this relaxation over your entire body. Move this feeling of relaxation that you have achieved in and around your eyes, to the top of your head. Feel the top of your head...move your awareness to your scalp...become aware of the skin and muscles on the top of your head...now allow yourself to release all tension in this area...allow your scalp to relax...good...now move this loose, relaxed feeling down to your forehead...allow the skin and muscles across your forehead to simply relax...just release any tension you feel in this area...good...now, allow this feeling of relaxation to spread down to your cheeks and the skin and muscles covering your face. Now allow your ears to relax. Maintain this relaxation as you allow your lips and tongue to relax. Continue to allow this relaxation to flow...like a warm wave...from your head...to your toes...slowly...allow this warm wave of relaxation to relax each muscle and body part as it gradually covers you from head to toe...allow this relaxation to flow and cover the back of your head and neck...now flowing and relaxing your neck and throat area. Allow this feeling of relaxation to flow over your shoulders and down your arms...one at a time...first relaxing your upper arm...then your elbows...then your forearms...then your wrists...then your hands...and finally, out your fingers and fingertips. Now, allow this feeling of relaxation to flow down your other arm...your upper arm...your elbow...your forearm...your wrist...your hands and fingers. Next, allow this feeling to flow down over your chest...over your back...down over your abdomen...covering and relaxing all the way down...now your waist is relaxing as this warm wave gently flows and covers you with warmth and comfort...your pelvis and hips are now relaxing...and now your legs...first one...down your thigh as you allow this part of your leg to relax...now your knee is relaxing...and you can allow your calf and shin to relax...and finally, relax your ankle...your foot...and allow this wave of warmth and relaxation to flow out your toes…now, the other leg…relax your thigh…your entire upper leg…allow your knee to relax…then let your calf and shin relax…then your ankle can relax…and finally, your foot and toes can relax as this wave of relaxation flows completely over your entire body…wrapping you like a blanket…allowing you to enjoy complete physical relaxation. Now that your body is completely relaxed, simply allow yourself to enjoy the peace, quiet, and comfort that you have achieved. You can imagine that you are wrapped in a warm blanket of relaxation. Now, with each breath you take, you will become more and more relaxed. Allow any sounds you may hear to simply add to this feeling of relaxation… deepening it more and more.

(End of Progressive Relaxation Exercise Script)

As you achieve and maintain this state of relaxation, you can give yourself suggestions, meditate, say affirmations, pray, or build imagery for yourself that you have designed to achieve specific goals (like giving a good presentation at work, or having a good athletic performance, etc…).

This relaxed state is a powerful state of mind that will enable you to achieve anything you set your sights on. Be mindful and never enter this state with negative intentions. At this level of mind, things have slightly different meanings than they do at the conscious level and they can have dramatically different effects, as well.

Just remember, love reflects love, and if you enter into this state with negative intentions; you will most likely reap what you sow. Use this method to achieve a relaxed state of mind from which your heartfelt desires can be issued forth with tremendous effect.

There are many good books that will give you further instruction and insight into hypnosis and self-hypnosis, but if you would like deeper instruction, contact the National Guild of Hypnotists, or look on the internet to find a hypnotherapist who can teach you self-hypnosis, or a certified instructor from whom you can learn hypnosis.

Appendix 2:

Prayers for Peace

As you read the prayers in this appendix, keep in mind that they were all written by different people, living in different times, in different lands and cultures, and in different languages. These prayers are all prayers for peace and offer an interesting perspective into the minds of humans. Despite the words we hang on our beliefs, all humans want essentially the same thing – peace. In fact, peace of mind is probably a better way to put that.

Even those bent on doing violence move in the direction of setting things in order according to their own beliefs. Some people may actually seek peace of mind at the cost of the lives of others. Peace, however, is the common denominator and seems to indicate that all is in its proper place in the universe of our mind. A nation, for instance, probably doesn't find comfort in the slaying of innocent humans; but if the act was in retaliation for some affront perpetrated against that nation, they may very well find peace of mind in the act of righting a wrong, or vengeance, as some may call it. We use apparent differences to create and justify such rifts between ourselves – even when no real differences exist. But we can not erase the underlying truth of whom and what we are. When one comes to the realization that "It is only skin...," this curtain we hang between ourselves and the rest of humankind, then it becomes easier to see the Light within and realize that we truly are *one*.

When you consider that these prayers were indeed written by so many different cultures, cultures that continuously war against one another, you may find it difficult to reconcile the similarities between the *inner* thoughts of people that appear to be so *outwardly* different. Look carefully at the references to celestial and beneficent beings, to light and love, and to the similarities in references to war, separation, suffering, and seeking higher states of awareness to cure these ills of humanity.

Now, compare these concepts and principles to those of your own religious or spiritual belief systems. I believe most people will find more similarities than differences. I have labeled each prayer as to its origin; but try to read these prayers with no consideration given to *where* they came from and you may see how difficult it is to label truth or beauty with nationalism or discrimination. Try using the technique in Appendix 1 to achieve the ideal prayer state before reading these prayers.

"We're all speaking the same different language."
—Alice Hurley

Prayer of St. Francis

Lord, make me an instrument of your peace.

Where there is hatred…let me sow love.

Where there is injury…pardon.

Where there is doubt…faith.

Where there is despair…hope.

Where there is darkness…light.

Where there is sadness…joy.

O Divine Master,

grant that I may not so much seek

To be consoled…as to console,

To be understood…as to understand,

To be loved…as to love,

For it is in giving…that we receive,

It is in pardoning, that we are pardoned,

It is in dying…that we are born to eternal life.

Shinto Peace Prayer

Although the people living
across the ocean
surrounding us, I believe,
are all our brothers and sisters,
why are there constant troubles in
this world?
Why do winds and waves rise in the
ocean surrounding us?
I only earnestly wish that the wind will
soon puff away all the clouds which are
hanging over the tops of the mountains.

Hindu Peace Prayer

Oh, God, lead us from the
Unreal to the Real.
Oh, God, lead us from darkness to light.
Oh, God, lead us from death to immortality.
Shanti, Shanti, Shanti unto all.
Oh, Lord God almighty, may there be peace in
celestial regions.
May there be peace on earth.
May the waters be appeasing.
May herbs be wholesome, and may trees and
plants bring peace to all. May all beneficent
beings bring peace to us.
May the Vedic Law propagate peace all
through the world.
May all things be a source of peace to us.
And may thy peace itself, bestow peace on all,
and may that peace come to me also.

Buddhist Peace Prayer

May all beings everywhere plagued
with sufferings of body and mind
quickly be freed from their illnesses.
May those frightened cease to be afraid,
and may those bound be free.
May the powerless find power,
and may people think of befriending
one another.
May those who find themselves in trackless,
fearful wildernesses –
the children, the aged, the unprotected –
be guarded by beneficent celestials,
and may they swiftly attain Buddhahood.

Zoroastrian Peace Prayer

We pray to God to eradicate all the
misery in the world:
that understanding triumph
over ignorance,
that generosity triumph over indifference,
that trust triumph over contempt, and
that truth triumph over falsehood.

Jewish Peace Prayer

Come, let us go up to the mountain of
the Lord, that we may walk the
paths of the Most High.
And we shall beat our swords into ploughshares,
and our spears into pruning hooks.
Nation shall not lift up sword against nation –
neither shall they learn war any more.
And none shall be afraid, for the mouth of the
Lord of Hosts has spoken.

Sikh Peace Prayer

God adjudges us according
to our deeds,
not the coat that we wear:
that Truth is above everything,
but higher still is truthful living.
Know that we attaineth God when we loveth,
and only that victory
endures in consequences of which no
one is defeated.

Native African Peace Prayer

Almighty God, the Great
Thumb we cannot evade to
tie any knot;
the Roaring Thunder that splits
mighty trees:
the all-seeing Lord up on high who sees
even the footprints of an antelope on
a rock mass here on Earth.
You are the one who does
not hesitate to respond to our call.
You are the cornerstone of peace.

Jainist Peace Prayer

Peace and Universal Love is the essence
of the Gospel preached by all the
Enlightened Ones.
The Lord has preached that equanimity
is the Dharma.
Forgive do I creatures all,
and let all creatures forgive me.
Unto all have I amity, and unto none enmity.
Know that violence is the root cause of
all miseries in the world.
Violence, in fact, is the knot of bondage.
"Do not injure any living being."
This is the eternal, perennial, and unalterable
way of spiritual life.
A weapon, howsoever powerful it may be,
can always be superseded by a superior one;
but no weapon can, however,
be superior to nonviolence and love

Native American Peace Prayer

O Great Spirit of our
Ancestors, I raise
my pipe to you.
To your messengers the four winds, and
to Mother Earth who provides
for your children.
Give us the wisdom to teach our children
to love, to respect, and to be kind
to each other so that they may grow
with peace in mind.
Let us learn to share all good things that
you provide for us on the Earth.

Muslim Peace Prayer

In the name of Allah,
the beneficent, the merciful.
Praise be to the Lord of the
Universe who has created us and
made us into tribes and nations.
That we may know each other, not that
we may despise each other.
If the enemy incline towards peace, do
thou also incline towards peace, and
trust God, for the Lord is the one that
heareth and knoweth all things.
And the servants of God,
Most gracious are those who walk on
the Earth in humility, and when we
address them, we say, "PEACE."

Baha'i Peace Prayer

Be generous in prosperity,
and thankful in adversity.
Be fair in thy judgment,
and guarded in thy speech.
Be a lamp unto those who walk
in darkness, and a home
to the stranger.
Be eyes to the blind, and a guiding light
unto the feet of the erring.
Be a breath of life to the body of
humankind, a dew to the soil of
the human heart,
and a fruit upon the tree of humility.

Peace is the only way to peace — in your mind, and in the world.

Namasté

"He does not believe that does not live according to his belief."

— Sigmund Freud

Appendix 3:

Affirmations and Affirmative Prayer

Affirmations are simply positive, or affirmative, statements of truth. The tricky part is that the truth of the affirmation need not be a "present reality;" it can be a future reality you truly wish to create. By declaring this future reality in positive, definite terms, you are tasking your conscious and unconscious mind with finding this new reality. It is important to consider that, when your prayer is answered, it will be now; so, the proper way to "declare a thing" and make it so is to offer thanks NOW – in this moment – for your desired reality as if it had already happened. Your emotional guidance system will seek to recreate the experience of being happy for having achieved this particular goal; and it is likely to do it by bringing that goal to fruition.

Life is a continuous series of changing circumstances. Our thoughts help us make sense of this ever-changing landscape; and they help guide us from one event to another along this path to future "now's." Along the way to your future, you are continuously asked to offer thought as a way of generating your future realities. Change happens with or without your input; but you can create affirmative change with affirmative thought. Consider the following words from two great teachers of this path of positive thought and affirmative action:

- *"Be the change you seek to create in the world."* – *Gandhi*

- *"Do unto others what you would have them do unto you." –Jesus*

- *"Declare a thing and it is so." –Jesus*

- *"As a man thinketh, so is he." –Jesus*

- *"Our thoughts become our words as they become our beliefs; our beliefs become our actions as they become our habits. Our habits become our values as our values become our destiny."* – *Gandhi*

- *"Whatsoever you desire, when you stand in prayer – believing – will be given unto you." –Jesus*

Believing in a thing is affirming it – it makes it firm, or physical. As you think about a thing which has sparked your interest or curiosity, or which has become desirable to you, your thoughts will naturally want to return there. As you think of a new thing, you will begin to notice that new thing in your world where you haven't noticed it before. You will also begin to look in new places, read new books and magazines, and perhaps begin doing research or study in this new area of thought. As you give more attention and thought-energy to these ideas, you will develop mental imagery and additional ideas.

The imagery and new ideas you experience, while giving thought to your new desire, will make you feel a certain way. If the feelings are positive, your desire will grow; if your feelings are negative the desire may also grow, but it will likely grow into that which you are afraid of. If your thoughts are positive, and they excite you, you will probably begin speaking about them, as we think and talk about those things which most interest us. These thoughts and words will then stimulate actions and behaviors. Affirmative thoughts inspire affirmative action. Inspired action seems to be effortless and always creates positive change and new realities.

Just imagine that you are programming a computer; you wouldn't tell the computer all the things you don't want it to do. You simply tell the computer – in a language it understands – what you want it to do; and then you tell it to do it. Your mind and body operate in much the same way; so, your self-talk – which is actually a type of self-programming – should always be affirmations of what you want to happen. Your programs should always be positive, affirmative, direct, and specific; but you should keep in mind that this is a process – and part of the process is exercising patience and a peaceful countenance. You may not master this immediately; so relax, and be of good cheer.

By thinking and speaking affirmative words, we can generate an affirmative mood, or disposition; an affirmative disposition is one which is free from stress. This state of mind and body is a healing state. Positive thoughts do not stress us out; that's because they do not cause or stimulate the release of the harmful stress hormones which we experience as "bad feelings." The way we phrase our words and intentions has a lot to do with the way our subconscious hears, interprets, and acts on those thoughts we hold so important that we took the time

226

and energy to turn them into words. When you turn a desire into words, it is one step closer to becoming a physical reality.

Imagine that you are ordering dinner and you tell the waitress what NOT to bring you. Do you know what you will get for dinner? Some people say that affirmations are not useful or effective because they affirm the lack of the thing you are affirming. In these cases, semantics are everything. Reframing your negative desires into positive affirmations may take some time and thought, but it is worth it. A declaration of what you do not want is really a "negation," and not an "affirmation."

By saying, "I don't want to be sick," or "God, please take away my illness," you are focusing on the fact that you are sick, or have an illness; and you are trying to negate it by thinking about it. This does not work. Though you may heal; it will be through natural processes that you could have sped up with an affirmation instead of slowing down with a negation. "Thank you, God, for giving me this wonderful health and strength so I can go for a walk!" is a much better prayer for restoring health and wellness than those listed above.

To create health, wellness, happiness, success, and prosperity, in all areas of your life, begin thinking positively and affirmatively. Think creatively and optimistically if you wish to create a new reality. Express gratitude in your affirmations; and try to feel the feeling of gratitude in your heart as you imagine the happy, new reality you wish to create. Continue to affirm only those things you wish to experience in your life, body, and experience. Below are a few examples of affirmative prayers for health, prosperity, etc; they will give you an idea of how effective thinkers effectively create using effective, affirmative thought. Affirmations need only contain gratitude, joy, and a positive intention. Try using the Relaxation exercise in Appendix 1 to achieve the ideal state before saying these affirmations.

- <u>Health</u> – *"Thank you, God, for giving me health and strength so that I might live fully and be a model of health and joy to others. Thank you for giving me the strength, courage, and willingness, to do the things that enrich and empower me..."*

- <u>Peace</u> – *"Thank you, God, for giving me peace. Thank you for giving me faith and trust and for quieting my mind so that I might rest and hear more clearly your will..."*

- Relationships – *"Thank you, God, for giving me the love and wisdom to see you in all your creation and to love all creation and all living things unconditionally. Love and harmony are alive and well in all my relationships."*

- Weight Loss – *"I am happy and peaceful here and now. I am safe and loved and create my own peace, security, and nourishment from the power from within me. I am free; and I release the past and others to be free now."*

- Prosperity – *"My good returns to me now in an avalanche of abundance; thank you, God, for prospering me in all my ways. Only good comes to me; and there is always more than enough to share."*

- Success – *"Thank you, God, for growing my good thoughts now. I give thanks for the wonderful insights and ideas which I have been given and are now coming to light. Thank you for all things going my way, favoring me with your blessings, and for benefiting all as your grace now benefits me. "*

"It's the repetition of affirmations that leads to belief. And once that belief becomes a deep conviction, things begin to happen."

– Muhammad Ali

"Belief consists in accepting the affirmations of the soul; unbelief, in denying them."

– Ralph Waldo Emerson

Suggested Reading

Joey-O, *Seeds of Wisdom: A Son's Promise Kept.* America: Joey-O. 2004.

Lipton, Bruce, *The Biology of Belief: Unleashing the Power of Consciousness, Matter, and Miracles.* San Rafael: Elite Books. 2005.

Aaron, David, *Seeing God: Ten Life Changing Lessons of the Kabbalah.* New York: Berkley. 2001.

Hawkins, David R., *Power vs. Force.* Carlsbad: Hay House. 1995.

Holmes, Ernest, and Kinnear, Willis, *The Spiritual Universe and You.* Los Angeles: Science of Mind Publications. 1971.

Holmes, Ernest, and Kinnear, Willis, *Thought as Energy.* Los Angeles: Science of Mind Publications. 1975.

Holmes, Ernest, and Kinnear, Willis, *Thoughts are Things.* Los Angeles: Science of Mind Publications. 1967.

Holmes, Ernest, and Kinnear, Willis, *Magic of the Mind.* Los Angeles: Science of Mind Publications. 1965.

Jaidar, George, *The Soul: An Owner's Manual.* New York: Paragon House. 1995.

Murphy, Joseph, and McMahan, Ian, *The Power of Your Subconscious Mind.* New York: Prentice Hall. 1963.

Ouspensky, P.D., *The Psychology of Man's Possible Evolution: A Great Modern Mystic's Essential Teachings on Consciousness and Spiritual Development.* New York: The Hedgehog Press, Inc., 1954.

Pearce, Joseph Chilton, *The Biology of Transcendence.* Rochester: Park Street Press. 2002.

Rushnell, Squire, *When God Winks.* Hillsboro: Beyond Words Publishing. 2001.

Walsch, Neale Donald, *Conversations with God.* New York: Putnam. 1995.

Wise, Anna, *The High-Performance Mind.* New York: Jeremy P. Tarcher/Putnam. 1995.